44 03?

D1759173

 University of Hertfordshire

Not of This Time, Not of This Place

Not of This Time,
Not of This Place

by Yehuda Amichai

Translated from the Hebrew by Shlomo Katz

VALLENTINE, MITCHELL
LONDON   1973

First published 1973 in Great Britain by
VALLENTINE, MITCHELL & CO. LTD.
67 Great Russell Street,
London WC1B 3BT

ISBN 0 85303 180 0

This book was originally published in Hebrew
under the title Lo' Me'Akhshav, Lo Mi'Kan.
Copyright © 1963 Schocken Publishing Ltd.,
Tel Aviv, Israel.

English translation © 1968 by Harper & Row,
Publishers, Inc., N.Y.

Printed in Great Britain by
Lewis Reprints Ltd.
member of Brown Knight & Truscott Group
London and Tonbridge

Not of This Time, Not of This Place

1

The evening breeze suddenly pushed the window open and the aroma of eucalyptus in bloom flooded the room. The eucalyptus was very late blossoming in this hot summer. It had a heavy and oppressive smell, the aroma of alien trees whose ancestors had been brought from Australia. Mina suggested closing the window, and coyly looked up after examining her fingernails.

"It was planted not more than twenty years ago, and it has already grown taller than my house."

"And when were you brought here?" Joel asked.

"I was brought, but I did not grow. I was brought little and I remained little."

Mina reached out of the window and pinched off an elongated leaf, crushed it between her fingers, and smelled them, then looked again at her fingernails with a concentrated and forlorn look.

It was one of those summer evenings when people talk to each other about their plans. Not only plans of the summer, but bigger plans, like the five-year plans of well-organized countries. Now Joel and Mina talked to each other. And though they were not lovers, the aroma of the eucalyptus tree affected them this night.

"Mornings the top of the eucalyptus tree swarms with bees. A persistent dense humming like that of a single giant bee, like a lion. And the tree swells with passion," Mina said. Then she laughed and added, "Such a big lover of a tree. Or is it a female tree? I am a little weak in botany."

She was silent and her lips curled. The noises from the rooms in this big old house became louder. There were persistent sounds of laughter, and indistinct music, and moving of furniture, but the sounds seemed remote and unclear and Mina and Joel stood between the rustling of the evening and the aroma of lust and did not know where they belonged.

"A woman too small in a house that is too big." She agreed, with a light sigh and a clownish pathetic look. Indeed, the old Arab house was big. Two pillars supported the ceiling in the room where they stood. Mina went up to one of the pillars and put her arms around it.

"A slim little Samson embracing the pillars," he said.

"Perish my soul with the Philistines."

"Who are they?"

"You, and all the rest. . . . You know, Joel, I can't master this house and all its rooms. There's one floor, and another, and an attic, and a basement, and the large workroom of my late father-in-law. It's like a museum, but Itzhak won't give it up. One day everybody will recognize his father's greatness; then the entire house will become a museum."

"But you have a maid."

"She, too, bosses me."

Again she embraced the pillar, but this time because of the love within her, and not in order to topple the house on everybody within it. And as she did so, her knees and a strip of her thighs became uncovered, dark and soft and fuller than one would have guessed when they were covered by the muslin and white silk of her skirts. She continued complaining to Joel: "Everything is too big. The cupboards are too high, and to reach some of the shelves I have to stand on a chair, like a child." Thus she complained as she stood there like a little girl in her mother's clothes. Her voice was clear as a bell.

"You have attractive knees."

"Oh, you archeologist! You have to uncover everything and determine its age and era."

"And put it away in a museum."

"Jars and more jars and scrolls and bits and pieces and some ashes and scraps and heads with chipped noses. That's all. That's your entire world."

Thus she chirped, and Joel exclaimed, "Stop fluttering your nostrils like a rabbit. Stop it." Mina glided away and vanished with a rustle of skirts, lightly, the way it is possible to vanish only in old houses. Strange Mina, destined to disappear, marked for the end—her end and the end of all the others, the end of the house, the end of the entire generation, of Joel and of Yoske and of Joseph and of Zeiger and of all the heroes of the past, and of Itzhak, her taciturn husband, who had brought her here some years before as one brings a tree from a faraway land, except that she stopped growing here.

Joel filled his glass and drank, then put it down on a small Damascene napkin that Itzhak's father had once received as a gift from a rich Arab. The more he drank, the more depressed he felt this evening. When a man is preoccupied, not even drink will give him a lift. He returned to the window. Outside, the street was silent except for some sounds from among the trees and from the parked cars. For some reason, he could not rid himself of a kind of apocalyptic feeling, as if the end of everything, the end of the world, was at hand, a sunset mood. Eat and drink, for tomorrow we won't even die. A remote ancestor of his must have been a prophet, one of those who come upon revelers and at once smell the end and prophesy gloom. Otherwise why should he be subject to moods like this now, when his life was a success? It has been some time since he went to a party. This evening, too, his wife Ruth has not come with him. Yet he is at the best time of life, at the height of his abilities, at the peak of his accomplishments and activity.

Early this summer, unexpectedly, an awareness of the end descended upon him. He noted a distinct resemblance to his father, who became despondent and began to sink and died in the arms of his wife Ruth before his time. Then, suddenly, Joel began to re-examine his life, like a general who reappraises his forces on the basis of new intelligence about the enemy's movements—and in doing so his life acquired a new orientation, the exact opposite of self-destruction. He was like a man who comes late to a movie and is guided to his seat in the dark with a flashlight. Only later, when the lights go on, can he see who has been sitting near him. He felt as one does during such an interlude, and this accounted for his thoughts and surprise at what he saw this evening. Who was with him? Where was Mina? Where was Itzhak? Where was his wife Ruth?

Through some open doors he caught sight of Mina. For some reason it seemed to·him that she, strange and confused as she was, could suggest to him what to do this summer. For something had to be done, but he didn't yet know what it was.

Most of the evening Mina had avoided him. "I must wait on the guests. Close the window. Joel, I'll see you on the large balcony. I'll see you by the pillars. I'll see you. I'll see you."

He put down his glass and opened a door. This was the

room of the Romans. Why Romans? Because all those in this room were men who looked like Romans, like Antony and Caracalla, the stern soldier, and others. And though they were now all drunk, their faces appeared earnest and their mood was grim like his own. These were his friends, from school, from the war, from the underground, or from the university. The witnesses of his life.

Again Joel caught sight of Mina. This time she stood in one of the corridors before a large mirror with a copper snake coiled about it. She stood there calmly, holding her shoes in her hands. She addressed him without turning away from her reflection: "It's necessary to open a door and a window—some prophet Elijah will come in—he must come and redeem us." Then she turned about and gave Joel her small shoes to hold while she combed her reddish hair to one side, so that her face looked as if threatened by a storm. Then she tucked the comb under the belt of her skirt and looked at Joel.

"You must fall in love, Joel. Don't look at me like that. Not with me. I know not with me. I know that already. But you must fall in love. Get involved completely, so that you forget your last archeological excavation, and the entire university. Don't answer me. You asked my advice. That's why you came here." This she said and went away, leaving him standing before the snake-framed mirror holding her shoes.

He considered Mina's words. He understood why she brought to her house all sorts of interesting people: Imron, the poet; and Meinzer, the painter; and Mr. Cohen, the American musicologist. And also him, Joel, the archeologist, she tried to encourage as a visitor. Now he understood why: to fill the void, to change one's life, to change oneself, to make a departure. All these slogans did not fit either his age or his status. But though Mina had said what she did because she was drunk, and because for a woman like her everything could be solved by a great love affair, he discovered that she expressed what was in his own heart—fall in love. But he loved his wife Ruth, who bore the name of little Ruth from his childhood days. And this was no accident. His life was organized and planned to the deepest level of consciousness. His life was marked out like the layers in an excavation of an ancient mound.

"Let's go to the roof! To the roof!" a group of revelers shouted as they dashed by Joel.

Two of them carried a plaster head of a stern-faced Beethoven, which they had found among the junk in the basement. Joel joined them in order to rid himself of his thoughts. The flat roof was spacious and for the occasion was adorned with colored lights that swayed sleepily in the breeze and spread a dreamy mysterious light.

Outcries were already heard from the roof, where mattresses and pillows lay scattered about amid low sofas and old bedsteads that had been brought up from the basement. In the center sat Morris, a black-eyed Jew from England, plucking at a guitar and singing songs of a faraway land: of an Irish girl who sold apples, or a Scottish king who murdered his wife, or of Negroes picking cotton or building a railroad. The girls and the women listened entranced. It was his big evening; everybody listened to him. He was escaping the loneliness that had driven him to come to Israel. "More! More!" pleaded the girls lying on their sides, the curve of their hips arching out from their bodies.

But when the loud revelers bearing the head of Beethoven reached the roof, the shouting drowned out the singing. Somebody called out, "What a wonderful Jerusalem roof! Let's play David and Bathsheba!" They put down the plaster head on a low table with crooked legs amid bottles and flasks and glasses. Joel put down Mina's shoes near the statue. The lights swayed sleepily. The breeze blew a large sheet of paper and plastered it against the railing.

He stood at the edge of the roof and his entire life was within him—all his memories, his childhood, his encounters, his conflicts, little Ruth and his wife Ruth, who during the war used to wait for him at the wadi in the Negev when he returned from night patrols. Joel always carried his entire life within himself like a circus. Acrobats and trainers, dancers and clowns and wild beasts. From time to time the circus comes to rest and everyone performs his specialty, his jumps or his clowning, his daredevil stunts or his dance. Then comes the time to move again and the whole circus packs up and moves on.

2

I had a dream. I dreamed that I was in Weinburg, my native town. Church bells tolled. I got up from where I was sitting, and I was big and grown up—not a child. I was overcome with a strange urge to buy new shoes. As I walked out of the house, my wife Ruth called out that the kitchen sink was stopped up. I paid no attention to her and walked into the street, which was festively lit with colored lights for the Christmas season. I had never bought shoes by myself. When I was a child, my mother went with me and later Ruth did. (I buy shoes impulsively and later they always turn out to be too big.) Near my house little girls played but, though in Weinburg, it was somehow my Jerusalem house. The house rested on three pillars, like a man resting his chin on his hands and thinking.

Little Ruth also played there. I told her to stop it, for we

were grown and she had been burned in the terrible crematorium. But she persisted and skipped after me with childish
jumps until we came to the illuminated street, which was
again in Weinburg.

We went into a shoe store. I told her: "You'd better go;
otherwise we will quarrel about every shoe I turn down."
Mother joined us and gave us sour candy. Sour candy is very
good when you are thirsty on a hike, she always says. I tried
on shoe after shoe, and little Ruth sat facing me, her face as
grave as an angel's. Her father, Dr. Manheim, the local
rabbi, stood on a ladder in his black robe and wrapped in
his prayer shawl that had a heavy brocaded silver crown
woven into it. He stood on the ladder as if he were about to
deliver a sermon in the synagogue. I paced back and forth
on the carpet to try out the shoes. Ruth suddenly said, "You
always look for comfort; the shoes shouldn't pinch. You even
married a wife named Ruth so you should be comfortable
and easy." In the end I was left with sandals on my feet.

I awoke with a sharp pain of longing within me. I suddenly wanted to be a child again in Weinburg, where I was
born.

3

Mina came up to the empty roof looking for her shoes.
David and Bathsheba games had scattered the people to
little rooms and hallways and closets. Mina stepped into her
shoes without touching them with her hands. Then she
asked, "Well, Joel? Have you found what you were looking
for?"

Instead of answering her, he told her of the dream he had some days before the party, and of his longing for the town of Weinburg, in southern Germany, where he wanted to be with his little dead Ruth.

"So you're lucky. Now you have a program for the summer," she said. "Return to childhood. Get involved with things that don't exist any more."

"But you suggested that I stay in Jerusalem and get involved in a love affair. Have you forgotten already?"

"I have not forgotten. You will do both."

"And what should I do first?"

"You can do both at the same time."

"You are drunk or mad."

"Both drunk and mad. So you will go yet stay. Then you will decide which is better and drop all the rest."

"You are imagining things."

"I'll arrange it for you. I am a specialist."

"You are a magician and a witch. In the Middle Ages they would have burned you."

"And now in the twentieth century I am burning all the time."

"You are mad."

"Like you, Joel."

She left and he remained alone. The breeze also died down and left him alone. In the dark he saw the illuminated face of a clock in one of the towers of the Old City. He sensed Jerusalem all around him, the Mount of Olives, Mount Scopus, the hills in the west, all waiting to see what would happen to him after this night.

Two came up to the roof, a pretty girl named Einat and Joel's friend Yosel, whom they called Yosel the Greek because he lived in an attic in the Greek quarter and because the beard that rimmed his face and his heavy-lidded big eyes made him look like one of the company of Ulysses. The two sat down on a mattress and Einat asked Yosel if he had also been a sailor. "Who has not been at sea?" he said. Einat then asked him about the mermaid tattooed on his arm. Where, in what port, was it done? Yosel rolled his eyes and caressed his beard. Yosel is Joel's best friend. He plays the violin in the Jerusalem orchestra and blows a big shining tuba in the police band. Only Joel, who was Yosel's commander during the war, knows the secret of the tattoo on his arm. The mermaid often filled Yosel's night with terror, for the scales and the tail of the mermaid covered five tattooed numbers. The numbers were not concealed but had been skillfully worked into the mermaid design. Why had Yosel covered up the number? In order to forget the past. Why hadn't he concealed it completely? In order to remember the past. Einat, who did not know about the number, insisted that he must have been a sailor, until he gave in to her and admitted that he was captain of a vessel with a strange crew. What kind of crew? Birds and mice. Einat indeed recalled having read in some paper about an American ship whose owners went bankrupt. Its crew abandoned it, and now it was anchored outside the port of Haifa, where it rocked on the swell and rubbed itself against the breakwater like a mangy dog. Thousands of birds and innumerable mice inhabit it.

"And do the birds and mice obey you?"

"I eat those that don't."

"And what do you do on the ship all day?"

"I think of you."

"And the mice?"

"They squeak."

"Take me there, please do."

"What is your name?"

"Guess."

"I bet you have one of those fancy new names. Shimrat?

Anat? Semodar? Osnath? That's what you girls call yourselves now. Where are all the girls named Leah or Rachel or
Ruth or Rebecca?"

"They remained in the Diaspora. Or they are over there,
on the Mount of Olives. My name is Einat."

And now a number of couples returned to the roof and put
on a record and began to dance. Einat was most in demand.
Her hair was cut short and her eyes were bright. Einat, the
country girl, danced with everyone, with the mustached
pilot and with the entertainment program director of the
radio station. The director wore horn-rimmed glasses and
was a whiz at improvising programs. Where hadn't he been
with his recording apparatus? He had broadcast the words
of a dying tramp, of a prisoner in his cell, a discordant music
lesson in a school for problem boys, the poet Imron improvising while drunk. He now invited Einat to the broadcast-
ing of such a program—a recording of the halting conversation between a young man and woman. Einat is conquering
Jerusalem. She was born among the orange groves of Sharon
and ran barefoot in the sand. Now, after being an officer in
the women's corps in the army, she has come to Jerusalem.
Her breasts are firm; her buttocks are round and firm. Tourists see her and exclaim, "She doesn't look Jewish at all."
They are proud of her and she is proud of herself.

Joel still stands near the railing apart from the dancers.
Every railing is like a railing on the deck of a ship. A man
who thinks thus to himself is like a traveler, even when he
stands still. Where is Ruth now? He was confused by
thoughts of little Ruth from his childhood and of his wife
Ruth, who came from a kibbutz in the Jordan Valley and
whose father was his commander in some of the Negev battles.

A bell tolled weakly from the clock tower in the Old City.
It summoned some to midnight prayer, and others to check

their watches, or to look at the face of a woman. Everybody looks. It is necessary to raise one's head.

Joel left the roof and walked down the fire escape that hugged the wall outside. He opened a squeaking iron door and went into a narrow corridor. Einat came toward him from a niche that held a little Buddha. "Why are you standing there like Balaam's ass?" she said, and poked him in the ribs. They went back up the stairs to the roof, which was now abandoned, and they danced to the rhythm of the swaying colored lights. She questioned him about Yosel, whom she liked despite the fact that he was from Poland. She was fed up with the talk about the Jews of Europe—all this literature about the *heder* and synagogue and Feierberg and Mendele that she had been made to study as a child. She was almost an anti-Semite, she said, and had her reasons, for she was employed afternoons in an office of former concentration-camp inmates. "They come to the office with the expressions of tortured martyrs, and pull out all kinds of medical certificates on bits of yellowing smelly paper. And suddenly all of them turn out to have been partisans; every one of them was blowing up German trains. I know one mustn't talk this way, but all the same there are times when I hate them. And yesterday one came and pulled up his pants leg to show some ugly scars. Exhibitionism." All this she said to Joel not knowing that Yosel, whom she began to love this evening, had been in a concentration camp and that the mermaid covered the tattooed number on his arm. Joel was silent.

"You are angry?"

"No. No. Get it all out of your system. It makes you look more beautiful. You'll be mad, you'll complain. Then you'll get to know Yosel."

"Take me to the excavation in the Negev sometime."

"Maybe."

Yosel appeared in the doorway and Einat went to him.

4

For a long time I was troubled by my dream. Why did I dream about buying shoes when ordinarily I am not fussy and not in the least interested in my clothes? As I thought about it, I encountered Mr. Mendelson, a margarine salesman who, like my parents, came from Weinburg. As a rule, I maintain no contact with the people from Weinburg, who are scattered all over the country. Mr. Mendelson gave me some information: he had heard that Rabbi Dr. Manheim had decided to settle in Jerusalem and to spend his old age here.

I tried to forget but did not know clearly what it was I was trying to forget. Perhaps I should tell my wife Ruth about my longing for my childhood and that I wanted to go to Weinburg alone for a few days. But how should I explain it to her? My mother had already received reparations from Germany. What would I do there? Perhaps I'll avenge little Ruth, Manheim's daughter, whom the people of Weinburg sent to the crematorium.

5

Joel finally decided to go to the Roman room to join his friends. He passed through a corridor and some plaster fell on his head. Itzhak and Mina's house was falling apart. He passed through the hall with the two pillars and saw a couple holding hands as their arms embraced one of the columns. He opened the door to Itzhak's room where the Romans were. They were deep in argument and paid no attention to him as he entered. Only Mr. Cohen, the sad American musicologist who always pretends to be gay, waved his hand in greeting and called out, "Hi!" Some plaster fell into Mr. Cohen's pipe. The house was coming apart. In the center of the room the other Romans sat around Itzhak, who looked like a Roman tyrant, his lean face deeply indented by vertical creases. Mr. Cohen explained to Joel that they were selling the house, every stick of furniture in it, and finally they would also sell Mina. "Itzhak is liquidating everything tonight."

Meinzer, the dwarfish painter, whose head was too big, and who kept on painting Jerusalem's alleys even after they were torn down and rebuilt as broad modern avenues, looked like a Roman landowner from the period of the decline of the Empire. Yoske was there, too. He also was an instructor in archeology. His nose was straight, his forehead high, his hair curly. Dr. Golgolos was appraising the house. His chin jutted out energetically and his deep blue eyes penetrated whoever looked into them. The drunken argument about the sale of the household goods was conducted with terrible earnestness. Who would buy the Beethoven head? And who the colored lights and the wine?

"And now Mina's white shoes! And now her toilet articles!" Itzhak was drunk. His head towered above the others. He noticed Joel and nodded to him from the clouds of smoke. Then he bent down, opened a drawer, and took out a large envelope from which he pulled out an X-ray picture. All crowded about him to look at the bones shining brightly from the dull flesh. From behind their heads streamed the light from a lampshade in the style of the late nineteenth century, held by a bronze angel. Zeiger's bald head glistened. Drops of sweat shone on Itzhak's forehead. The smile froze on the excessively large face of Meinzer. Itzhak rose and paced back and forth. The other Romans followed him with their eyes. Itzhak limps when he walks, but nobody knows the cause of his limping. Some say that he once wrestled with an angel at dawn and ever since then he had a limp. Mina knows nothing about it. All evening she did not go into the room of the drunken Romans. They are too grown up and hard. To counterbalance them, she filled the house with young artists and college students and poets and musicians and girls with bulging hips in tight skirts.

Itzhak raised the X-ray picture to the angel-held lamp.

"Sell it!" they all shouted. "Just a moment! One moment!" Joel cried, for he saw that Itzhak was crying inside.

Joel leaped to rescue his friend, but having cried out "Just a moment!" he had to say something more in order to put an end to the auction, and he did not know what to say. In the silence, he heard the voice of his teacher Professor Oren, one of the most prominent archeologists, calling to him: "Joel, come here!" Joel approached the ancient sofa on which the professor lay. He had not noticed him before. He looked like an old Roman emperor, though his face was lean and tanned from his recent trip of exploration in the desert caves. Oren waved his hat, his old hat from which he never parts. It is faded and crushed beyond repair.

Joel sat down on the edge of the sofa. Behind them the auction resumed. Above the group of heads, Mr. Cohen's pink babyish head popped up from time to time, his mouth open and shouting, "Hi!" "Hi!"

A commotion was heard at the door. A delegation from the young artists came in pale-faced announcing strange rumors; a demon had been found in the house; a bunch of beggars were knocking on the outside door insisting that a wedding was taking place inside and demanding to be admitted; there was a terrible quarrel in the hall of the pillars on account of Einat, who was cursing the Jews of the Diaspora.

Itzhak put away the X rays and opened an ancient Persian cabinet in which bottles sparkled in various colors.

For a long time Joel had avoided talking to Professor Oren, except on professional matters, because of his constant complaints that he was being persecuted and betrayed. Everybody was plotting against him, even his loyal student Joel, who had risen to become an instructor.

"You are concealing something from me," he now complained.

"I am concealing something from myself." '

"You will discover it, Joel, you'll discover it."

"Of course."

"You are now at a crossroads."

"There are other names for it: at an intersection, on the eve of a great decision, in crisis, before a great turning."

Then both drank. Yoske announced: "Now they are selling Mina." Oren said, "Itzhak acquired her only a short time ago."

Joel went up to the window. The hills of Jerusalem were relaxing and resting like tired dancers at the end of their performance. The lustful aroma of the eucalyptus assailed him again. When Joel thought of Mina, he became very tense, as if great things were about to happen in his life because of her mad advice.

He had first met Mina on a winter day when Itzhak had brought her to the country from the wide outside world. That day it had snowed in Jerusalem. She had sat curled up like a kitten on a sofa near the window examining her nails. The snow had melted the very next day, but it continued falling inside Joel. A crazy snow, Mina had said. All the snows of his childhood in Weinburg were within him, mad and ceaselessly insistent.

Now they were selling Mina in a drunken auction, together with all the other effects of this big old house.

"The house isn't worth a cent."

"It's too big."

"It's too close to the border."

"One can shoot into it from across the border."

Reuben-Rudolf, the banker, put on his tan pigskin gloves and announced, "I am buying the pillars."

They protested that if he were to buy the pillars and take them the house would collapse.

The door opened and Klein, the agile little newspaperman, slithered in. He looked over those present, noticed Joel, and called him. "Good that you are here. The only sober one among the drunks. I've been looking for you. That is, I've been looking for someone sober." Then he asked Joel to take power of attorney over his apartment in Talbieh. Klein was going abroad. His wife had already left and he would go in a couple of days. Where? Out to the big world. He felt restless. A blood bath was about to sweep the world—this was his favorite expression. Joel would have no trouble; he would only have to look in occasionally to make sure that the subtenant was taking good care of the apartment and the furniture. The rent had all been arranged for in advance. Klein only wanted the arrangement so that he could feel reassured, so that he could travel about in the world and enjoy the atmosphere of an impending blood bath with the presence of mind of a peaceful observer. No trouble at all for Joel. And he would have asked someone else, one of his closer acquaintances, but they were all drunk that evening and only Joel was sober.

Joel agreed, though ever since they had been students together their contacts had been infrequent. "And do you know why all the Romans are drunk?" Klein resumed after a brief break in the flow of his talk. "They are drunk, loaded, because Itzhak is drunk, and Itzhak is drunk because his Mina is going away this evening. Every so often she goes away to one of her faraway lands, and the evening before she leaves Itzhak gets drunk, and they all get drunk with him." Then Klein led Joel to one of the small rooms on the second story. Suitcases of different sizes stood in the room. Three were packed and stood upright with tags bearing the names of remote cities. The traveling room. Here was the source of the unhappiness in this big old house.

Jerusalem crossed the line at midnight in reverent silence. Jerusalem always floats in time, like a ship, from morning to noon and on through the nights, and there is no end to its motion. Mr. Cohen passed by the door carrying a tray of candy. He, too, is a sailor without knowing it. Everybody is a sailor in Jerusalem without knowing it, sailors or passengers, mechanics or captains, everyone according to the pattern of his life and character. And Joel knew at this moment that whether he remained in the city this summer or went to Weinburg to find burned little Ruth he would forever be on the move, forever a sailor.

Mina passed by him later that night. She was barefoot and looked for her shoes. "I am all barefoot, not only my feet." "Poor barefoot girl. Tomorrow you are going away." "You, too, are going away; and you, too, will remain behind."

The clock on the tower in the Old City showed two. From far away was heard the siren of a police car or a fire engine. True alarms and false alarms have deeply grooved the face of Jerusalem. Some of the Romans now sat in the garden and sang war songs and Hasidic songs. All the windows of the house were still lit, though most of the guests had already gone. Joel wished to go to the kitchen but found himself in Itzhak's office. Here everything was white and shining and orderly and severe, like Itzhak's face. The room seemed not to belong to this house. Surgical instruments glistened in a cabinet that was all glass and efficiency. Joel sat down. What is he expecting now, at the end of the fourth decade of his life? Others his age are already fortifying their lives. Others have long ago removed the scaffolding, convinced that the structure is solid and permanent. But tonight he is beginning to destroy all he has built and to scatter all he has gathered. A thin odor of medicine hangs in the room. His friend Itzhak's instruments are so shiny and precise, the various pliers and scalpels and all the rest which cut and tie and isolate—they are all so exact and decisive and final.

Mina suddenly appeared near her husband's large writing table. She told him that she had met an old friend, a certain Major Patterson, a New Zealander on the staff of the U.N., who came in his white jeep. She also said that Imron read her some wonderful new poems. In the evening she listens to poems, and at night she unravels them into feelings and sensations, loves and despairs. The next day the poets come and make new poems out of the parts she has disassembled, and it seems to them that these are new and original poems.

"Don't look at me like that!" she exclaimed.

"Like what?"

"Like an archeologist, as if I were some kind of jar or ancient idol made of brown clay."

Her eyes became hard and shining and precise, like one of her husband's surgical instruments. She passed her fingers over the glass of the cabinet, then bent her head down to examine her nails. Joel suddenly wished that everything was as simple as it had been in the past, when he was with Ruth in the Negev, when she left her parents' kibbutz to come with him. Mina abruptly raised her head as if her spirit had become alerted, like a snake that hears the sound of a flute.

"You must understand me," she said quickly, as all people say who are unhappy. "Why don't you go home?"

"There are parts of the house I don't know yet."

"An alibi. You don't want to go away."

"And you are leaving?"

"Yes. In an hour Itzhak will take me to the airport. The suitcases are packed. Do you know that there is a sea in Jerusalem?"

He smiled uncomprehendingly and she took him by the hand and led him to the yard where three cypresses stood in a corner of the garden. There they stopped. A breeze rustled in the trees. "Do you hear?" she said. "The sound of Jerusalem's sea. Listen."

"Yes, yes," he whispered and caressed her hand. And suddenly, in the beginning of the terrible summer, there was a smell of rain in the air.

"Come, Mina, let's go back to the house. You have to leave soon." But Mina answered, "I don't want to go back. I am afraid. Even the Yemenite maid scares me. And Meinzer the painter and Mr. Cohen and all the others frighten me because they know that something is falling apart. They buy everything."

They returned to Itzhak's office. Mina opened a drawer and took out a large sheet of paper and began writing on it. Joel sat down on the sofa.

Einat joined them and collapsed wearily in a chair. Yosel, following her, rested his head on her knees. Einat was beautiful, as when she was a schoolgirl and danced at the first-fruit festivals. At that time she used to wear a long gown and her schoolmates would bring baskets of apples and squash and onions and tomatoes and oranges. They would also bring doves and a lamb, and they would pile all these things about Einat on the stage as she stood happy and beautiful in the midst of the bounty.

Later, Mina stood in the small room and caressed the packed suitcases. A gaudy Mexican hat fell down from a shelf, a reminder of the past Purim. Solitary voices came from all over the house: "Let's go! Home. Somebody do me a favor! A last favor! I am dying! Where is the bathroom? Where's my coat? My scarf? Where are we?"

Rapid steps to the outside doors. Some returning because Itzhak had already locked some of the doors. From a remote room came the sound of a typewriter. Mina stood before the mirror that was gripped by a snake and her lips mumbled something.

Joel emptied his pockets of the accumulation of the evening: addresses of people written down on cigarette packages, other addresses on napkins written in pen and pencil and lipstick. A telephone number. "Wednesday between three and four, fourth entrance." All these he threw away. "Where is Mina?" And why shouldn't he fall in love with her this summer? But two halves like us don't make a whole, he decided.

Mina came down the stairs wearing a light traveling coat and Itzhak followed her carrying the suitcases. A key dangled on a string around her neck. What will she open? What will she lock? Where was she going?

Itzhak put the suitcases in the trunk. Mina stood near Joel.

"Do you think Itzhak will sell the house while I am away?"

"Why should you care? You are not happy in this house."

"The garden is so neglected. In the fall we will fix everything. I am afraid to go and I am afraid to remain."

"Yet you advise me both to go and to stay behind."

"You are a hero."

Itzhak said, "Come, Joel, come with us; you won't sleep tonight anyway." And Joel readily agreed. He loved airports at night: the passengers, the people who came to see them off, the loudspeaker making its announcements that penetrate even to the washrooms.

They started out and the clock on the tower in the Old City showed quarter to four. Itzhak drove and asked Joel and Mina to sit in the back. Joel was surprised but said nothing. (For Yours is the kingdom.) To go, to part, to sever oneself slowly from all that was. They left the city and Itzhak drove faster on the winding road. Mina was silent. Joel became aware that they had left the main highway and had taken a side road that climbed steeply into the hills. Olive groves passed by them. A jackal ran by. He cried out to Itzhak, "You're on the wrong road! You're drunk!" Itzhak turned his face toward him and it was tormented. Blood trickled from the corner of his mouth. Earlier, Einat had thrown an ashtray at him when he tried to calm her during a quarrel about the survivors of the holocaust. Joel did not understand where Itzhak was driving, but he realized that his friend was not drunk. The road kept climbing.

A gate appeared before them suddenly, and the car passed through a neglected orchard and pulled up before an old Arab house. The windows had iron gratings. An iron door opened and a woman in a nurse's uniform and two powerful men in white took the suitcases and escorted Mina inside without a word. The heavy door closed behind her. Itzhak turned the car around. For a moment he stopped and wiped the blood from his mouth with a handkerchief. Then the two friends returned to Jerusalem. The sun rose before them in the east.

6

I went down the street at noon and met my mother coming up. Why was she out at this time? It was best she should stay indoors when the sun was hot. The doctor had advised her to rest after lunch. She asked me what I was doing outside, and I asked her the same so that I shouldn't have to answer her question.

We stood at the edge of the sidewalk and I looked at her wrinkled, flushed face. Women walked by on the way from the food store. On the sidewalk lay scorched pieces of board and tin cans covered with soot. The smell of a doused fire hung in the air. The night before, there was a fire in the store. Every so often there is a fire in the store. A big police dog barked sharply.

Only now my mother answered me: "I can't rest." Then she added in a whisper, "This mad construction. It's reached our neighborhood, too." Just then there was a shout "Blast! Blast!" and a man waved a red flag in our direction. "They'll be blasting down there." Window shutters were closed and the street waited for the sound of the explosion.

I pulled my mother around the corner and we stood near a wall and cast short shadows. The man with the red flag stood farther down the slope. I asked him how late they worked, and he said till four. After four my mother will be able to rest from the mad construction that has seized upon the city. People who have lived peacefully in their homes for years are taken with a fever to find luxury apartments. "On this location a house will go up. Apartments for rent. Four rooms. Three and a half. Apply to . . ." Everybody believes they'll have it better. But at night the store goes up in flames. And the top of the hill has been sliced off as one cuts off the top of a soft-boiled egg.

Then the air compressors went into action and the man holding the compressor trembled, and his shoulders shook like the shoulders of a man weeping disconsolately. Another man was now holding the red flag. It had been cut from the flag of a political party after a demonstration. The offspring of the revolutionary flag now warned people against the explosion.

"Why are you so mean to Ruth?" my mother asked suddenly.

I did not know what to answer, and at first I wasn't sure whether she meant my wife Ruth or little Ruth who was burned in a crematorium.

"Why aren't you kind to Ruth? Why don't you take her with you?"

"Where to?"

"To your excavations, for instance. You won't change; you can't."

My mother is always afraid I will change. She never got used to the idea that I was always changing as I grew up, as I went to war, as my adult teeth grew in, as I ran around for purposes both good and evil. It seems that she also didn't know that despite all this I didn't really change at all. Now she continued complaining about the building boom. Her home, too, had been affected. The outside wall of the kitchen and laundry room which held water pipes and smoke vents had always faced on a court, and now the building on the other side of the court had been torn down and the wall was bared to the sun like a grub under a stone that had been rolled away.

"You know who arrived?" my mother asked. "Dr. Manheim."

"So soon? Wasn't he supposed to come a month from now?"

"He came ahead of time. He's afraid he will die."

"Where is he?"

"In Talpioth, in the Pension Schluss."

"Maybe I'll visit him later."

"Don't think that Ruth will tolerate all this indefinitely. She won't sit around crying. One day she will pick up and go back to the Jordan Valley."

"Anyhow she hates Jerusalem and its stones and its quarries."

"And what will you do?"

"Ruth will be all right."

I took my mother away from the mad construction, and we sat in a café among the buzzing of the customers. I ordered cocoa for her and coffee for me. There was a time when she used to order cocoa for me and coffee for herself. Now my heart is strong but hers has weakened. She took out some rolls from a paper wrapper that rustled. When I was a child, I used to feel embarrassed whenever she brought rolls or sandwiches to a restaurant. "Mother, don't. People are watching us, the waiter and that woman across." Now I took the roll she had baked and I ate it. My dentist looked in through the window and smiled. His office is right over the café. He has a chart of my teeth in his desk. There are documents about me all over Jerusalem, all over the world. My mother saves my report card from the first grade. Everyone who knows me opens a file on me, a real file or one in his heart. Photos and documents. Now that I am about to take a trip, there are additional documents about me in a number of offices and consulates. But even if they should all combine their files about me, they couldn't reconstruct me. The result would be a caricature, a vague giant, a slow-moving whale, a mob. For my footsteps are scattered throughout the world. The best bloodhounds couldn't track me. And now Rabbi

Dr. Manheim came here to bid farewell to the world. He had already made many preliminary farewells. In the end, all of these add up to the one final farewell that has but one taste and one ache.

With my mother I had reached the final endless desert of speech. Everything had already been said and asked and answered. And anything that might still be said will not be understood either by her or by me.

Zeiger, the photographer, and his assistant stood outside the photo shop. My mother noticed that I was looking at them.

"What are you looking at?"

"Mr. Zeiger the photographer."

"What is he doing?"

"He is opening the showcase and taking out Oren's picture."

"Professor Oren?"

"Yes."

"You don't get along with him any more?"

I didn't answer. My mother senses everything. Zeiger closed his showcase, which now had an empty, naked space. He is shrewd and always knows whose picture to display. Some of the photos look at you straight, like the Japanese woman whose picture was displayed for a month. Then Professor Thema died, and Zeiger displayed a picture of him bent over his books. Two weeks later, the dead professor gave up his place to a little girl with round eyes. After her, Zeiger hung the portrait of Professor Oren, in honor of his sensational discoveries at the site of an ancient port. Whose picture will be hung now? Who died? Who accomplished something?

The construction workers were going home. The building boom would stop for a few hours. My mother, too, decided to return home. I asked her a second time to come with me to Dr. Manheim. "The way I took you to school the first time?" She took a few paces, then turned back. "Be good to Ruth," she said. "It's enough that you are leaving her here while you are away." It occurred to me that I never saw my mother's profile, only her large round face. Now, too, I saw only her round, perspiring, flushed face, and then her retreating back.

I took a bus. I remembered Dr. Manheim dressed in a black robe, square hat on his head, a white tie on his stiffly starched collar. The bus passed by the railroad station. The sign on the station said, "JERUSALEM," as if people didn't know it anyway, as if it could be otherwise.

But I am already apart from the others and prepared for my journey to Weinburg, and my trip begins with Dr. Manheim. I passed by the building of the government printer who prints laws and rules that also govern my life. Soon it will be evening and the grass will remain dry, and night will bring no relief. I passed by the power station, then the wall of the monastery whose gate is always locked, and beyond is no man's land. I got off the bus well before the Pension Schluss. Mr. Rosenbaum, who is also a native of Weinburg, came toward me. "I heard you are going there." He does not want to go back; he only asks those who do to take care of all sorts of matters for him there. He gives them telephone numbers and addresses and all kinds of carefully filled-out forms. He is used to people forgetting the errands with which he entrusted them, or losing the numbers and the forms. He never got married because of the many things that he still has to settle in Weinburg. For instance, what happened to his parents, whose fate is unknown, and to his house and the plot on which it stood, and the reparations he is entitled to? He sells sewing supplies to convents. He is tranquil, and they are tranquil. He is a bachelor and so are they. His eyes are like those of a gentle dog during a time that has the face of a raging mad dog. Time allots faces to all: to the good according to their goodness and to the evil according to their evil. This could have been a quote from one of Dr. Manheim's speeches.

I took another bus and got off at Talpioth, exactly in front of the pension. Once I had friends in Talpioth, but no more. During the war, soldiers entered their homes to observe the enemy. Some fired, others were fired upon, and the trees continued to grow and to crack the concrete paths in the gardens with their roots. From a distance one sees no houses in Talpioth, because of the trees. The ground is sinking. The floors sink and cause cracks to appear in the walls and ceilings, and loosen tiles which clink when one steps on them. That is why my friends moved out. A sinking earth is a more stubborn enemy than any other.

The pension, strictly orthodox, stands near a military cemetery. Here are buried Indian soldiers of Allenby's army who fell during World War I. There are some graying stone benches, and rocks and tall pine trees and Jerusalem in front. There is a big monument with an inscription in English and Hindustani. I saw neither child playing nor couple courting. Only the pines rustled but said nothing. It is said that on moonlit nights everything is understandable.

The door of the pension opened slowly and automatically, and I found myself in a dim corridor. A woman whose head was wrapped in a turban stuck her head out through an opening that wasn't quite either a window or a picture frame. "Mrs. Schluss?" "Yes, what can I do for you?" ("Schluss" means "the end." In that case, Hello, Mrs. End. What will your end be? How does one end differ from any other?) "I want to see Dr. Manheim." The woman came out into the corridor and wiped her big red hands on her apron. "I think he is sleeping. Wait." Then she looked quickly at my uncovered head. "All our patients are napping." Still, she knocked on a door. She cautiously opened the wicket and signaled to me to wait. Then she motioned to me to come closer and put a finger on her lips: "He is praying. He is sitting down. He mustn't stand up even for the eighteen benedictions. You can see him without going in."

I saw only darkness, and after the darkness a dim twilight, and after the twilight the weak flash of the reflection from his glasses. The old man sat in a well-upholstered chair near the window. He did not pray loudly; even his lips barely moved. Mrs. Schluss handed me a black skullcap. "There is a Torah here," she whispered. I saw Dr. Manheim move his head a few times, a symbolic motion that was intended to take the place of the few steps backward at this point in the prayer. Then, as if continuing his prayer, he asked, "Who are you, my son?" (Genesis 27), and then, "Sit down, my son" (there is no such phrase in the Bible, and I wasn't his son, but little Ruth who died was his daughter and I no longer had a father). "I have grown old," he went on without turning his head toward me. "I can't turn my head; because of a chill, I can't turn my neck. My neck is stiff. I have become stiff-necked [Deuteronomy and elsewhere]." I told him that a grove of trees in memory of Indian soldiers was before his window. He coughed suddenly and asked, "Who are you? Yes, you came to the old shlemiel Manheim. My son, I owe you something." I did not know what he meant. I looked at him carefully and saw his gray eyes which were greatly magnified by his powerful glasses. He removed his glasses and wiped them. "I owe you the speech I had prepared for your Bar Mitzvah. You were no longer in Weinburg, and the page is lost, but I remember the speech."

Dr. Manheim used to deliver an oration to each Bar Mitzvah boy who faced him at the east wall of the synagogue. The congregation would be seated; he would stand on an elevation and the boy faced him from below and listened to words he did not understand.

I bowed my head as I recalled other boys used to do on
these occasions. But now he sat lower than I, and he began
to recite in precise German: "This day you stand before this
holy congregation. Generations of your forebears are proud
of you this day. . . ."

Then came remarks about the portion of the Torah for the
week. As luck would have it, the portion for the week of my
Bar Mitzvah dealt with impurities of the body, and Dr.
Manheim delivered himself of sentiments on the subject of
purity and impurity of body and soul and the symbolism
involved.

Mrs. Schluss appeared in the doorway bearing a tray.
When Dr. Manheim concluded his oration, she said "Amen"
and handed us glasses of tea. "In honor of the Bar Mitzvah,"
she said, smiling, "though belated by many years." The
synagogue in Weinburg no longer exists; I have grown up
and Dr. Manheim is relieved of the duty of remembering.
Away with speeches, away with words, away with the heavy
clapper of language, away with the belated sermon, away
with it, out of the window, to the rustling of the trees, to the
tombstones of the Indian soldiers who died in a strange land.
Lucky Dr. Manheim! He can now forget. He can release the
beasts of memory from their cage. We were silent and permitted the sun to set in the west. We did not mention Ruth.
Then he said, "I heard that you are an archeologist. It is a
good deed to dig in the land of the Bible and to uncover
proof for the Holy Scriptures." I told him a little about my
diggings. He smiled and said, "You don't have to shout. I can
hear very well; only my eyes are dim." I opened the window.
A white U.N. jeep stood outside. Mrs. Schluss said, "Across
the street lives a Swedish officer from the U.N. He came
from the north." "From the north," Dr. Manheim repeated
(Jeremiah 1).

I noticed that the thorns outside grew high and reached to the window sill. After the thorn plants die, the thorns harden; they cause all their hurt after they die. They avenge the thirst from which they suffered. Mrs. Schluss nodded and I rose. Dr. Manheim said, "I heard that you are going there, to Weinburg. Deal graciously with me [Genesis 43] and look for my collected sermons. They were hidden in a trunk. When they came to arrest me, I locked them up. Then they looted the house, and later the house itself was destroyed by an American bomb. Maybe my friend the Bishop saved them. We used to play chess together. And now go, my son, go your way [Genesis 12]." With this he finished talking. Again he sat as if frozen, as I found him when I came in, immersed in an endless inner prayer, like an eternal hemorrhage where one does not see the blood. Perhaps I should have talked with him about gay little Ruth. I suppress everything in silence: the summer, the stones of Jerusalem, my good wife Ruth, who came to me from the plantations of the Jordan. I felt that I was becoming so remote from everything that I could reach the very heart of my life, and there occurred to me the possibility of being apart and beyond everything.

Mrs. Schluss moved back into the twilight that pervaded the house as in a Rembrandt painting. From the dimness she said, "Be careful outside; you mustn't stumble—the tiles are not even." The ground is sinking. The sun is sinking. A final light illuminated Jerusalem like a strong sweet pain, like the last wail of a great lust. Walking down the cracked pavement, I was so overcome with the imminence of the future that I nearly fainted from its sweet hurt. I got off at the station near Zeiger's shop and noticed that my friend had already put up a new picture in the empty space. In the dying light, I saw the profile of a woman facing north (Jeremiah 1), her hair piled high on her head, her nose long and somewhat tilted; the one eye that showed in the picture was both penetrating and profoundly sad; her lips were full. Looking at the picture, I became convinced that I would indeed have to go away. Even this strange woman was telling me to go north and, like her, to turn my face to the wind, on the deck of a ship or in a railway station or at a big airport. But a second thought warned me to stay in Jerusalem.

7

Joel stood in the hospital corridor waiting for Itzhak, who came out after he had finished an operation and changed his clothes. Joel asked about Mina, and Itzhak told him that a few hours after they left her she no longer recognized him. The attack had begun almost at once, and it was just as well that they started out at dawn and drove so fast. No one aside from them knew about her illness. So far as all the rest were concerned, she had gone abroad as they were accustomed to seeing her go every few months. When the attacks become more frequent, it will be more difficult to conceal the truth. All her friends and acquaintances receive picture postcards from different countries. Itzhak has arranged it all in advance; he has contacts with doctors in many capitals. Mr. Cohen received a picture postcard of the Eiffel Tower, and Yosel received a letter on the stationery of a café in Saint-Germain-des-Prés. Only Joel knew the truth about her travels.

Later Joel went to Mamillah Street, where Einat lived. At

the end of this street a high wall faces no man's land and the Old City. Many children played in the street and life was turbulent and noisy. Where Joel excavates the layers of earth, it is peaceful. One generation covers another like a blanket. Each generation puts its predecessor to sleep. Thus it came about that Joel could come thousands of years later and drive in stakes and stretch ropes and determine ages. Generation sleeps upon generation, and the living generation is like foam upon the deep.

Einat lived in the basement of an old house. In that very basement, a British and a Turkish general signed the surrender of the Turkish Army that was routed in the hills of Jerusalem. Joel banged on the door with the iron knocker. "Right away," he heard from inside; then Einat appeared clutching her unbuttoned dressing gown to herself. "Hello, General," she said, smiling. "Did you come to sign your surrender?" But Joel had had enough of documents and agreements. They sat down near the surrender table. Einat's hair was uncombed. She brought coffee. "What did I say that crazy night? Nonsense. A lot of nonsense. I am getting to know Yosel. He is wonderful. Come, let's look out the window. From the back you can see the wall of the Old City. And there is the Tower of David. Why am I so excited? Soon I'll go to Yosel, to his other room, not the one in the Greek quarter. I play the piano there. That's the piano Mrs. Minkus lent him. She is mad at me. Do you see that little girl outside? That's Vicky. She is my favorite. I am trying to educate her. Her parents are irresponsibles. They live near no man's land."

Einat's outburst on the night of the party was like that of a student who had studied too much and too quickly. Now she is with Yosel, and sometimes accompanies him on the piano. She is learning; she is also learning to love, and this angers Mrs. Minkus. Yosel has already revealed to her the secret of the mermaid tattooed on his arm. Einat listens to him and swallows every word of what happened to him and his friends. At night she reads books about the holocaust in the room where the weary Turkish general surrendered.

8

I was in my room in a small hotel in beautiful Zurich. The flight had been pleasant. Aside from my dentist, who turned up unexpectedly, all the other passengers had been strangers. I opened the window and saw the light summer mist turn to a thin drizzle, like a veil. The chambermaid came in and said, "Bad, bad weather." But I thought, Good, good. After the dry brightness of summer in Jerusalem, I came to mist and rain. To grayness and mercy and moisture.

I walked by one of the university buildings; it was empty except for some people in gray smocks in a laboratory in the basement. A girl came walking down a broad stairway. It was warm and the thin rain did not stop. When she reached the sidewalk, she took off her shoes and sang as she walked barefoot.

This is my system. Whenever I come to a new place, I drop my things without arranging them and at once go out into the street. Whatever happens to me during this first walk is a sign and an omen for the future.

I came to a quiet street in the university quarter on the slope of a hill. Ancient chestnut trees were in glorious bloom. The rain did not stop and the day did not stop, for the afternoons in Europe seem never to end. The houses were nearly invisible among the trees. The street was named after some philosopher. I knew that someone had to be playing the piano. And when I became aware of this, I heard the playing. For me this was the wonderful and incomparable Europe: a fence, trees, a garden, a house, a drizzle of rain, playing the piano, and a man like me coming from afar, a wanderer, alone, deep in thought and full of memories, walking on a street named after a philosopher. When the music stopped, I walked up to Leonora Street. I said, "This is the street of my beloved Leonora." I said it as poets do, for poets speak of their beloved even when they don't have one.

Then I came to a street where most of the houses were inhabited by all kinds of soul healers. There was Dr. Charlotte Schtiz, the psychologist; and Dr. Buler, the neurologist; and Professor Bruner, the psychiatrist; and a variety of other titles, and all of them healed sick souls and lived among chestnut streets and were set in the midst of music and were concealed by heavy curtains. A woman's dress hung on a balcony. A man came running. A red roadster sped down the hill. I stopped and wept inwardly over the destruction of my life and the destruction of Jerusalem.

The rain fell harder and the streets emptied. Only a Jerusalemite like me enjoys staying in the rain and turning his face up to feel its softness. This was not a savage downpour such as we have at home. This was a warm rain like a caress, a velvety touch, a civilized rain at the end of the summer, without bloody self-laceration for sins committed.

I crossed the ancient bridge and walked to the square which had once been a fortress and is now a small public park surrounded by linden trees. It is called Lindenhof. There were no unoccupied benches, so I sat down near a couple of twilight sitters. The Swiss speech sounded like Yiddish.

Why didn't I go directly to Weinburg? I decided to come to Zurich first in order to become accustomed to German speech from the lips of people who did not persecute Jews. I now recalled the parting from my mother and from my wife Ruth, who will stay with her parents on the kibbutz during my absence, and I suddenly knew that if I return from Weinburg our life together will be good again. Until the very last moment, I could not decide whether to go or not. This confused many people and it also raised a kind of smoke screen behind which I now travel. I am sure there are people in Jerusalem who would swear that I am still there.

And for what purpose am I returning to Weinburg? It began with a dream and grew with a great longing for a lost childhood. Now all these feelings have merged into a passion to avenge what they had done to little Ruth. I heard of many horrors from Mr. Rosenbaum, the son of the Jewish butcher in Weinburg. Some hours before I left, I visited him in the institute where documents about the Nazis are preserved. He has a night-watchman job there. He also, of course, sells sewing supplies to nuns, and New Year's cards. He asked me to look into the matter of a lot he owns in Weinburg. He is involved in many things and he told me much about the troubles of the Jews of Weinburg.

Thus I sat in Lindenhof, the fortress of days gone by. Peaceful people sat on benches and on the wall. In Jerusalem we do it differently: public gardens are turned into fortresses. The bell on the Grossmünster Cathedral rang. I thought, as I usually do, I will stay here; I will not go back to Weinburg to close the door on my longings; I will not take vengeance; I will stay here until it gets dark.

9

The evening was well along and Joel was still alone. The evening was sifting the crowds in the street. Some went home, others gathered in groups of two and three, and then these, too, were sifted in the evening sieve until everyone was left by himself and alone for the night and for sleep and for the dreams that decided matters. (For Yours is the kingdom, and You shall reign forever.) He walked till he came to the Klein home in Talbieh. He went up a couple of steps and rang the bell. It had been some time since he had visited this friend. Now Klein came to the door, smiling, and said, "There he is, my agent, my redeemer. Welcome." Joel entered and stepped over a suitcase. Everything was in disorder and prepared for change. They sat down near a desk fixed to a wall, and Klein showed him receipts and accounts for electricity and water and the deed to the house and his bankbook, and then he brought out the power of attorney. Some papers fell to the floor and revealed a letter of appreciation from the Foreign Office commending Klein for his fine journalistic work, and also the last letter Klein's parents sent him before they were deported to the extermination camp: "Dear son, we are going to a place from which there is no returning. May God preserve you."

Joel glanced through the power of attorney which empowered him to do all things in Klein's name, to sign papers in his name, and to collect the rent and withdraw money from his account. And there were many signatures on the paper, and Joel added his.

Then they climbed over the suitcases and went into the kitchen, where they drank tea. Klein said, "Please stop in sometime to see if everything is in order. These Americans are terribly careless and don't take care of furniture and things. I haven't told you. The tenant is an American woman. First they were a couple. He is with movies, or some magazine sent him to make a film, and she is a doctor, sent here by some health organization to do research and practice medicine. But when she arrived, she came alone. Who can figure out the doings of these Americans? They are Christians. You're looking at the picture? It's a poor reproduction. Blue horses with long necks. When will this Miss Patricia take over? She's an interesting woman."

They were silent, for they had nothing to say to each other. The refrigerator hummed. Joel leaned on it and some of the tremor of its motor passed through him. The cups tinkled as they were put down on the saucers.

Suddenly the bell rang loudly. "The bell is out of order," Klein said, and went to open the door.

10

The European summer afternoon finally came to an end, and when it got dark the drizzle stopped. Girls sitting nearby shook droplets of rain from their hair. I passed a finger over one eyebrow to squeeze out the water. The neon lights went on and danced over roofs and on walls. I walked over the bridge that spanned the river close to the water. Automobiles turned on their lights and the mountains retreated into their remote night. And now my prolonged stay at Lindenhof has become a memory. Memories consume me like acid. When there are too many memories and not enough places to remember them in, the memories devour the man himself. Unless he engages in some new action, there is no telling whether anything would be left of him.

In my pocket I felt the envelope given me by Mr. Rosenbaum. It was still sealed. When I return to the hotel, I will open it at leisure and see what is in it. I guard this envelope as if it contained secret orders. It was handed to me in the institute to commemorate the holocaust during a quiet after-work hour. The building which houses the institute was specially constructed to facilitate remembering. On the walls hang pictures of Nazi atrocities and photostats of expulsion orders and extermination instructions, so that the officials in charge of remembering should not forget even when they went down to lunch or to perform private functions. I now returned to the hotel. In the coffee shop on the ground floor sat students from many countries. I was remote from them in age and education, but their presence comforted me. I found an empty table in a corner and took out Mr. Rosenbaum's envelope. In it I found a map of Weinburg. I marked on it various arrows and circles. Here was our house, and here the house of Rabbi Dr. Manheim, little Ruth's father, and here the synagogue that has been destroyed. I made other marks on the map, like a general; I measured distances and drew lines, as if I had an army at my call. In addition to the map, the envelope also contained various photographs and documents, and the deed to Mr. Rosenbaum's lot on the Square of the Four Centaurs, the sale of which I was to arrange; and I was also to collect his restitution allotment.

The pictures were of the synagogue and of the last group of Jews to be deported from Weinburg. A number of these unfortunates were crowded on the steps of the Weinburg railroad station. A crowd stood about them. One man laughed with his mouth wide open and pointed at them. I will have to find this man and avenge little Ruth for his laugh. But meantime he has probably changed, or perhaps the Russians have preceded me in taking revenge. In addition to these pictures, there was a photostat of the expulsion order: "The Jews are to appear . . . The railroad management is to supply . . . The court is to provide an official to take care of the cancellation of the citizenship of the last exiles."

I stayed on, and was not aware that the students had left the coffee shop. I folded my map and went upstairs to sleep.

After breakfast the next morning, I sat down again to prepare my plans for entering Weinburg, plans of direct invasion and plans of first surrounding the city. From which side should I approach it? Should I make a direct assault upon it, or should I infiltrate it like a secret agent, whose shirts and trousers and even the handkerchiefs in his suitcase are really explosives? Should I come to it with the sadness of an adult who returns to the scenes of his childhood, or should I burst into it like an avenging god? Should I go at once to court? What should I demand? To whom should I turn? Or should I take up my residence with the American troops who, according to Mr. Rosenbaum, are stationed nearby? But each time I tried to arrange my plans, Zurich softened me and filled me with joy. The bells of the Cathedral drowned out my thoughts of revenge, the waters of the Leman swept away my strategy, the drizzle covered everything, and the green of the mountains confused my plans.

Much stuff piled up on my table, as on the table of a military staff: brochures about Weinburg from the German Tourist Office, maps of bus lines, leaflets about historical sites, the story of Weinburg and of its final destruction at the end of World War II, when the *Gauleiter* went mad and ordered the city's defense to the last bullet and it was destroyed within a single hour. Also a book of photographs of the ruins of Weinburg and of its restoration, a house for a house, a street for a street, an eye for an eye, a tooth for a tooth. An inscription on the title page read: "Weinburg Restored. Let Us Remember the Dead. Let Us Remember the Destruction Which Human Foolishness Brought Upon Us."

To all these I added some of little Ruth's letters, including the last one which was sent through the Red Cross at the very peak of the destruction: "Today I am calm. I reached the final conclusion, after which there are no more. I often read our beautiful prayers. In a little while I will follow in the path of all the others."

I went outside knowing that this was my last day in Zurich.

11

The bell that was out of order suddenly rang very loudly, much louder than Joel had expected. He waited and was beginning to hope that nobody would open the door. Some days had passed since he had been here to sign the papers Klein had handed him. Now he pinched one hand with the other, waited, then waited some more, and went down the stairs. Below he noticed Klein's mailbox, and over the entire battery of mailboxes an electric meter attached to the wall, and within it a small wheel turning and humming. When the echo of his steps died down, he looked back and saw that the window in Klein's apartment was pushed partly open, and he went back and rang the bell again. Now he heard an indistinct voice from within: "Come in. Come in." And when he did not open the door, the voice, now with a definite American intonation, called louder, "It's open! It's open!" He went in and remained standing in the foyer. The voice directed him: "Come in, straight ahead, whoever you are, come in." Joel walked forward and heard the sound of a body splashing in water. "Who are you?" she called to him, and when he announced himself he heard her gay laughter. "Oh, you, the agent, Mr. Klein's representative. I'll be right there," and her voice was lost in the noise of the rushing water.

He went into the room and sat down in his friend Klein's faded chair. Some distinct changes were now apparent in the room. The bed had been changed to a sofa covered with a red blanket. An American record player stood in the corner and the soft chair had been moved from its accustomed place. On a small round table lay thick medical books and thin volumes of poetry, some letters and hairpins, the kind a woman holds in her mouth as she combs her hair.

Again the bell rang shrilly, and before Joel knew what to do he heard the woman's voice: "Please open the door. It's for me." Joel opened the door. He already felt a part of the establishment. He belonged to her. He needed her. Some roses were delivered, and Joel signed for them. The roses filled his arms, and he shouted to the bathroom, "Where shall I put the flowers?"

"What? Flowers again?"

"Red roses."

"Put them on the mantelpiece," she called from the roar of the water. He went into the kitchen. The sink was full of unwashed dishes. The mantelpiece was covered with various cans of preserves, full and half empty, as if this woman didn't rely on Jerusalem's stores and received all her supplies from America. On the wall hung the picture of the blue horses and Joel remembered Klein, who was dashing about the world looking for a place where he could think.

Suddenly Joel felt very happy in this apartment; his heart was flushed with warmth and the head of an unseen woman talked to him through soapy water.

When he re-entered the living room, he almost hoped that she would never emerge. Then he heard the door open, the sound of bare feet on the floor, and another door slamming.

Now she came in. "Hello. Anything new? Any word from our friend?" She was drying her hair and begged to be excused. She begged to be excused because the hospital smell clung to her. Joel got up from the upholstered chair and she sat down on it. Then he reminded her of the flowers, and she went out and returned with a vase. She had on very short shorts and her thighs were swarthy and firm and somewhat fuller than the prevailing fashion called for. He asked her whether everything about the apartment was in order. "Yes," she said. "The electric bill came, and some printed matter for Mr. Klein." Joel took the papers and stuffed them into his pocket without looking at them.

She combed her hair. She piled all of it in front of her eyes until her face was hidden, and she said, "I am glad you came; you are a dear, and very considerate. How does it feel to be in authority? A secretary? An executive? A major-domo? An agent? And what will you drink? The water is boiling already."

Again he noticed how her thighs were fuller than style approved, and stopped himself. Whose style? Who decreed that a woman's legs must be like those of a stork?

She laughed. "I shouldn't be wearing shorts. This won't do."

Her hair was beginning to dry and was combed down to

her shoulders. It was black and her eyes were daring and almond-shaped. He thought he had seen her before, and told her so. "Of course," she agreed. "Of course you saw me. My picture is on display in Zeiger the photographer's showcase. And the flowers are from him, too; that is, from him and from poor Mr. Cohen. There will never be a shortage of flowers."

Then she rose and brought in the tea, which tasted of smoke as it always does in the desert. He sensed that she knew his past, and the deserts he had traversed, where tea always had a taste of smoke. Her hair was almost dry now. She closed the window and pulled the curtain shut. For some reason he became chivalrous and said, "I hope I am not intruding," or something of the sort.

"I am glad you came," she said.

"Why glad?"

"Because," she said vaguely. "What are you thinking about?"

"I think that you are meeting me at a time of musing."

"It's a good time to meet, a time for errors."

"That's why I am often silent."

"My hair has dried. I must go. Tonight I am doctor on duty."

"Is that hard on you?"

"Why do you people in Israel have only one day of rest a week?"

"You own such thick books."

"Oh, these? Silly books."

She shook her hair and put a finger to the tip of her nose. He leafed through one of the volumes and saw the cross section of a wound in colors, yellow for fat, red for muscles, the veins blue.

"I heard you are an archeologist," she said. "Is that more interesting?" And it seemed to him that he had just un-

earthed her from the sand and that it was necessary to brush
her off carefully. She sat opposite him and there was gaiety
in her eyes, but her mouth trembled like that of a child
about to cry.

"Where did you live before?" he asked.

"In the Poriah Hotel."

"The one with the jasmine?"

"Yes, I was literally covered with jasmine."

"And before that?"

"With friends who went abroad for a couple of years. I
always return to the Poriah Hotel when I can't find an apartment for myself."

"Unsettled?"

"Unsettled."

"How long have you been in this country?"

"I am ready. Come. Escort me to the hospital. . . . Over a
year."

"How is it I never met you all this time?"

"You were musing. You were busy with your diggings.
You were deep in the earth."

"And all this time you were in Jerusalem?"

"Most of the time. In hospitals. In alleys. Near the border.
I love the place."

They walked out together. There were stony hills near the
house. She pointed out to him happy stones and sad ones.
Then she asked him whether he was always busy musing
and making errors. He answered that the land of error was a
broad one and that he was a permanent resident in it. They
walked down the steps and she untied her bicycle from the
railing. He walked alongside her, the bicycle between them,
and she looked at him sidewise. Suddenly she took off on her
bicycle, her hair flying behind her, and left him standing
near the big sign that announced: "A LUXURY APARTMENT
BUILDING WILL GO UP HERE."

Joel returned home. He made several circuits, like a plane that cannot find its landing ground; he met some acquaintances and passed by some stores where he used to do his shopping. In his mailbox he found a letter from Mina. The envelope bore a French stamp and a Paris postmark. It said: "I rented a room in a little alley. I fell in love with a young painter. I can see a bakery outside my window. I am happy. In two weeks I will go to Amsterdam. I don't want to go there but many things have to be done unwillingly. There is the great will, and in it decreasingly smaller wills. You will understand me, I am sure. When are you going out digging again?" She also wrote many other things, how her days are spent and how the nights hold back the days, like so many terraces on a hillside that hold back the soil. They hold back the days from being washed away into the sea of time. He would understand. She had written this letter, together with many others, while she was still clear of mind. And now, Joel thought, he would do as she had done. And he knew that he would not return to Weinburg this summer.

12

It is impossible to return to the place where I am returning. I am only going there to shut a door in my life which refuses to close, a door that hangs loosely in its frame and disturbs my sleep in Jerusalem. It is possible that this door disturbs my sleep only when I am in Jerusalem. How often a man is troubled because it seems to him that he left a door open, a fire burning, a faucet turned on.

So now I am on the train to Weinburg. The landscape is

passing outside. A low tree, and a post, and more trees, and behind them slow-moving low hills, like mourners returning from a funeral. Other things passed through my mind. I sat alone in a compartment, until I discovered that it had been specially reserved for cripples. Among the signs which warned not to spit, not to lean out of the window, there was also one: "THIS COMPARTMENT RESERVED FOR CRIPPLES—FOR THE BLIND, FOR INDUSTRIAL CRIPPLES, FOR PEOPLE SUFFERING FROM WAR-INCURRED DISABILITIES." The conductor came in and pointed to the sign. I went out without a word and took a seat in another compartment. I could have given him a list of my disabilities: I am blind; I have an artificial soul; I came here not to love but to hate. I stood by the window and my thoughts leaped out of me like fugitives who jump from a running train; they tumbled and rolled down the embankment to the river. Yet nobody called my attention to it; nobody said, "Excuse me, but haven't you lost something?"

And regarding the door which I was returning to close—could it be that someone had already closed it? Of course, I knew that only I could shut it. Perhaps the house had been destroyed? I had heard that many houses had been blown up during the last day of the war when the *Gauleiter* defended it in his mad gesture of blood and fire. He waited for the American attack in the St. Maria fortress. This fortress had three towers, a round one, a square one, and one that was lopped off. At the time of the peasants' rebellion, the knights fought the peasants who came upon them with pitchforks and hoes, and then discovered that plows and pitchforks are fine weapons while swords and spears are good for plowing.

The city was destroyed in a single hour. The house with the door loose in its frame was also destroyed. In my dreams I sometimes see the ruins of this house, with the door hanging on a single bent hinge. Perhaps I will put an end to the curse of this dangling door and it will instantaneously turn to dust with a low sigh, and will be no more. Or perhaps they have taken the door off and used it in another building? The couple opposite me speculated on what they would find in the resort they were going to: sea waves, and tides of people, and breakers of waiters constantly serving food.

The names of the stations were called outside, my father's stations. My father had been a traveling salesman. He sold everything a woman needed for sewing aside from the cloth itself: buttons and buckles, needles and thread, lace, black ribbons for mourners and colored ribbons for people who were not mourners, veils and wraps, hair nets and decorative buttons, and many more kinds of buttons, and hooks and safety pins, and pins that were not safe, and little pieces of fur to trim collars with, and lining for jackets and winter coats, and scissors and foxtails, and rabbit ears, and black dummies, minus arms and sex organs, filled with straw and sawdust. All these my father had in his store. My uncle used to stay in the store. He would sit on a high chair near a pillar and keep the books, and when there was no bookkeeping to be done, he would sit in the café and play cards or chess. My father used to tell me about the towns he passed through, and now these names rose up within me as if they were also my father's names. He had a different story for each station. I ordered many thoughts into my head so that there should not be only a single one. I caused the earth to be empty of people and I left in it only myself as a child, and little Ruth and a few others from my childhood, Dr. Manheim and kind Henrietta. The train stopped and there was whistling. People said that it was good few trains now smoked. Most trains are powered by electricity. It is not good to see smoke rising.

Late in the afternoon a big sign in one of the stations announced: "VISIT WEINBURG FOR THE INTERNATIONAL SKATING COMPETITION." So there is a purpose in my returning to Weinburg. I am going to the skating competition.

13

Joel planned an outing to the Jerusalem hills, to the last remaining spring that had not gone dry. These days he felt as if the sea of time had receded from him and exposed all the days of his life like so many shells, stones, scurrying crabs, and dead fish. He wrote a letter to Mina, tore it up, and rewrote it: "I, too, am now abroad," but he did not say where. Once, he went with Itzhak to the hospital in the hills. He sat in the waiting room while Itzhak went in. When Itzhak came back, he said, "I saw her through a grille. She read your letter at once. But the doctors advised me not to go in; she is undergoing a change." "We are all undergoing a change," Joel said. Itzhak pushed his skullcap down on his head. The cap was like a father's hand on the head in the act of blessing. The friendship between Itzhak and Joel was now closer, perhaps because of this paternal skullcap, and certainly on account of Mina, who was in the hospital but sent letters and postcards from all over the world. Some days later, Joel decided to invite Patricia and some of his close friends to the outing. She would probably come wearing the broad-brimmed hat he had noticed in her closet; his friends would wear khaki caps to remind them of the old days. But Joel was not one of those who sighed for the old days.

14

At the next station some young people who looked like dancers got on the train. One tall curly-haired young man wore shorts and carried a suitcase covered with stickers from many countries. Two young women were with him. One was auburn-haired; her wide mouth constantly laughed, and tight slacks gripped her hips. Her laughter filled her entire body and burst from her under pressure. The other, golden-haired, with high cheekbones, had her back turned to me and argued with the porters.

The dancers passed by my compartment. The girls stopped talking about themselves and one remarked to the other, "That's Binder, the internationally famous skating artist."

The conductor passed and I decided to return to the quiet compartment reserved for invalids. One man was there, but he was engrossed in watching the landscape and paid no attention to me. I sat down at the other end of the compartment and thought about my mission.

The landscape was now becoming familiar. (Do not weep for the departing; weep for him who returns.) Vines lay facing the sun on the terraces of passing hills. I went to the dining car and sat near the dancers. Someone remarked that this was the border area between wine drinkers and beer drinkers. People living in this region drink everything, and their drunkenness is coarse and heavy when they drink beer and gay and witty when they drink wine. Soon I would see the river of my childhood. In fact, after the next range of hills the river approached in a gay loop that aimed to embrace me. Then it fled and disappeared behind a forest. But I knew it was there and that it would return. The river of my childhood was the only one who came to greet me and to look at my face, which had been spoiled and deformed by life. The telephone wires rose and fell continuously. The lower wires rose to meet the upper ones. I watched for their meeting, but a high pole cruelly slapped them down again, and those who were to meet never did meet. But the wires did not learn their lesson and again yearned upward until another pole slapped them down. Those not destined to meet never will meet. Who learns from experience? Nobody. Who returns truly? Not even I.

15

The train slowed down, but the river still remained out of sight. An Indian passed by me wearing a white helmet. His eyes were dark and earnest. Indians come to Europe to learn sciences and to compare them to their own world. Or perhaps he is going to the skating tournament. I had seen him earlier, sitting near the dancers. How can one skate when one has such earnest eyes?

People prepared to detrain. The bells that a little girl wore on her shoes jingled, and there was the sound of the scraping of heavy luggage. I suddenly felt that this was a train going to the front. Who was with me? Who? Only a small part of my forces knew that the front was near, perhaps only the Indian and the dancers and the man in the invalids' compartment, who had disappeared and did not return. Now the river returned burdened with heavy barges. The engine belched loudly. The man from the invalids' compartment had apparently deserted. And now the train ran on the river plain. The vine-covered hills at times retreated suddenly and made room for small villages with red-tiled roofs. Quarries exhibited their white wounds. Smoke rose from chimneys.

I felt that I was being observed, and not only from the side of the river. One of the dancers stood behind me. Her head was outlined against the expanse of the widening river; it seemed almost as if her head floated on the river. Bathers shouted. I recalled little Ruth. Once, she and I were knocked down by Nazi boys. I will find the ones who knocked her down when they were boys. Perhaps they have been killed in the war, but if by a miracle they remained boys I will recognize them. At that time I had felt as if it were the end of the world. Some weeks later, we parted when my family left for Palestine. Ruth's father, Dr. Manheim, then delivered an oration in the synagogue in my father's honor, and blessed him, and all those "who go to find new hope in the ancient land of our fathers." Some stations before Weinburg, peasants from neighboring villages boarded the train. I made a last survey of my forces and plans. When I get there, how should I enter the city? Stealthily? Like a saboteur? Or like a conquering army? I surveyed my troops. The Indian was doubtful, for he probably came only to study but not to act. The dancers would be too busy rehearsing for the tournament. The dancer with the golden hair and the high cheekbones sat immersed in her thoughts. Her suitcase did not have a single label on it. I decided she would be my staff adjutant.

The train rounded the last sharp turn and the valley of the city of my childhood opened up and revealed itself. I saw a hill with a path on it. I saw many towers. I swallowed the scene in one great gulp without distinguishing names of

streets or churches or parks. A great hurt came upon me and
I at once projected it onto the world outside, for I had sworn
to be indifferent when returning to Weinburg. Beloved, beloved, I am leaving you here. Beloved, crown and glory of
my life, I am returning. Little Ruth, your time has come.
The train stopped. The old railway station was destroyed
and its ruins were still visible. A new building, all color and
sparkling glass, had risen. Few passengers got off—the
dancers, some peasants, a number of Englishmen, the Indian, and I. Also the little girl with the bells on her shoes,
and her parents.

16

Patricia would appear suddenly. Better still, she would already be there, as if from the beginning of eternity, waiting,
as beautiful animals wait.

Joel had on his back an army bag, surplus of the U.S.
Army, ready for the hike. He passed by the Roma Café,
where they had agreed to meet, and did not see her. He
went in and was given a note: "Itzhak can't come." Then he
was called to the telephone: "Yoske is busy; he's having some
trouble and won't be able to make it."

Now he hoped that no one but Patricia would come. He
had already forgotten how many of his friends he had invited. A girl came out of one of the banks across the street
and informed him that her boss wouldn't be able to come,
and ordered a glass of coffee for him.

The tailor across from the café opened his shutter. An
unfinished suit is always on display in his window. No fin-

ished garment catches the eye the way a suit does that still shows the white basting stitches and has but one sleeve. It is possible that Joel, too, was like that, unfinished. But only Patricia, the American, who looked in through the café window, realized that Joel's life was incomplete, despite the fact that in age and status in society he seemed completed long ago. She went in, and when he turned around he noticed her gray skirt and sleeveless blouse loosely tied at the neck with a golden thread. She came toward him like a ship in full sail, and her face was like the painted faces of women that adorned the prows of ships in years gone by. And in fact she began by saying, "This skirt is made of sailcloth." She anchored and sat down beside him and smiled and lifted a questioning yet threatening finger: "Where are all the others? The gang? The people? The friends?" And he gave her some sort of answer, and she smiled slyly and knowingly.

They got up and went to the Hills of Judea station and boarded a bus. Patricia's hair was loosely coiled around her head, yet one could not say that it had been done carelessly. Everything she did had about it a sense of completeness and finality. She probably dressed quickly, too, not like most women. Without a doubt, she got out of bed unwrinkled and was at once wide-eyed and neat. Her hair was held in place by a number of pins, and a comb that looked like a buckle and supported the entire mass from the back. The bus moved off and he offered her a green candy.

"Not now; later. What's so strange about me that you stare at me like that?"

"That you are here and that we are on the way."

"And that your friends didn't show up."

"You American. Do you know that here America has become a synonym for exaggeration? Peddlers announce their goods by shouting, 'America! America!' Even when they sell oranges or cucumbers. The public responds."

"You, too?"

"Is your hair dry already?"

"It's been dry for quite a while. I'm glad I am outside. Maybe I'll get rid of the hospital smell."

"Will you remain here much longer?"

"I don't think so. I have to finish my assignment, a study of hospitals in Israel. Part of a world-wide study."

"International Health Organization?"

"Yes, my friend. I will have to go back."

"Where?"

She didn't answer, for it is possible to return in two directions, just as when going out it is possible to take one of two directions. Returning is a form of going away, and going away is a form of returning.

"I was in the hospital and gave blood."

"Strange. I was on duty but didn't see you."

"Anyhow my blood won't help. It is only coursing for a while in somebody else's veins, then it returns; it must return."

Patricia laughed and raised the palm of her hand. He pointed out to her the dam where the water refused to stay, seeping away and leaving the great wall towering uselessly, and the terrible Castel; he told her of robber villages on the way to Jerusalem and battles of the Crusaders and of Israel's War of Independence. And he said, "This piece of the road is called Seven Sisters, because it has seven hairpin turns." Where the road started climbing, they left the bus and were alone. The sun was fierce over their heads. She squatted down and her skirt covered her feet. From a small basket, she took out a pair of tennis shoes in two colors with broad white laces, put them on, and skipped like a little girl who had been given her freedom, until they came to a ruin and he pointed out to her the tower over the grave of the prophet Samuel, and the radar installations and the ruins of Castel over them. Yes, everything here is of gray or pink stone, everything. They descended and passed the wreck of an auto which the police had placed beside the road as a warning to drivers. They should have put some people there who had erred, to warn the others. But people who made mistakes, Patricia argued, don't always look crushed.

A busload of children passed by them, and a song rolled down the hill. Joel pointed out to her the young trees of newly planted forests and explained how the native forest had been destroyed first by conquerors and then by flocks of goats, enemies of the land. She liked the expression "enemies of the land," and she laughed, tossing her head backward, and asked many questions about the enemies of the land, and laughed again.

The layers of the hill showed distinctly and they were assailed by the odor of the blood of the land. They did not walk alongside each other; from time to time she skipped forward and her leaps were like her outbursts of strong laughter. He ran and caught up with her and explained to her the veins showing in the rock, and he said, "Look, seeds flying in the air, seeds of thorns. Be careful that they don't land on you; thorns, too, are enemies of the people." Then he pointed out all the springs in the vicinity and most of them were dry. And who was she? he asked. Where did she come from? Was she an enemy of the land and of the people? Did she come like the floating thorn seeds? She laughed heartily and gave confused accounts of herself, of a father who was a commander of a warship and of a mother who was an Alaskan Eskimo. And then, no, she was the daughter of an Indian chief, the kind one sees in the movies sitting by a campfire, but her mother was a Mexican who came to California as a farm worker when Patricia was an infant and carried her in a basket on her back. Then, again, her father was a black-haired Irish priest who betrayed his vows and married a Jewish woman from New York; or she was a daughter of the South and grew up in an old mansion that was about to collapse. And then she asked whether all these stories satisfied his curiosity. Enough, enough, enough. "You have a wonderful country. I will stay here."

When they reached a bend in the road, the valley of Kiryat Anavim and Abu Ghosh opened up before them, an ancient green valley, a blessed blessed valley surrounded by forested hills and parceled into gardens and orchards and houses and towers. On the slope above them was a dead forest. Gray, nearly white, pine branches sifted the light into a net of shadows. A moon forest, a forest of death. How had it come about? Had the enemies of the land destroyed this forest?

They turned in to a narrow path between the ledges of rock toward a place called Aqua Bella. During the time of the Crusades, a convent stood here. Now there were only ruins and the spring was dry. He told her of the Crusader castles scattered throughout the country, of all the places that had been conquered and were lost and now stood in ruins, shriveled by wind, rent by clouds. When a place is conquered, the ceiling collapses and no pillars or arches will sustain it. The arches remain to the last and gather a bit of earth, and sprout some grass and green moss and thorns. Joel and Patricia lay down in the shade of tall pines on a soft layer of brown needles.

They talked to each other in broken English and halting Hebrew, and when they wanted to say words that come from the heart they resorted to their mother tongues and sat facing each other in an ancient arch of a window. The thorns about them towered above their heads. Joel suddenly noticed her hand in the shade of the drying grass and lifted it. She did not protest, and only held her breath. It was the hand of a very mature person, grooved by lines of fate and creased every which way, like the garden of a mad king. They were silent a long while, as if the contemplation of the hand had deprived them of speech. And as the afternoon grew upon them, a great and unfamiliar passion arose within them, a passion not of his homeland, or of hers, or of this land, but springing from remote depths within them.

17

All at once the station was abandoned by the trains. This seldom happens. The trains had left on their way and the loudspeaker fell silent, for it had nothing more to announce. All the "rams' horns" which are usually sounded fell silent, for in stations every day is a day of decision.

It was noon. I had come to Weinburg. Signs announced that Fersil cleans everything and Odol whitens teeth and kills germs. The few people who had gotten off the train with me had been absorbed by distant doors and tunnels and passages. Only I and my suitcase remained, and I was barren of feeling and thought.

I put down my suitcase and remained standing in the empty station. Then I picked it up and entered a tunnel. My steps evoked twin echoes. The sparkling tiled walls of the tunnel were covered with timetables in different colors. A train rumbled to a stop, and at once the tunnel was filled with people who swept me along to a landing lighted by colored lights. Here were a number of billboards and a map of the city. Odol whitens and Fersil cleans everything. There was also a list of hotels in which I would not stay, and another of barbershops in which I would not have my hair cut, and still another of films which I would not see. The police were seeking a woman suspected of murdering her husband. Over one door it said "MEN," and I went in. A woman dressed in a shiny black linen smock received me and handed me a neatly folded towel as one hands the city flag or the keys to the city on a white satin pillow to an alien conqueror or an honored guest. I handed her some coins whose names still rang in my ears from childhood. I looked into the mirror and saw that I was not prepared for battle. My army of dancers had scattered through the city, and the army of my dead was busy with being dead and with illusions of resurrection. Undependable. I went out and the door swung behind me. I recalled the door which I had come to close. If I were deeply in love, this would be the right time to forget. Forgetting a door is the same as closing it, the same as forgetting the future, as forgetting the past. I decided to check my suitcase to lighten my movements. I went up the escalator. People moved up and down like sad and silent angels. I could act with greater ease without my suitcase. What was in it? Some clothes and a pair of shoes and some books. I could do in the city what I wished and deceive the inhabitants so that they would not even guess that I had arrived. "WELCOME NEWCOMERS! WELCOME RE-TURNEES!" an elegant sign proclaimed as I emerged from the depths. A shoeshine stand was in the upper passage. I sat on the throne and the man bowed at my feet as if he were about to crown me.

More trains passed with a dull rumbling over our heads. A great calm descended upon me. It will be necessary to re-examine everything anew. I had not imagined that there could be such peace, or that all my plans would be so confused. I had thought that my excitement would provide the fuel and the ammunition so that I could come at once and conquer the city, divide it into quarters, and seal off its approaches to prevent the fugitives from fleeing. I had thought that only after that would I be calm and able to deal at leisure with the problems of occupation, supply, transport, organization, and retreat back to Jerusalem.

The shoeshine man asked if I had said something. I hadn't said a thing. I felt the brush through the thin leather of my shoes.

Then he pulled the two pieces of cardboard from my shoes and I got off the throne. A woman dressed in black, seemingly a widow, took my place. Everything on her was black. Her underwear must have been black, too, but then black underwear does not signify mourning. I held out the money to the shoeshine man, whose face I could not see because he was already busy shining the shoes of the black queen, and he only said, "Put it in the box."

I left the upper passage and went into the big concourse. I saw at once that it was quarter past one. In Germany there are clocks everywhere; they are stuck into walls or suspended from above or stretched out like arms into the streets. There is no need to look at a wristwatch. An attractive woman again announced from a wall that Fersil cleans well and a shiny-toothed child proclaimed that Odol keeps his teeth healthy. I raised my head to see who called me but saw only a clock. All the clocks tick away, but time is not filled by them.

I went out of the concourse. I had not remembered it like this, new and modern, but soot-stained and smelling of rust and adorned with many strange and ancient carvings on the pillars and parapets. I pulled out document No. 1. It was a snapshot of our family taken the day we left Weinburg for Palestine. Suitcases and all sorts of bundles lay about us, and Father held a small briefcase containing some documents. Children in emigrant families are always loaded down with small bundles and coats. A grownup says, "He can carry this coat and the briefcase and the small basket." In the end the child is almost invisible under the small parcels the grown-ups load him down with. Many friends and relatives came to see us off, and we were all bunched in one tight knot, so that a bystander couldn't tell who was leaving and who staying behind. Only when the train whistled in anticipation of its departure did we part as cream separates from milk in a separator.

I checked my suitcase, then asked about some train that goes to a place outside Germany. Railroad stations are extra-territorial homelands of the wanderers of the world. They are the embassies of those who have no home, or have left their home and find themselves in a state of profound forgot-tenness. Two men wearing badges around their sleeves came up and asked whether I had come from the Communist East and whether I needed assistance. I did not answer them, even though I was in need of assistance. Thus two men must have approached Ruth when she was being led to the crema-torium; only they must have been younger and worn a different badge, with a swastika. Ruth was badly in need of heavenly assistance and must have been helped by someone nearby as she skipped on one foot, for she had no doubt already been deprived of her crutch. Little Ruth had known many sorrows long before the troubles descended on every-one else. Her leg, which she had lost in an accident, had been burned long before the rest of her body. I saw the dancers disappear through shining glass doors. Big signs di-rected people to registration desks for those who came to the international skating tournament. Are you here for the skat-ing tournament? No, I came to a different tournament.

All at once I was in the large square before the station. In the middle of the square, as always, stood the statue of the city's patron saint, Saint K., his hands uplifted in a gesture of blessing toward the doors of the station. He stood in an elevated stone basin from which water flowed to a lower, larger basin. Curtains of water fell quietly downward so that one could hardly discern their motion, and only the light reflected from the sheet of water told of its falling. The Saint's hands are always raised in blessing. His hands were also raised in blessing when the last Jews of Weinburg were taken away, though it is possible that there was no water in the fountain then, as a wartime measure, to conserve water to put out the fires.

Four American soldiers passed by. I was glad to see them, but they were not glad to see me and proceeded on their way to the milk bar. The people of Europe have decided to be good, and in order to become accustomed to this new state they have milk bars, and milk saloons, and milk taverns. The drinking young men of Europe sit on high chairs and sip frothy milk mixed with all sorts of colored juices and ices and fruits. I ordered an extra-fine milk shake and was given a mound of froth and colors and tastes. I calmed down as I sucked it. A streetcar passed with a screech. It was an old car and probably remembered me from the past. The ghost of old Professor Freud sat on the unoccupied chair next to me and said, "You suck? You suck again?" I answered him, "You are right. You are right again." I would gladly have added him to my forces, even though he would not advance the action because of a too close examination of the motives. The four Americans, one of whom was a Negro, would probably not cooperate with me. What do they know? By the time I explained everything to them, they would be due for rotation and sent back home.

Behind the heads of the Americans was a window and through it I could see the small park where stood a statue of Pestalozzi. As children, this strange name amused us no end. I continued sucking at the straw. Church bells were ringing heavenward. Heaven listened. When I was a child, I used to listen to little Ruth's footsteps. There she comes; her eyes are gray and gay; her pigtails are thin and still short. What should we play today? Sometimes we made so much noise that Dr. Winniger would send the maid to quiet us down. Dr. Winniger was the owner of the house. The house was built early in the century and was a medley of styles. It had big towers and strange little towers and pillars that served no useful purpose, and heads of women that supported balconies and other stone images and gargoyles and birds' heads and griffins, and more and still more projections and windows and grilles and niches, and patient giants with sad faces of beasts of burden supporting lintels. Because of all these decorations, the house was always dark inside. Dr. Winniger was a professor of classical Greek. His only daughter was a pretty girl and attended the St. Sophia Lyceum. On Saturday afternoons, when I suffered from the Sabbath depression common in the Diaspora, and Dr. Winniger used to get spells of headache, his daughter would emerge from the house, all in white, and go to play tennis, proudly swinging her racket.

Once, before Hitler came to power, Mrs. Winniger invited me to a Christmas party, at least to come and look: "Nobody will eat you up." I was dressed in a blue velvet suit with glass buttons and an ivory-colored lace collar. The Winnigers' apartment was brightly lit. I stood in the doorway. Her hand on my head, the Winnigers' beautiful daughter encouraged me: "Come, come in, little Jew." She had a broad, powerful hand. Her friends filled all the rooms. A decorated Christmas tree stood in the middle, its branches dripping silvery powder, and little angels and sparkling balls swayed in the hot air. I stared wide-eyed and proceeded to create a world of my own in the midst of the noise and the lights and the hubbub, as children always do. Then I smelled the aroma of heated wine spiced with cinnamon. A

pinch of the silvery powder fell on my hair. Little Ruth
envied me much because of that evening.

The soldiers got up and walked out. I heard the ring of the
coins they threw on the counter, a tip for the waitress, and I
knew that I, too, had to leave, for I was beginning to build
myself a home here in order to avoid acting, though I did
not know yet how I should act. Now I saw Saint K. in profile
and his hands were no longer raised to bless me. He had
lost interest in me. He was all involved in the miracle of his
survival on the day Weinburg was bombed, when he remained unscathed.

18

He held her hand long and read in it all her life—not only
her character but all the days and nights of her life, even his
own life with her, as in a map of prophecy and of love. "Why
do you hold my hand so long?" she said. "Is it something
antique? Or perhaps an ancient scroll?" And she laughed
and teased him, until he squeezed her hand powerfully so
that she cried out, her head bent backward with pain, and
she struck him in the chest with all her might. She was
strong and had known how to tame unbroken horses without
a saddle. He handed her a piece of candy, as one does to a
child.

"Where do you want to go?" she asked.

"To a bigger forest, a pine forest."

"Dead pines? A dead forest? Like the one over there?"

"No. In Kiryat Anavim there is a big forest."

"Is it far?"

"No."

"It's a trap. I know. You are setting a trap for me. All the same I will go with you. It will be a pleasure."

And she talked of her last night on duty at the hospital and he told her of all sorts of conferences he was organizing, and they made fun of the study seminars and symposia and conferences that filled the calendar to overflowing throughout the country.

"How long will you remain here?" he asked, but she did not answer.

They rose and walked up the path. They passed by a spring whose water was now stagnant and greenish, and swarmed with all manner of water insects. There was a tangle of raspberry bushes near the spring, but the berries would not ripen till much later. The air smelled of dust and figs. Patricia's mouth trembled.

They walked in the ravine along the watercourse which was hidden by bushes. It was past two in the afternoon. The aroma of sage overlay the smell of dust. The sage grew here amid dryness and despair and its aroma confused the senses. When they came out of the ravine, they found themselves among patches of grass on the slopes of the hills. Cairns marked the borders between the fields. They would forget the borders; they would forget all boundaries; they would not remember their countries and their languages.

They turned off to an ancient Roman road beside which there was a deep water hole in the rock and a wine press carved in the stone, and as they walked the two of them were like those who trod the grapes, but they did not know it, and the wine streamed and intoxicated them. They came upon ruined houses among ancient trees, arched doorways and vaulted windows that had remained standing. He told her the names of the places about them and of the places that were not near, the Gate of the Valley, and the

Gate of the Winds, and he showed her where the mill had stood and explained about the upper millstone and the nether millstone, and she wanted to know which of the two was male and which female. They reached the orchard of a kibbutz where cows lay silent in the entranced afternoon. He asked if she was tired, and she laughed and pointed to her sturdy legs. Then they turned off into a draw and came upon a narrow path which became a forest trail, and sticks and small branches crackled under their feet. The path was suddenly covered with feathers and down, and dead birds lay about, so they called the place the forest of the dead birds. Some of the feathers fluttered in the light breeze and were caught on the branches and the thorns of the bushes, and thus marked the path. Then they entered among pines which here grew close together and shaded them. Their clothes caught on branches and they freed themselves carefully so as not to injure a branch or rip their clothes. A bird fluttered, a dove called mournfully, a stone rolled down the slope.

They found a narrow spot on a ledge and sat down to rest. She gave him a bread roll and it crumbled between her fingers. Then they lay on their backs and looked at the golden pine needles that reflected the sunlight. She said, "This is indeed a great pleasure and joy." They hung their shoes on branches and, seizing each other's hands, they rolled around and wrestled, and she said, "Careful, now, I am strong and I know many holds." "That's all right," he said; nevertheless it cost him an effort to hold her between his arms and to lock her thighs between his knees. "Enemy of the land," she whispered, and laughed as they knocked down one of the dangling shoes. He heard her heavy breathing and she said, "I give up." He almost regretted that she had weakened and that now it would be necessary to free her, and he exclaimed, "Weak Amazon!" Then she lay at his side, and he shoved some earth under the nape of her neck but did not tell her that it was customary to do so to the dead. And as if to demonstrate that she was still alive, she suddenly began to choke him with her ancient evil hands until he grasped them in his own. Then she said, "You must be patient with me."

After they had rested and eaten something, they played a game of hide-and-seek and their pulses quickened, and when they had rested again he told her of mountain faults and domes within the earth and folds and depressions, and of the broken pottery he unearthed and of oil that was being drilled for not far away. They lay down and inhaled the smell of the dry earth and the aroma of the pines, and rose again like pieces of paper that are lifted and tossed about by the wind. In the distance they discerned the road descending in a breathtaking hairpin turn. Cars moved upon it blowing their horns and shifting gears, but these sounds reached them from afar in a strained and purified mutter.

Her clothes rustled as she prepared to return. He must be patient and wait. She put on her shoes and placed some small items in her handbag, and they returned by the path of the dead birds. The day was coming to an end, and when they entered the kibbutz she began looking for a washroom like a little girl out on a hike. He waited for her to return, thinking how half the human race is made up of women and this world is full of love and the promise of much happiness. When she returned, they walked slowly. Their parallel shadows lengthened. Amid a cloud of dust, a small truck stopped for them and they climbed into it. Long pipes protruded from the truck and a red rag fluttered at their end. The pipes vibrated and his hand was on her bosom. Her hand was held against her forehead. And as they sat thus, Joel felt that the restraining wall in his life was breached. Some go on journeys to shut doors that were left open, but for him new doors were being opened.

Through the rear of the covered truck, they watched the pavement recede, becoming narrow and bluish in the distance and merging with the landscape, the olive trees and the fig trees, the terraces and the vineyards and the abandoned quarries. They passed the first house at the entrance to the city. It stood on a cliff and a small boy stood on the roof, naked and swarthy, his skin gilded by the setting sun. Whoever enters Jerusalem comes into a besieged city, always, in times of peace as well as war. There are always Nebuchadnezzars and Tituses and Crusaders ringed about it. One who lives in this city is always besieged. And Joel knew that for him the siege was lifting, and when they parted he said, "I'll pick you up at the hospital."

19

From there I walked down Kings Street, which no longer has any kings. I crossed Kaiser Square, though there is no Kaiser. There was no street named after Ruth, and she, too, was gone. St. Magdalene Alley joined the Capuchin Order Street. I walked down a street that was not named after me. I saw nothing and heard nothing, and walked with the assurance of a blind man in his darkness. I crossed the Street of the Good Well, which had regained its name after having been called Adolf Hitler Street. The Good Well was also not there. Most of the houses had been rebuilt after the destruction. In the big Palace Square, the fountain which I remembered from childhood still stood. Here, too, a stone man dispensed water from his palms, but he was assisted by a number of bulgy-cheeked Tritons and some fish that spouted water. I did not go into the Palace Park; I saved it for another occasion. Instead I went up Courier Street. To justify the name of the street, I ran. I ran so that I should be breathless, and tired, and simply in order to run. A traffic cop stood at the place which had once been a playground. This, too, was a change. He came up to me and said, "This beats everything. You saw me. You know it is forbidden to cross here." I paid the fine and walked by a stationery store where as a child I used to buy pencils and notebooks. The closer I approached the place I wanted to approach, the more I was troubled by questions one usually asks in a strange city: Where should I check in for the night? How many days should I stay here? How should I leave the city and where should I go? Should I stay each night in a different hotel so as to cover my tracks? Or should I curse the city from different hilltops, like Balaam? The first night at a hotel, one is asked formal questions, the kind whose answers are in the passport. One is given a key on a large plastic ring, or some other weight. The second day, one is observed quietly. The fourth day, one is met with smiles and one rapidly slides down the slippery incline to friendliness. And as for pronouncing curses from hilltops, it is no longer done. The only useful curses are those with which a man curses himself and which clog the ducts of the heart.

I dashed through streets which were like panting breaths. It was a running amok that caused no casualties. Hit and run, hit and run, but those who were hit did not know it. It was necessary to inform them: "Mister, you have been hit." "Madam, you wife of the S.S. officer, you have been hit." As in an army maneuver, where labels are pinned to soldiers, "Wounded." Here is the statue of the boy feeding birds, and here is the playground just as it used to be; here is the newsstand, and the little park. I went on and bit into every place, as one bites into apples, one after another, leaving teeth marks upon them. A man asked me what was the name of the street and I knew the answer. This calmed me. But suddenly I was overcome with a yearning for the hills of Jerusalem, to walk on the parched earth as pebbles and thorn seeds collected in the cuffs of my pants.

Three American girls walked behind me and sang a song: "Honey, oh, honey,/Don't meddle with the bees,/Come meddle with me." I let them catch up with me. They wore tight blue cowboy jeans. Then they let me catch up with them, and then I let them catch up with me again. They were gay and I tried to guess their ages. When Ruth was burned, they must have been about five or six years old and playing with dolls and balls.

Through the loudspeaker inside me, I announced to myself, "We are approaching the place where my house used to be." I repeated this announcement, the way it is done on ships or planes when the destination is approached. But I still didn't know where I was going. I approached the place roundabout, and on the command bridge inside my head various thoughts rushed about and collided. The girls disappeared. Perhaps they wanted me to show them the city. But then I would have had to explain to them the purpose of my coming to Weinburg and they would have been bored. I approached the last street. Here is the store where my mother used to buy her groceries, and here the wall covered with vines, and now the drugstore. I reached my street.

Aside from myself, there was not a soul around. My feet seemed to recall that a steep climb was due here, but the street ascended gently. My feet remembered that it was necessary to walk fast and far, yet here I was facing the square and the spot where Dr. Winniger's house had stood, the house in which we were tenants. Now the house was gone, together with its little towers and carvings and gargoyles and the heads of women supporting balconies. In its place was a slick modern building. A broad staircase led to a wide entrance and many young people went up and down the stairs, like the angels in Jacob's dream. "International Student House," read the inscription over the door. I thought of going in and dropping plumb lines at a certain spot and proclaiming: "Here was the bedroom." "Here is where I used to sit." But I reconsidered. Why do it when the house is no longer what it was? Red roses wide open to the point of coarseness stood in the vestibule, and also a symbolic statue: a Negro, a European, and a Chinese intricately interlocked their arms. Perhaps I should spend the night here. But I am no longer a student. I have finished my archeological studies. I am now a teacher.

I pretended to be a newspaperman and took out a small notebook and wrote in it three times, "Ruth." The kitchen was in the basement. Once, it had shelves on which my mother put up apples. The sacks of coal stood nearby. Suddenly I noticed the Indian. He coughed politely and asked whether I would take part in the skating competition or whether I was only one of the trainers. I was flattered that he mistook me for a trainer, and I neither confirmed nor denied it but only remarked that I was looking for something. "We are all looking for something," the Indian said. "I knew you'd say that," I told him. "As a matter of fact, I am a student." He invited me to visit him at the university hospital. "Which department?" I asked. He smiled and said, "I am doing a special study in all departments, something between philosophy and psychology, between yoga and synagogue. I'll explain it to you when I have a chance. Why are you looking into the basement?" I told him it was a matter of world outlook, which is the same as looking into a basement. He understood everything, he assured me. A bell tolled. "That one is from the Church of Our Beloved Lady," I said.

The Indian said, "No, it is from the Dominican Church." We argued about it like a couple of Asians tossed up on the steps of Europe, until a girl student came by and said we were both wrong, that it was from the Church of Mary. "Strange," I said. "What's strange?" she asked. "They must have put in a new bell," I said. She confirmed this and the three of us sank into mutual contemplation until the tolling stopped. I left the Indian and went to Ruth's house.

I walked a little way up the street to the corner where the house had stood. I found a ruin. It was the only house in the neighborhood that had not been rebuilt. Through the broken frame of an arched window, a tree put out a branch like a hand stretched out in greeting. Beyond the arch had been Ruth's room. Now the tree lived in her room and greeted me. I stood for a while; then I walked around the ruin till I returned to the wrecked window. There were no shutters which I could close. During Crystal Night, the window of Ruth's room was smashed with stones thrown from where I now stood, and the blanket on her bed was covered with splintered glass.

The fence surrounding the small garden was undamaged but the gates were blocked with heaps of wreckage. Children probably came here to play hide-and-seek. Why hadn't they rebuilt Ruth's house? One window had been blocked halfway with stones. Near this house the inner city comes to a halt and there begin the suburbs, which are called Rose Hill, Monk's Mountain, and the like. A deep ravine separated the inner city from the suburbs. The railroad, which circles the city after it leaves the station, passes through this ravine whose slopes are overgrown with a jungle of raspberry bushes and walnut and chestnut and plane trees. I sat down on a bench which faced the ruin, my back toward the ravine. Trains passed and I did not see them. When we were children, this jungle served us as an excellent place to play

both permitted and prohibited games. Parents always worry
when their children find a jungle.

I recalled Heinz, the son of the rich widow, a pretty and
pampered boy. I was his protector from the persecutions of
the other boys. I protected him not out of kindness but so
that he would become my slave and property. I looked
around and, seeing no one, quickly ran and disappeared in
the undergrowth. After some searching, I found the big tree.
Heinz used to pray and bring offerings to this tree. We had
persuaded him to believe that the tree was a god named
Holifotz and, like other gods, was always angry and had to
be placated. I suggested that he make it offerings of chocolate. Chocolate and walnuts, that's what the god loved most.
Toys, too, were acceptable to this angry deity. Like true
priests, we had made up solemn rituals accompanied by
songs and lifted hands and circling the tree in procession.
Heinz would leave his offering on the exposed roots of the
tree and go away, and then we would gobble up the chocolate like true priests.

I now recalled Heinz's face. His skin was delicate and the
shade of olive. His brown eyes slanted a little. He had a
straight long nose and his hair was smooth and long and well
groomed, not like the rest of us whose hair was tangled or
coarse like hair brushes. Where is Heinz now? Once I met
his stepsister. Heinz was burned. Now the tree was a true
place of worship for me and I recalled that which can never
be again. I placed my memories on the roots of the tree.
These were my first acquaintances in Weinburg who I could
be sure had not murdered Jews—the tree and the American
girls. It was now clear that I had loved Heinz. I was always
with Ruth but I loved Heinz. We used to wrestle frequently
on the soft carpet in his mother's house. He begged me to
wrestle with him even when I told him to choose someone
not as strong as I was, for it was no fun to win all the time.

He would not answer and only pleaded with his brown eyes, and I could not resist him and again we rolled around on the carpet and held tightly to each other.

I went back to the street. The memory of the strange love I had felt for Heinz filled me with a sharp pain. I had not known that I had loved Heinz when I was a child, and now there was no returning to it. This pain was suddenly interrupted by the recollection of the face of the strange woman in Zeiger's showcase—the elongated nose, the flared nostrils, the smooth skin, and the dark slanting eyes.

I followed the street which bordered on the ravine on one side and had a row of houses on the other, until I came to what had been the Jewish hospital. I entered the yard through the ruins of the gate. The building was razed to the ground and its basements gaped open. The big walnut tree loomed taller than ever, because there were no walls to dwarf it. The walnuts were green. A bird fluttered among the leaves. I stood there for a moment, pure and calm, like the dead on the day of resurrection. Like them, I had come to examine a world I had not seen for a long time. A little girl looked at me through her hair, then leaped wildly away and disappeared. Out of habit, I walked around the path that surrounded the hospital. I could have walked right through it, for the place had been swept clean. No wild bushes grew here as on the ruins of Ruth's house. Just the same, I walked along the outer path out of respect for the building that had stood here. The area of the hospital seemed very small now that only the foundations remained —the same as with man. He takes up much room while he is alive, and the moment he dies his absence is not felt and he and all his doings shrink to insignificance.

I walked up flights of stairs that led nowhere, and I descended flights of stairs that came from nowhere. I turned the corner of a building that was no longer there and found myself in the garden of the Home for the Aged, which had not changed. The railroad passed above the parapet surrounding the garden. The same tracks which farther back had been in the ravine now emerged onto a fill, and to those in the garden it seemed that the trains ran right above them. It was five in the afternoon and the garden was peaceful and pretty. Some people sat scattered between the fruit trees and the flower beds. Each was immersed in himself and there was no communication between them.

I saw Henrietta under the apple tree and recognized her at once, although she had aged much. She knew that I would arrive sometime during the summer, and every day she sat in the garden waiting for me. She had no one else to wait for.

I did not want to startle her, so I walked around her cautiously. She had a black Sabbath dress on. Her heavy breasts hung loose. She had never had a child. Henrietta had tended me like a mother, she and her now dead aunt. An apple dropped to the ground and she did not stir. During the war, she had been in Theresienstadt. I completed my circuit and looked at her face without her seeing me. Her eyes were deep and Jewish, and her fat heavy legs suggested all the bitterness of exile. Henrietta was a prophetess sitting under an apple tree in the Home for the Aged in Weinburg. She did not give vent to her prophecies and they turned in on her and caused her pain. She became accustomed to the pain and forgot that she was a prophetess and God, too, forgot her and her pains.

I now beheld her sitting under the apple tree as in a children's story. She raised her head and saw me standing before her. She wanted to get up but I lightly pressed my hand on her shoulder. She wanted to say something, but could only call my name, which she repeated many times, and after each time she shed a tear, so that there came into being a strange necklace consisting alternately of my name and of round tears.

I bent over the old woman and put my cheek against her damp one. Her skin was rough and stray hairs grew on it.

"Every day I waited for you."

"You thought I wouldn't come?"

A train passed. The same train seemed to be passing and repassing, like an actor who regularly appears at the back of the stage. An old man walked by carrying a tin pan. As he passed, he looked to see who was visiting Henrietta. She whispered in my ear, "This is Mr. Cohen. He breeds dogs. He picks up the leftovers in the dining room for his dogs. He sells the puppies. He was in Auschwitz. His dogs keep on barking and nobody dares say anything about it."

Mr. Cohen went up to a little shed, and when he opened its doors there was barking and the yelping of puppies. Henrietta's veil fell to the ground. I reached for it, but the wind picked it up and blew it against a bench on which sat a hunchbacked woman. She cackled like an angry hen.

When I returned to Henrietta with the veil, she told me that the hunchbacked woman was a Mrs. Goldenheim. "She's terrible," Henrietta said. "She hasn't been in any camp. She came from Eretz Israel. Nobody talks to her and she quarrels with everyone. If Dr. Zelig were here, he wouldn't let the likes of her stay in the Home. He was a very good man. We were together in Theresienstadt."

"Who is the director now?"

"Hush. Quiet."

I bent over toward her and she whispered in my ear, "Mr. Metzman. Don't say anything. Dr. Zelig, he was director of the Home, and head of the community and also rabbi and cantor and doctor."

"And how many are there in the community aside from the residents in the Home?"

"Only one. Mr. Binsheimer, the merchant. He is now head of the community."

"One Jew in the city and he is also head of the Jewish community?"

"Yes."

"And the Home—doesn't the community run it?"

"Yes and no. That's what the big fight is all about. When Dr. Zelig died—he knew my Oscar, of blessed memory— that's when the quarrels began. What? You don't know who Oscar was? That was my husband. I married him in Theresienstadt. Both of us were well over fifty. He suffered from diabetes. For an entire week I took care of him in the attic. For a week we were husband and wife. And then they sent him away. Oscar of blessed memory and Dr. Zelig were friends. He arranged the marriage ceremony for us. Quiet, now. Here comes Metzman."

Mr. Metzman approached. He came out of the door as if he were looking for something; actually he was driven by curiosity to see who was visiting Henrietta, for no one ever had. He came up. I rose and extended my hand. He said he already knew I had arrived, and then he added in Hebrew, "So what's new in Israel?"

"Lots," I said.

"Lots and plots." He grinned knowingly.

20

"A pity I have no time now," Mr. Metzman said as he picked up the fallen apple. "In Israel the grapes must be ripe already, no? A pity I have no time. All day it's Mr. Metzman, the accounts; Mr. Metzman, a new bed is needed for Mrs. Greenberg. The books, the accounts, milk for the Sabbath, coal. And complaints about Mr. Cohen's dogs."

He walked away with bowed head, as if afraid someone would give him a punch on the chin. Henrietta was deathly pale. "What's the matter, Henrietta?" "Better don't ask. He's a scoundrel. He wasn't in the camps. He was in Palestine during the war. Ran a Hungarian restaurant in Haifa. Then he switched to Oriental foods and went bankrupt. And now he has returned to Weinburg to resume his old tricks. He outsmarted everyone. He pulled the wool on Mr. Binsheimer, too, who is rightly the head of the community because he lives outside the Home, and Metzman is only its director. Everything is so mixed up. Come, my boy, come let's go to lunch. Oh, if only Dr. Zelig were alive. And Oscar, my poor Oscar, peace be with him."

A train rumbled by and Henrietta raised her voice to make herself heard over the din, and some gray locks came loose on her forehead.

"I used to cook for them," she went on. "For nothing. I enjoyed it and everybody enjoyed my cooking. At that time everyone here was from the camps. Bergen-Belsen, Buchenwald, Theresienstadt. And now? Four came from America and seven returned from Israel to collect their pensions."

"They're lonesome, Henrietta," I said to her.

"I am lonesome, too," she said. "Come, my boy. I heard that you have a wife. Why didn't you bring her?"

A small boy suddenly burst out from among the trees and bumped into us. Henrietta's face underwent a change. "Here is Heinrele. Come here, Heinrele—come, come here."

Heinrele, about three years old, stood motionless.

"Heinrele. Heinrele."

The child moved away. "I have candy for you," Henrietta shouted after him, but he ran to the hunchbacked Mrs.

Goldenheim. She gave him a little red car and he at once started playing with it. The hunchback looked triumphantly at Henrietta, whose face fell. I was mad at the little traitor. I caressed Henrietta's aged cheek. Tears rolled from her eyes.

"Every time I see Heinrele, I think of you as you were. I have nobody left alive. Heinrele is a bright boy. I taught him to speak German. When he was brought here about a year ago, he could speak only Polish. His parents brought him. They were on the way to Israel and remained here. His father thought there was easy money here. Now Heinrele belongs to all of us. Be careful of Mr. Metzman; he will try to get around you with all sorts of sweet talk and get you involved in the affairs of the Home. Here is his wife."

A rolypoly blond woman came out of a side door, all smiles and curves and buttocks. Her buttocks also smiled. She cast a sly and lustful glance in my direction. Her entire body winked at me, and she disappeared shaking her behind.

"Mrs. Metzman—she is his second wife. He married her there, in Israel. She's a native of Israel. Mrs. Metzman! Mrs. Metzman!"

The woman reappeared in response. Apparently she had stood behind the door waiting to be called. Henrietta introduced me to her. "Here is a man from Israel. Came to see me. I've known him since he was no bigger than Heinrele."

Mrs. Metzman slapped me on the back. "*Ahlan,*" she greeted me in Arabic, and repeated the greeting again and again. "*Ahlan, ya Sheikh.* How do you like this place? Fantastic. No? The mostest. And what do you think of these characters? A bunch of clowns." And she laughed. Heinrele stood by us like a puppy and took it all in, oblivious of the toy car in his hand.

"Say '*Ahlan,*' Heinrele! Say '*Ahlan!*' " Mrs. Metzman urged him.

Heinrele, whose name was also Henrik and Zevi, said, "Allan, Llan," or something like that and everybody laughed. Mrs. Metzman was convulsed with laughter. Her fat arms, her nipples, and her buttocks shook with laughter. Her entire body rocked and her face reddened deeply.

Another train roared by. So many trains, passenger trains and freight trains. Henrietta told me that the last deportees from the city were sent on this line, and when they stood on the platform waiting for their train a band played "I must, I must my city leave/And my beloved leave behind." And at the time this last shipment of Jews from Weinburg waited at the station, the American girls whom I saw earlier played ball and knew nothing and their parents knew nothing. Today they wear cowboy Levi's and sing about their honeys.

Heinrele became bored and started running around among the flower beds shouting, "Allan! Llan!" And from all sides hoarse old voices called to him:

"Heinrele, come here!"

"Heinrele, who's there?"

"Heinrele, look what I've got!"

And by my side Henrietta's low voice: "This boy Heinrele. He breaks my heart, the little bandit." A car drove in through the gate and stopped on the gravel. Mr. Grinfeld, a tall, fat, ruddy-faced, gray-haired man, stepped out. His mustache was made up à la Emperor Franz Josef, with two rounded brushes to each side. His American car was brand new, and its uptilted trunk suggested its being in heat. Of all the Jews who had lived in the surrounding villages, he was the only one who returned after the war. A cattle dealer, some seventy years old, he was still in his prime. He walked by us jingling his keys. "This is he," was all Henrietta said. Later I learned that he had resumed his cattle trade and had friends among the village women on whom he showered gifts.

I escorted Henrietta to the stairs. She leaned on me, for it had been a long time since she had leaned on anyone. She was very proud that Mr. Cohen and Mrs. Metzman and Mr. Grinfeld and the hunchback saw her thus, her old arm linked in mine. I told her I would come back soon, and I returned to the garden and from the garden to the hospital grounds. When little Ruth's leg was cut off, she stayed in this place many days and nights until the amputation healed over and was ready for an artificial limb which squeaked and banged. She would sit in the garden under the apple tree bedded in pillows and blankets and lording it over the other children, a fair, black-haired queen. Her hair was loose and no longer worked into the thin little braids that were called mouse tails. Her body was covered with a blanket so that it was not apparent that she was missing one leg. Ruth's father, Dr. Manheim, was the local rabbi, and delivered his sermons to Bar Mitzvah boys and his eulogies over the dead in the magnificent temple, dressed in his black robes. He would refer to the dead with all kinds of poetic expressions, such as "they who have been gathered to their Father," and "dwellers of a fairer world," and "sleepers in the bosom of our kind and beloved God." When Ruth died, nobody recited "The Lord is God" seven times or "Hear, O Israel." Before her misfortune with her leg, the grownups used to say about Ruth and me that we would be bride and groom. Heinz, whom I loved, also said so. Later a boy from the Hitler Youth kicked Ruth cruelly, and the echo of those kicks beats in my head and in my blood. Since that time, I have heard many violent collisions between bodies, iron striking earth, metal striking metal, iron striking stone, stone colliding with stone, steel with flesh, flesh with flesh. All these sounds dimmed in my memory. But the sound of the brown-shirted boy's foot striking Ruth's crippled body has grown stronger instead of dimming, until it has become the thunder in my life.

Once, I waited with Ruth before her father's vestry, and I

saw how he pulled off the heavy robes over his head and remained standing in white shirt and black trousers that were held up by black suspenders. The rigid five-sided cap which he wore during the services he would put away in a special container, and the beadle later reverently wiped its soft velvet.

Ruth was eighteen, or perhaps nineteen, when she was murdered far away from me. Here, in this garden, she was a fair queen. Her gray eyes were the eyes of an adult and she was unlike us though she was only eleven. I remained a child but she was already grown and had known pain—she was an ambassador from the realm of the adults.

I returned to the Home for the Aged by way of the gate that was no longer there and by imaginary stairways. I sat down in the waiting room where stood a number of uphol- stered chairs and where newspapers were scattered on tables. One wall was all glass and through it I saw some of the old people sitting at their tables waiting for dinner. I hung my head like a lantern in the doorway to the dining room and found that Henrietta had not yet arrived, so I returned to the waiting room. The sound of a typewriter assailed me and I knocked on the door marked "Office" and walked in. Metzman's wife sat there typing a letter. She smiled at me and began explaining what she was writing even as she rocked up and down and sidewise in her chair— all about the Home and its management and the disputes between Mr. Metzman and Mr. Binsheimer, who was head of the nonexistent Jewish community in Weinburg, and how the trials had been going on for over a year, and many letters had been sent and arguments presented and protests signed by former camp inmates submitted. A long and confused business. And the German judges were afraid to reach a decision lest they be accused of anti-Semitism. While she was talking, Mr. Metzman himself came in and his face glowed as he saw me: "Come and have dinner. Waiting for Henrietta? Good, good. What do you say to all this business? I only came here temporarily to straighten things out. The poor old people; there is nobody to look after them. And, between ourselves, Dr. Zelig was no genius. There was much disorder, a real mess. They begged me to come here with my wife, a real native Sabra, blond but a true Sabra, by birth, a Sabra from her mother's belly."

And as he said "belly," his eyes lit up and glittered, for she no doubt had a belly rising like a mound of wheat, as the *Song of Songs* says, and to change the subject he stuck his hand into his pants pocket and pulled out a silk skullcap: "Here. Put it on. Here it is customary to eat with covered head. I'm not so terribly religious myself, but I know what is the right thing to do." And he walked out after slapping me on the back and saying cheerfully, "See you. See you."

Heinrele ran past but did not notice me. His mother ran after him, a plate in her hands, calling, "Henrik! Henrik!" I returned to the waiting room and began studying the announcements and the large portrait of Dr. Zelig.

Henrietta came down the stairs wearing a festive black dress in my honor. I went to meet her and extended my arm to her. She put her arm in mine and I noticed the camp number tattooed on it. As for myself, I generally cannot remember serial numbers or other identification numbers. "Let's wait for Mrs. Munster," Henrietta whispered to me. "She is the most pitiful of us all. She lost thirty-three relatives. When the Russians came, only she and her youngest daughter, Clara, were left. And then Clara, too, died, on a train, or in the snow. Talk to her. Be nice to her."

Mrs. Munster came down. Her little black eyes were fixed in the great distance where her daughter Clara was endlessly sinking into eternity. The old woman's eyes were set in a number of rolls of pallid fat, a Lot's wife who turned her face to look at her last daughter, Clara, and became a pillar of white fat. Strangely, her hair remained shining black and was now stretched tight into a bun at the back of her head. She moved heavily in our direction. Henrietta pushed me toward her, as she used to do when I was a child and she wanted me to greet someone.

I went up to her, moved by reverence for her great sorrow. She had been there and had returned alone.

She smiled at me. "I heard that you came. It's good that you came to see our Henrietta. When we returned here, she took care of all of us; she cooked for us. Isn't that so, Henrietta? Isn't it so? Love your neighbor like yourself. Who's rich? He who is happy with his suffering. Isn't it so?"

I pressed her hand and resurrected it. Her hand came to life in mine, and her eyes, too, looked up from their pockets of fat and shadows.

"You came from Israel?" she asked.

Henrietta breathed heavily and her eyes were filled with terror and warning.

"You studied in school here?"

"Of course, Mrs. Munster, up to the fifth grade."

"Was the late Mr. Kleinman your teacher?"

"Yes, yes, of course."

"And did you know Clara?"

"Clara?"

"Yes, my Clara."

"It seems I don't remember."

"You attended the same school as she and you don't remember Clara?"

I said nothing. Henrietta nudged me. Mrs. Munster stared at me with terrible anticipation, like a hungry dog.

"Just a moment," I said. "One moment," and I touched my forehead as if trying hard to recall. "Clara? Clara Munster? The one with the smooth black hair?"

"Yes, yes, my Clara. Now you remember?"

"Of course. Of course. She acted in the school plays."

"Rebecca at the well. Do you remember?"

"Yes, and also Eliezer."

"They pasted a beard on her."

Mrs. Munster was crying in quiet reconciliation. "I lost everything. I go on living only in order to go up and down these stairs three times a day. It's hard on my legs to go up these steps. Sometimes Henrietta helps me. All my family were killed. On every landing of the staircase, one of them sits, and there aren't enough landings for all the dead. My daughter Clara sits on the lowest landing. You remember what she said when she played Rebecca at the well? 'Drink, and also your camels, and also your heart—love your neighbor.' "

A door was opened and a sudden gust blew in. Something, a midge, got into my eye. I shut my eyes tight and killed the little midge, and Henrietta removed the black little corpse from my eye. Then she said, "Come, let's go to eat." She was proud of me as a veteran is proud of a recruit who has stood the test of the first battle. I opened the door for her and she entered before me with dignity.

The dining room was modern. Most of the tables were already occupied. A glass wall faced the garden. The room was new and shiny but the diners wilted, as at the end of the Day of Atonement when one cries out with one's last remaining strength, "Open the gate for us at the time of gate closing, for the day has passed." The dining room was large and impersonal, like the waiting room of a railway station where one goes to meet someone, or to see someone off. There were not many diners and they sat at round tables. At some of the tables three of the chairs were empty, as if the diner, alone and bent over his plate, were partaking of a meal with his dead. One man sat chewing his meat in terrible silence. The dead said not a word, and the only sound made by the living was when their forks scraped against the plates. Thus I came in, together with good Henrietta, to an underworld with big windows and pleasant, smooth furniture. Why did I come here? I came like Odysseus, who descended into the nether world to commune with the spirits. I came to have my future foretold.

On a shelf along the wall at the right stood a television set flanked by framed drawings of Chaim Weizmann, President of Israel, and Theodor Herzl. The drawings must have been copied from photos by an amateur among the old people whose hand shook, and they were a little crooked. Above the threesome of the TV and the two statesmen hung the flag of Israel and some wilted wreaths placed there on the last festive occasion. In the corner was a serving table with plates and pots and saucers which were sent up from the kitchen in the basement in a hand-operated elevator. Every time the dumbwaiter platform came up, a number of heads turned toward it with curiosity and envy and suspicion. A Catholic nun quietly ladled the food into the plates. After this quiet came a deeper quiet. She was accustomed to living among the dead. She was atoning for the sins of her people by handing out food to the dead and the old. When the lift is delayed, the nun waits with lowered head, her fingers interlocked, as if reciting some special prayer. *Kohanim* bless the people with outspread fingers, but the nun interlocks hers. She is old and shriveled and more pale than the dead whom she feeds as atonement. Her black habit is faded and the thick-lensed glasses she wears cut into the bridge of her thin nose. The food has no flavor. The food has no taste. The food of the dead is dead, and there is no atonement for the dead. She takes the bowls and ladles the food out into plates. I was told her name. I walked up to her and said, "Sister Maria. Sister Maria." She was startled and said, "Quiet, please. Don't shout." I hadn't shouted. I whispered, "Sister Maria, where is Sister Elizabeth now?" She said, "She is sick in the hospital."

"Which hospital is she in?"

She told me in a whisper. We heard a chair being moved. An old man got up and left without looking at the others; only his lips moved, since he was always talking with his dead. The dead are close to him, and he to them; therefore he can talk to them in a whisper.

"Why do you want to know where Sister Elizabeth is?"

"She took care of little Ruth when they amputated her leg."

"I know."

"That was a long time ago."

"I know. We are all from a long time ago."

The old man returned to the dining room and went up to Henrietta's table. He bent over her and whispered something. Henrietta listened a moment and then struck the table with the flat of her hand as if in great and pleasant surprise. I remained near Sister Maria.

"Why did you come? Ruth is dead and Sister Elizabeth is very sick."

"I came on account of hate."

"It's a long way from the Holy Land here."

"How do you know?"

"I know those who come from the Holy Land," she said. And after a while, "Have you learned to hate?"

"Not yet. Meantime I listen to the stories of the old people."

"And the story of little Ruth who died."

"She was burned."

"I know. The smoke blew here, like the smoke from the train engines."

"We stood on the overpass once, when we were children."

"Now, sit down and eat. For hate, too, one needs strength."

She sank into the depth of prayer and did not rise from it. I returned to Henrietta's table. Sister Maria brought us plates. I remarked that the plates were made of clay. She said we would return to earth. Henrietta muttered something to herself, repeating the word "ingrate," so that I should ask her what she was saying. But I did not ask. She told me that the old man was Mr. Levinger, and that he guided people around the cemeteries in the neighborhood. He helped them remember, and knew by heart the names of all the people of the community in the past.

I thought, How will I hate? I sank into my memories as one sinks into forgetfulness. Time was passing and I still didn't hate. I will have to leave the Home and walk about the streets and look into people's faces. All those over thirty had murdered Jews. I calculated mentally how many Germans there are and how many had passed the age limit I had set. I indulged in reckonings as one does on Passover on the night of the Seder: Ten plagues at the sea and all the other mysterious calculations of numerology.

A man rose from a neighboring table and Henrietta told me that he was Dr. Messer. He got up, but his wife continued eating. Her face was pale and delicate. For years they hadn't talked to each other. Her lips trembled as she ate the stewed fruit. Mrs. Metzman came and said, "What do you think of them? Characters, eh? Every single one of them."

"Now we will find a hotel for you," Mrs. Metzman said. "I have a file in the office. We want to be sure that the hotel isn't owned by one of the synagogue burners, and also that there aren't night clubs on the ground floor where they will sing and bawl."

No hatred would come into my heart. Instead I felt a great weariness. Dr. Messer's wife walked by like a corpse and hummed something indistinctly. I patted Henrietta's cheek. She said she'd wait for me in her room and meantime get tea ready. I said it would be getting dark by then. But she assured me that it wouldn't. In Europe it doesn't get dark till late in the summer. The people of Europe are lucky; they have two evening hours of happiness. In Europe darkness comes from forests and rivers, and not from a merciless desert as in Israel.

I went into Mrs. Metzman's office. Many filing cabinets lined one wall. Portraits of Weizmann and Herzl hung above them. These must have been the photos from which the amateur artist drew his inspiration. The two statesmen looked severely at Mrs. Metzman. Indeed, she was acting strangely. She rocked in the chair behind the desk. She shook her thighs and declared again and again that it was warm. She undid a button of her blue smock and disclosed the swell of a flushed bosom. "If you only knew how glad I am to see an Israeli here, someone who . . . from that time." And she looked at me, encouraging a response.

"Yes, yes," she went on. "So you came here to remember and to hate, but you know that psychologically speaking loving and hating are the same thing."

"That's right, Mrs. Metzman, only I'd prefer to start with hating and get to loving afterward."

"Yes, you want the name of a hotel," she said, displeased, and buttoned her smock. She took out some files and glanced through them. Everything that is ends up filed away in an office. The card files of this Jewish Home for the Aged, for instance, resemble the card files of spare parts in a factory. Mrs. Metzman went into action, turning cards over and making phone calls, short questions, short answers. "With or without bath? Pity. What? No? For how long?" I didn't know what to answer. "Very good." In the end she suggested the Savoy Hotel, near the railroad station, whose owners came from another city. I consented because I love to stay near the exits of a city. It gives me a feeling of security; in case of trouble I can get away. The chair I had been sitting on was comfortable and it now cost me an effort to get up, for Henrietta was waiting for me. Mrs. Metzman staged a final assault. She disclosed fattish thighs and heaved her breasts close to my face; then she brought out a little snapshot. Recognize? There was a blond girl in a British Army uniform, a British officer next to her, and in the background the pyramids of Gizeh. As I walked out, she whispered, "Come again. I am simply thirsting for Hebrew talk." And she returned to her files with a great show of energy.

Mr. Cohen walked by carrying a puppy. "I knew your father," he said. Then he returned and said again, "I knew your father." I wanted to tell him that my father had died, but he anticipated me. "I know that he already passed away. We served in the Imperial Army together. Last Yom Kippur I commemorated him."

On the Day of Atonement they commemorate the dead in the Home, and the list is so long that they had to skip part of the noon service. Here they called it the Ritual of Souls. When I was a child, they used to chase us children out of the synagogue during the memorial service. Only Heinz, whom I loved, was permitted to remain, because his father was already among the dead. We envied him, for we didn't know what was done during this service. Ruth's father no doubt addressed the mourners with words of consolation. When we returned to the synagogue from our games outside at the end of the service, we found many eyes red from weeping.

I went up to Henrietta. From a room came two quarrelsome voices, male and female, about some letter from America that had been lost: he blamed it on her and she on him.

I knocked on Henrietta's door and entered. Mrs. Munster

was with her. Her face became animated when she saw me.
She offered me an ornate girl's comb. "Here, take it, as a
memento. It belonged to Clara." I tried to refuse but she
would not hear of it. It belonged to me, she said, because I
had remembered that Clara had played Eliezer at the well. I
went out on the porch. Mr. Cohen was in the garden playing
with his dogs and puppies. Mrs. Munster said, "We don't
talk to Mr. Cohen on account of his dogs; they are soiling
the house."

An engine raced by outside. It pulled no cars and was free
of all responsibility.

The two old women began talking excitedly about "that
ingrate." Finally one said, "It's all right to tell him." And I
heard the tale of an orphaned little girl who was picked up
in camp and then was brought here and taken care of and
educated. The late Dr. Zelig took care of her like a father,
and when she was twelve years old she was sent to Israel
with a group of children and she grew up in some kibbutz
whose name Henrietta had forgotten. One day they heard
that she had run away from the kibbutz. Now it was
rumored that she had returned to Germany, that she had
joined a traveling circus as an acrobat or a clown. Mr.
Cohen, with whom one doesn't talk because he breeds dogs,
swore that he saw her take part in some performance and
that she hadn't too many clothes on. It was also rumored that
she came to Weinburg to represent Germany in the skating
tournament, and that it was a scandal and a shame and a
blasphemy.

I did not tell them that without a doubt I, too, had seen
her. From their description of her, I recalled that she was
with me on the train, that her hair was beautiful and her
legs strong. At once I felt happy. Things are beginning to
move. One thing impinges on another. The confusion is as-
suming form. And I was overcome with a strange sense of

remembering things that were about to happen.

I sat and drank tea and ate cake. My right thigh began throbbing. My blood began pulsing in an unexpected place, like a bird that suddenly bursts into song among the branches. The blood pulsed in my thigh for no apparent reason except impatience. I thought perhaps my leg had fallen asleep and I moved my weight to the other side, but the throbbing continued.

Bells were ringing from the Church of the Good Virgin and from the Dome and from St. Michael's.

I left Henrietta and the mother of Saint Clara. I promised the two women to return soon, and went down to the garden and from there to the yard of the hospital. I went up and down imaginary staircases. I saw Heinrele hiding among the ruins of the foundations of the house. No other child was looking for him and the old people had locked themselves in their rooms. The child began following me, but I waved to him to stay where he was, to stay, to stay.

21

I saw that once more there were horses in Mr. Kleiman's yard. He had been the most Germanized Jew in the Weinburg community and owned many horses. It was told that an aristocratic lady in the neighborhood fell in love with him on account of his purebred horses. When as a child I had been put to bed, the gossip of the grownups about Mr. Kleiman rustled over me like a breeze murmuring in the summits of trees. He had a daughter named Lore. She was in my class. Her eyes were green and her skin was tanned and she could ride her father's horses.

Bells began ringing. These are from St. Magdalene's; a wedding is being performed there. A little girl near me said, "There are horses here." I asked her, "What is your name?" "My name is Lisel, and sometimes they call me Lise. There are brown horses and black ones, and also a white one."

Many bells were ringing and I thought, There must be many weddings. But the little girl was gone. I tried to avoid the tempo of the bells and to follow an inner cadence, but the ringing came from so many bells, from the church of the monastery, and the Church of St. Francis, and the Church of Our Dear Lord Jesus, that I could not overcome their rhythms. I stopped and waited till the ringing ceased. In another hour or two it would be evening, even in Europe in the summer. What will become of me? What have I discovered so far? That once again there are horses in Mr. Kleiman's stables, and that Sister Elizabeth is sick in the hospital, and that a new building had been put up in place of the old station, and that the snapshot taken of us that day on the steps of the station no longer fits the present. My time has passed; my sacrifice is in vain. Behind a wall I heard children playing hide-and-seek. I heard them scampering about and seeking hiding places. I heard one of them counting: "Ninety-eight, ninety-nine, I'm coming." Tense silence and the terror of being sought filled the early twilight. In my pocket I fingered the comb that had held Clara's hair. Mrs. Munster had taken it from the head of her dead daughter: Clara's black hair tumbled down, her dead body collapsed, and she was buried alongside the road where the trucks of the Red Army moved westward. As a child, Clara had played Eliezer at the well and a beard was pasted to her chin; she had played Rebecca at the well and had worn gypsy earrings; she had played Hannah with her seven sons, and Antiochus and Judas Maccabeus. Now I stood like old

Eliezer at the well. I had made no vows, nor did I seek a wife. I looked for Nazis of the past, like the one who had kicked Ruth, and the one who had taken her artificial leg, and the one who had laughed, and the one who was silent, and the one who took snapshots of the last Jews, and the one who sang, "Now I must/ Now I must leave my native town/ But you, my girl, are staying here."

I went into the yard. The ground appeared well trampled by horses. From the door opposite the entrance came an old man. "Yes?" "I am just looking." "You are not from here?" "No." Some of the horses stuck their heads out of their stalls. I asked, "What do you need horses for now?" And he said, "For the police, and for some of the new aristocracy. They come here to learn to ride—the daughters of Eckman, the contractor; and Wenckle, the agent; and Mayer, the owner of the factory of motorcycle parts. The girls come here dressed like cowboys. They drink gin-and-tonic. Me, I am an old man; my time is over."

As he talked, the head of an old horse appeared out of a stall near him. At first the man tried to shoo the animal back; then he patted its head. "This is the mare Falada," he said. ("Falada, Falada," the princess in the children's story said to the mounted horse's head that hung over the gate.) "Falada, Falada, what happened to Mr. Kleiman?" As I said this, the old man began to weep bitterly. "You know everything. You come from far away and you know everything. This mare was born that terrible day. She had just been born, and stood trembling coltishly near her mother, Farina. My hands were still covered with blood and mucus when the gate was opened loudly. I raised my hands as two storm troopers entered and ordered me to give them the keys to the stable. They cursed me and called me a Jew's dog and a swine. Jesus! Everything would be different from now on, they said. Mr. Kleiman came out of the feed room, and he was a strong and proud man and his hair was white. When they saw him, they shot him dead. Jesus, forgive my sins! And the door of the stable opened and the young lady, Fräulein Lore, came out riding on the wild bay horse. She had green eyes. 'Careful, the horse is mad!' I shouted to her. But she galloped right up to the two S.S. men, and one of them was knocked down by the horse and she dashed on to the gate. She had lost control of the horse, and as it dashed through the open side gate her hair was caught in the arch and she was left hanging by it. The S.S. man who hadn't been hurt emptied his Mauser into her, the entire clip, and so she remained hanging, as in a butcher shop, the blood pouring out of her. They didn't allow us to take her down. As it says in the Bible, 'for the bird of the sky and the beast of the field.' That S.S. man, the one who was kicked, was hurt in the crotch. He was about to get married and now there was to be no wedding. Jesus! Jesus, forgive us the terrible joke. Blood and soil! Strength through joy! What do you say, Falada? This man came from the Holy Land and he knows all about you." I reminded the old man of the places in the Bible where horses are mentioned. "I know the Bible well," he said. (Their surge is as the surge of horses. A host of horses. Open the gate for us at the time of the closing of gates, for the day has turned to set.)

The old man opened the small side gate and gave me a business card which read, "Anton Schmiding, Expert on Horses, Diplomate Riding Instructor, Second Lieutenant, Cavalry, During World War I." Falada! Falada! What an end for little Lore who had been my classmate. "What are you whispering, my dear sir?" the old man asked. "I am remembering things," I said. "You remember by whispering?" I tried to recall whether Mr. Kleiman had *mezuzoth* nailed to the doors of his stables and storerooms and offices, for he had lived there, too. Lore had a friend, also from our class. Franz was his name, and he, too, is dead; I was told he was burned. A refined and dark-complexioned boy. His parents were Spanish Jews and their name was Laredo. A foreign boy, from another world. Lore, who was green-eyed and strong as a boy and had a muscular body, used to take care of Franz with a strange love. Lore—like Absalom— died while suspended by her hair. The old man stamped his foot. "You hear? Hollow underneath. The wine cellars are under the city. Some Jews tried to hide among the barrels and their blood mixed with the wine." Then I went out and the side gate was closed behind me.

Now I have lost my last chance to forget. From now on I won't be able to forget. There is a time for remembering and a time for forgetting, a time for opening doors and a time for locking them. But with the last chance to forget gone, all the details came to life within me. My heart has become a necromancer and all that was buried is brought up by it to the surface; even the face of the unknown woman in the store window of Zeiger the photographer—all, all are now attached to my heart with terrible hooks.

I will go to the railway station and from there to the hotel on the square. The city is now fully lit on this glorious summer night. Where should I begin? What should I do? Who is with me? Who?

22

The wind was practicing, like a child learning to use its teeth. In Jerusalem the wind, too, has teeth, especially near areas of no man's land, which are themselves sown with the broken teeth of ruins and tank obstacles and barbed wire.

Vicky sat in a spot sheltered from the wind. This was her domain, the area opposite the Old City wall and the Tower of David. She lived with her family in a wrecked hotel near no man's land. Her mother and father, since Vicky led her brothers and sisters in revolt, had not slept in the same bed. They had decided that eight living brothers and sisters, three dead ones, and three miscarriages were quite enough, and now, whenever the parents were together, even if they were only talking to each other, and especially in the afternoons and on holidays, Vicky organized a standing guard over them. In any case, there weren't enough beds for all of them. All the children did guard duty, except the baby and the brother who was serving in the army. He was busy guarding the borders of the country, and it was he who taught Vicky how to maintain an effective guard over the parents, for he was a private first class. Vicky herself did not sleep in the same room with the rest of the family but occupied an outside room through whose breached walls she could see the Old City.

Joel surprised her as he approached from behind the high walls that had been built as protection from snipers. These walls have openings for tourists to look through to the enemy side. The tourists peep through, then take snapshots of each other near the sign which proclaims, "Danger! Border!" in English, French, and Yiddish, in addition to Hebrew, so that there would be no mistaking it. To avoid any final possibility of error, the sign has a skull and crossbones painted on it. At one time Vicky added a mustache and glasses to the skull, but the danger remained the same. Over the years people got used to it and the picture of the skull no longer frightened anybody. Joel brushed the cuffs of his pants and, standing on a pile of trash, he called to her loudly. But Vicky slipped away. One day she will fail to return from no man's land and then it will be necessary to call Major Patterson, Mina's friend, to get her back. Or she might step on an old mine. Now he heard her calling him and saw her head outlined in the window of a ruin, her hands holding on to the frame. Away on the other side, the head of a young Bedouin soldier of the Arab Legion appeared over the edge of the Old City wall. Joel shook his finger at her and ordered her to get down. He was about to go into the ruin to get her, but it turned out that it was the only wall left of a house, like a stage decoration, and when he went behind it he saw that she was hanging from the window sill and her legs dangled like the legs of a doll. He whistled to her and Vicky jumped down, her wide skirt ballooning out like a parachute. He noticed that her panties had been made out of a British flag. (During the War of Independence, Vicky's father came across a cache of British flags and used them to make underwear for all his children.) She leaped at him and curled herself about him like a kitten and begged him to tell her the end of his stories, two of which he had once started telling her and left unfinished, one about the god Osiris, who was rent to pieces, and the other about little Ruth of his childhood, who was injured in an accident in the street.

"And your wife's name is Ruth, too."

"How do you know?"

"I know everything. I also know that the lady doctor is at Meinzer's."

They went to Vicky's room, which had once occupied a corner of the hotel and looked out in three directions like the bridge on a ship. They sat in wrecks of upholstered chairs of which only the creaking springs remained. Vicky ceremoniously served him a glass of water on a wooden crate marked "Suleiman Bros., Damascus." Then she brought out a dented and blackened tea kettle, a doll with a broken head, and a book which Joel had once given her. She was full of questions. What happened after Ruth's leg was cut off? Did they make her an artificial leg? And did Osiris come back to life after he had been rent to pieces? And what happened to Ruth later? The children outside became so noisy they couldn't hear themselves talk. The children played hide-and-seek, war-and-peace, skip-and-jump. One day there will be so many children near no man's land that they will rise up and kill all the grownups.

Vicky showed him her palm, which bore the inscription "No." Then she smiled and showed him her other palm, which said "Yes." Joel said nothing. The world agreed with him and was silent, too. Then Vicky wrote on her thigh "Go." He was about to do so, but she pulled him back and showed him her other thigh, which said, "Stay." Then she walked with Joel down the corridor, and he left.

Joel went into the huge old house where Meinzer had his studio. The building sprawled between more modern structures, which were mostly schools and movie houses. Where is the entrance? Where the corridor? Could you tell me? Does he live here? It consisted of units haphazardly added to older units, like a wild hornets' nest. In some of the cells, they had no doubt buried the dead, in sitting and standing postures. Through the window on a half floor, the feet of a tailor could be seen, but his head was on the floor above. Joel passed through a shop where an old man sat making rubber stamps, shaping letters backward so that in the end they should read forward. Where is the roof? Where is the entrance to Meinzer's studio? A long explanation, confused as the house itself, followed. A couple of frightened cats dashed out of the way. Joel heard the footsteps of a crowd of people coming out of a movie house where the picture had ended, but he could not see them. A dozen times he said, "Excuse me," to frightened people. He picked up two children on whom he had almost stepped. He broke off a piece from a shaky railing and overheard an indistinct quarrel from an apartment somewhere deep in the recesses of the house.

Finally he came to a small court on which Meinzer's studio opened. The bell on the door was a head of Buddha, the lintel was Greek, and a tin weather-vane cock swung overhead. As he opened the door, he activated an entire battery of bells and whistles and fifes. He passed through a room that was decorated with African spears and Chinese masks and Japanese hara-kiri daggers. A soft melody was heard. All kinds of sound amplifiers were concealed in the rooms, under the sofa, in the bathroom, between the springs of the chair. Low tones emerged from thick books and higher ones came from the refrigerator. One took a glass of cold water from the refrigerator and the tones became louder. Guests were seated in a half circle and Meinzer was showing them his latest paintings. He set up a painting and gingerly stepped back to assess the effect. The guests responded appropriately—mouths gaping with enthusiasm, eyes staring with excitement: "Wonderful! When was this? What is that? Unbelievable! How the colors blend! The space values, so perfectly handled! How it projects the background!" Joel saw at once this was a Grade C showing. Meinzer showed his work in three categories. In the lowest category the viewers sat on the floor. (Good for young romantics.) He would show his most modernistic, shapeless, and even abstract work. To the accompaniment of music by Tchaikovsky and Brahms, he would toss cheap cigarettes and peanuts into the excited and uncomfortably seated audience. There would be no buyers here, in any case.

In the middle category of show he would also display some of his collection of Chinese paintings and Indian sculpture. The music would be punctuated with rare items of medieval composition. Then he would lead the men to the corner where the bookshelves were and show them some classical Japanese pornography—a man held between two women as between tongs, or a Japanese woman committing hara-kiri with the erect penis of a man against whom she leans. The women would ask: What is it? What is going on there? And the men would smile conspiratorially. Then Meinzer would treat them to imported English cigarettes and roasted almonds dipped in brown sugar and also to tales of his adventures in Paris, where he had been, and in the war, where he had not been. Thus he entertained intellectuals, people of educated taste but with not enough money to buy his pictures.

For the rich, especially rich tourists, he gave a Grade A showing. On these occasions Meinzer would dress up in a medieval monk's habit and don a knight's steel helmet flaunting a red feather. In his hands he would hold African dolls. On his feet belled sandals from the South Sea Islands. In a solemn and portentous voice he announced the opening of the show. An automatic device closed the shutters and simultaneously lit a red light in the head of a Chinese dragon. Into the hands of his surprised guests he placed slender Mexican candles, warning them not to burn his studio down. The smell of incense filled the place. He sat on the floor among his amazed and confused guests and, removing his helmet, began to hum Hasidic songs, for he is also an ardent Hasid. This would be followed by the flashing on and off of colored lights in unexpected places, producing the effect of fireworks. And now was also the time for whiskey and vodka and all sorts of mixed drinks and for rare recordings: the talk around an operating table, a dialogue in a confession booth, and other unusual occasions. His guests cheered by the liquor, Meinzer would tell them of the kibbutz where he had been a member, and of his exploits in the war, where he had actually done only camouflage work.

Finished with his assault on the religious and Zionist sensibilities of his guests, Meinzer would attack their other sensibilities. He would bring out pornography works more outrageous than the ones shown to category B: now it would be three men with one woman, or two men and two women contorted in a knot from which a tangle of innumerable limbs project. But he would not let these brochures be looked at too long, and quickly gathered them up the way prayer books are gathered up at the end of a service. Now came the turn of coffee and tales of Bedouins, and recollections of life in the Palmach commando units and their songs. The coffeepot runs over, the fire hisses, a woman cries out because she doesn't realize that it is all part of the program. Then Meinzer goes out to the bathroom, as if by chance, and opens a small wall cabinet which contains a pair of earphones. He listens to the whispering of his guests recorded by a concealed microphone, and from their remarks he decides when to stage the final assault on their wallets. Even his bathroom is stylized; heads painted everywhere, and comic sayings on the walls. An original man, Meinzer, a true artist, a bohemian.

Meinzer paints many pictures because he suffers from unrequited love. As a consequence of this abundance, he makes much money and has many new loves. He sowed one frustrated love and harvested many in its stead. For he, too, is an angel of the Lord and very efficient in the ways of fate. On summer nights he presents Jerusalem to his guests. He announces: "Behind this curtain stands my beloved." His visitors impatiently expect to see a beautiful nude. With a dramatic gesture he parts the curtains and points to the night city, the suffering humiliated city. Fate loves him. Fate loves the smell of his paints, his stretched canvases, his strange masks, his idols, his bells from Burma and Angola, the teeth from the Congo, the tiger claws, the buffalo horns, the wooden dolls from Java, the stuffed falcon, his brushes and the works he fails to complete, his collection of Chinese poems which say, for instance, "I sit with a quill in my hand; the cherry tree is in bloom; last summer I wondered, What will be this summer; and this summer I wonder, What will be next summer. What will be? What will be?"

"Where is Pat?" Joel asked Meinzer in the adjoining room, threatening him with a West African spear which he had taken from the wall. Meinzer at first pretended not to know, then gave up and pointed: "Over there. There."

Joel went into Meinzer's studio. The room was dark and silent, except for the scratching of the needle on a record; the sound box was in the other room where the guests were. Joel turned on the light, which was inside a skull. Patricia slept on a couch, covered with an African blanket. Her clothes were tossed on a chair. A number of pictures stood on easels, all nude portraits of Patricia, prone and crouching, her hair loose and merging with the dark background, her breasts small like those of a young girl. All the pictures were done in a conventional style and that may have been why Meinzer did not exhibit them.

Joel sat down and watched her waking, and his heart contracted. Her fist moved to her temple, then slowly opened. A smile spread over her face. Joel rose and she opened her eyes.

"You here?"

Her face paled and her mouth trembled. "I love you. . . . Meinzer? He only paints me." And she laughed. "He is hollow, like a hollow Easter egg with a face painted on it. Why are you standing?"

She got up, wrapped in an African robe. Erect, proud, she walked to a wall cabinet and brought out a bottle. Her eyes fused with his and he touched her. She whispered, "Wait till we are in my house. I promised you. You don't know me yet.

I will be your servant. I will wash your feet, you antique Oriental. I will prepare delicacies for you. I will tie a napkin around your neck. You will be my king."

She laughed and they drank.

"And you have yourself photographed against the background of the Old City."

"Silly. Are you jealous of Zeiger, too?"

"Who knows who you hang around with in no man's land."

"I can go there. I am American and Christian."

"How much longer?"

"Some weeks."

"Pat!"

"What?"

"Nothing. Are you tired?"

"You always think I should be tired. I never tire. I saw you pass by my house this morning and called you, but the gravel machine made so much noise you didn't hear me."

"This savage construction."

Pat—who came from afar, who never tires, who had promised him a night, who is a Christian and in Jerusalem, in all of Jerusalem, in all its no man's lands.

23

A city built on a river is totally unlike a city that has no river. Jerusalem has no river. Weinburg, my native town, has one. It is true I had decided to go to my hotel near the railroad station, but I went to the river. Where do lovers and people tired of love go to in Jerusalem? On what bridges do they stand watching the dark stream below? By what parapet will a man stand when he is alone? By what bank will he sit to watch what is being swept away never to return again? In Jerusalem people go to face the desert; they sit on the edges of dry ravines. In Jerusalem people lean on rocks.

Here in Weinburg there is a river. It is not a big river, as rivers go, nor does it flow directly into the sea. First it flows into a bigger river, and only then does it add its share to filling what can never be filled. On this evening the sound of recorded music alternately came and went, suggesting someone opening and closing a door. As a child, I used to press my palms against my ears and create a weird melody with a strange and broken rhythm. Now I was thinking, During the war they didn't take people to their death on this river, because it flows west. It is therefore innocent, unlike the railroad tracks that go east.

On this evening the river flowed rapidly. It occurred to me that a river flows faster and its murmuring and rustling near the grassy banks between the boating clubs are louder in the dark. There was something about the flowing of the river that suggested a confusion of seeing and hearing, so that one could almost see with one's ears and hear with one's eyes. This river is bordered all the way with fertile hills and towns and villages. It is spanned by hundreds of bridges, ancient bridges resting on many pillars and modern ones consisting of one swift arch. Some of them have been bombed to ruins, some have been rebuilt, and others are completely new. It has been a well-harnessed river for a long time now. Castles and churches and monasteries on its banks have lent many legends to it. There were the robber barons, who used to stretch ropes from their castles across the river, and boats trying to pass at night bumped into the ropes and alarmed the robbers, who descended upon the boatmen and robbed them and murdered them and drowned them. One can judge the width of this river by the lampposts on the opposite bank and the volume of the sounds coming from there. I heard a man call to another. A dog barked interminably. And these sounds recalled to me the width of the river. That is why I came here, to measure distances, to remember and to recall and to remind, to hear again the sounds of childhood by which I could measure the true distance to that time and that place. The voice of dead Ruth and the voice of Henrietta, still alive in the midst of her prolonged dying. Now I heard these voices and I wasn't sure whether I was calling to them or they to me. But I did know that the distance was greater than I had supposed.

Standing thus, I was not an avenger; I was like any other man who returns to the landscape of his childhood. My vengeance was like a wax sword. A great sadness descended upon me because I was empty of vengeance, for it was for its sake that I had come here all the way from Jerusalem, for its sake I left my work and my wife. As a matter of fact, I had been sent here from Jerusalem by all my friends and acquaintances. My colleagues and my pupils had decided that I must go. I was tense and nervous and given to black moods, like King Saul. My wife would say, "You are melancholy." She surmised that I had to return to Weinburg for a while to do my vengeance. My best friend said, "Either you will go there and get rid of your tension, or you will end up by betraying your good wife, and you'll become involved in all sorts of adventures of the flesh and of the blood which can only lead to heartbreak and tears and unusual deaths." To such an extent had I been tense and planning and plotting and gloomy before I came here.

I brought up little Ruth from the depths of the river, and she walked alongside me and was sad as on the day they amputated her leg. The nerves in her head then still pretended to feel the pain in the leg, but the leg was no longer there. I brought her up from the river, together with other shades from the past.

The bridge was lit up and empty; only the solitary saints in niches waved their censers and swords. Not even romantic couples used this bridge. Suddenly I saw the intense face of Lore Kleiman, the daring horsewoman, and my heavy-eyed friend Yosel, who had been in the camps and whose upper lip did not fit the lower so that they made a sucking sound as if they had not sucked enough in infancy. I also saw the face of my wife, whose eyes are brown and whose skin is smooth, and Dr. Manheim's lean, furrowed face. Faces of the living and of the dead came up before me in confusion on the bridge, and some of them were lit up and others were dark, immersed in inner dialogues of death and oblivion. Some faced each other and others gave themselves over to honeyed pain and the buzzing of the bees of sorrow. There were shades of lovers and enemies, wearing halos or wrapped in hatred.

I left the bridge and went along the bank to the place where once there had been a small marina. It had been moved farther upstream, and in its place tennis courts had been fenced off. They were dark except for one that was brightly lit up. A big sign was also visible: "SCHMIDT & SONS—WOOD AND COAL." Here sons inherit, and even when they are killed their names remain. Here the traits of parents are transmitted to their children even after war and destruction. Everything is inherited, shops and the color of the eyes, habits and talents. With us it is different: the troubles and the wanderings and the peculiar deaths provide each one with a physiognomy of his own. I don't resemble anyone in particular. Neither does Zeiger the photographer, nor does Mina. And Yosel—even if he should resemble his parents it cannot be proved, for they were burned as were their photographs.

I walked past the sign of Schmidt & Sons till I came to the illuminated tennis court. A number of people stood along the high fence and watched in silence. The court was flooded with light. A young woman skated. She circled calmly, then stood on one leg spinning slowly as in a dream. Her eyes were shut. She lowered her leg and again circled almost without moving a limb, borne by the breeze, borne by her dreams. She wore a short red pleated skirt and underwear of the same color. The light was strong and her movements seemingly hypnotized the few spectators. Nearby the river flowed but nobody paid any attention to it. From time to time, when the pirouetting of the dreamer became more daring, the spectators came to life and cheered. She squatted or stretched her leg straight out before her. To one side, a young man leaned on the wall of a wooden structure, a bath towel hanging loosely around his neck. I recognized him as having been on the train and raised my arm in greeting, but he did not see me because of the blinding light, and my arm remained suspended and clutched the wire fence like the tendril of a creeping plant. Some people came in a truck and began throwing off boards. Each board, as it fell, made a report like a shot. Nearby someone said, "They will work all night to set up more bleachers." The flagpoles were already up. The girl was still circling dreamily. After I had heard her story from Henrietta, I called her The Girl from Israel. Absent-mindedly, my hand picked a leaf. Nearby flowed the river which gave me strength, which reminded me and also made me forget. I went into an enclosure, together with the laborers, who began banging away with their hammers. The girl came toward me, her skates suspended on her back, the way children do in Israel. I saw her but she did not see me because the light was behind me and blinded her. I said, "*Shalom.*" She raised her head. "Who are you?" she asked, also in Hebrew. And then added: "Come, come with me to the dressing room." We went into the dressing room, which smelled of fresh lumber and rubber and soap. A number of the participants in the tournament sat about tables, dressed in strange tight-fitting clothes or wearing woolen sweaters on which were knitted all kinds of emblems: beasts and flowers and designs that adorned the robes of the High Priest. They paid no attention to me. They were accustomed to hearing foreign languages, for this was an international competition. We sat down on a wooden bench like the ones they have in mountain inns. Her hair was in long golden braids and her eyes were somewhat green and somewhat blue. Her face was the face of a terrible angel and her legs were long and powerful.

"What do you want of me?" she said. "Are you one of those who are trying to reform me and return me to Israel?"

"I am one of those who return themselves, not others."

"An emigrant going back?"

"No."

"Then why the philosophizing? Will you have a cold drink?"

"Beer."

She went to the lunch counter and fetched the beer and asked me to be her guest, though she still suspected that I had been sent by the women from the Home for the Aged to influence her.

"How long will you stay in Weinburg?"

"Not long. My days are numbered."

I said this and was alarmed. I had meant to say that I had much to do in a short time. I realized that I would never persuade this waif who was now free in the world.

"How many days?"

"Four or five."

"Will you come to see me at the tournament?"

"In whose name are you appearing? I mean, which country are you representing?"

"As an individual."

"And how do you earn your living?"

"If I didn't know that you are from Israel, this question of yours would tell me as much. Just the same, I'll tell you. I am a model. You must have seen me on a poster where I stand against the Rhine, a castle behind me, my hair flying in the breeze. 'Visit Romantic Germany,' it says. From time to time I skate. I learned it in Israel and specialized here. You saw me spin. Have another beer." I consented and she brought another. I tasted the bitter foam and she said, "One learns to spin and to dream."

I said, "I, too, spin in a dream."

She said, "But you don't appear before an audience."

Then I suddenly told her that I had come here to settle. To her amazed question, I replied that I wanted to immerse myself deeply within myself. She warned me that I shouldn't drown within myself because of too much philosophizing. She got up and shook her braids, which were golden like the frame of an antique picture, and whispered, "You can always find me here. Ask for Leonora." I asked her what she was called in Israel, and she said Tamar. "And who named you so romantically, Leonora?" She had picked the name herself. Henrietta used to call her Rosie. Mrs. Munster called her "my Clara." Henrietta also called her Roselein, when she was in a good mood, and Roselie when she was angry, and sometimes also Rosichen.

She stood there, her names and nicknames humming in her head. She spun the skate wheels, which rattled metallically. Suddenly she said, "You, you probably intend to offer me your help. You will say that there is something helpless about my eyes, something that calls for assistance. You'd better know—I don't need any of this sort of thing." I assured her that I had nothing of the sort on my mind, that I had simply been walking along the bank of the river and had come here by accident, and that I had already noticed her on the train. Then we were both silent and the table stood between us. I almost reached out to stroke her hair. She could have been my elder daughter, if I had a daughter.

Leonora returned to the illuminated tennis court, and the few people there applauded. She resumed her circling. She, too, was a river, a river that flowed in circles. And I returned into the darkness. I walked up the flight of stairs leading to the bridge of the saints. Leonora had taught me what to do. A bell tolled a late hour. Most people were at home and didn't know that I was passing by outside—a man who returned carrying his vengeance like the gilded sword in the hands of the saint who fought the pagans. Who is with me? Who?

Like Leonora I, too, almost sank into circling dreams. An electric trolley passed, ringing lightly. It was yellow and brightly lighted. I noticed that the houses on the street had been restored in the old style. Only in the corner there remained a big dark heap, a heap of rubble, the remains of two houses that had not yet been cleared away. I walked up to it and felt like a spy, like a detective who has to examine every suspicious spot.

When I walked by the heap of rubble a second time, I noticed lights coming from it. I went into the mound of wreckage through an illuminated tunnel, like the subways in big cities. Show windows lined both sides of the tunnel. In one of them well-dressed men stood motionless, their hands upraised and a smile on their faces. One man, dressed in black evening clothes, had his hand delicately raised in a gesture of blessing, like Saint K. in the square before the railroad station.

Another blessing was vouchsafed me in the city that I came to curse.

In a neighboring show window a child in sport clothes stood holding an airline bag. His face, expressing delight, was turned to his father. The father, too, was dressed in sport clothes and carried a bigger suitcase and an umbrella. In the background were airplanes and a control tower and sleeves showing the direction of the wind. The wind, too, was pointed in. Near the two stood women waiting for the plane, women in gray dresses of English tweed. One of them shaded her eyes with her hand and another carried a short jacket on her arm. Other people in the show window waved their hands from a train window.

It is in the nature of a show window to reflect the image of the person looking into it. Thus I appeared among the suitcases and the ladies about to emplane for a long journey, but my image was indistinct and transparent. My traveling equipment should have been of another kind: a dagger and a pistol and a submachine gun and a bottle of poison and maps and Ruth's last letters and snapshots and slivers of glass which covered her on the day the synagogues were burned.

Archeology consists only of digging and restoring. A destroyed city is uncovered and soot is found on the bricks and stones, and one says that this city has been conquered; this city has been burned; slaughter was done in this city. But there is neither compassion nor desire to avenge. I, too, had reached this point, as if the purpose of my coming here was merely to reconstruct Ruth's last years.

In the third window stood a living man rearranging the display. Heads and other parts of bodies lay about him, as in Ezekiel's vision of the dry bones. I proceeded in the tunnel and forgot that I was walking under a ruin. In a window I saw Ruth's face as it was when she turned toward me when we both lay on the ground, the boys of the Hitler Jugend holding me fast, and I heard one of them kicking her and her artificial leg gave out the dead sounds of wood and metal. When Ruth was burned, revenge was burned, too, and the country remained empty of mercy and of vengeance and of man. Her face is the eternal light for my actions and, like all eternal lights, her face is exerting a calming effect on me and fills me with melody and happiness and sadness, instead of driving me to acts of vengeance.

In a neighboring show window, an automobile stood against the background of a savage landscape. The car was stained and its windows were dust-covered. A sign near it proclaimed that it had traveled through the high Alps on Grades C and D roads without requiring repairs and it won a prize. Everything is clear in show windows. There are no secrets. Like the open skies in the visions of the prophets. And everything is useful and plentiful. And there were other windows displaying cornucopias of jewelry and clothes and fruit and bottles. Should I now smash the windows and the lights and rend the garments and spill the wine and tear to bits the pennants and kick the manikins around, I would accomplish nothing.

Like Leonora, I aroused myself from my trance and noticed that opposite the display windows was a modern café set back into one of the caves in the heap of rubble, all glass and shiny with glistening metal, and adorned with cloth of modern design and a flight of stairs leading to a second floor where some people sat. A fountain sprayed water which fell into an attractive mosaic basin. Birds hopped in cages along the walls and brightly colored fish swam aimlessly in tanks. A big bar extended diagonally in true modernistic fashion. An espresso machine and some utensils gleamed like surgery tools. And there was a cage with a yawning parrot and taps for beer and for milk, and spear points impaling slices of bread for toasting, and bread-slicing machines and toasters and bottles made up like scrolls of the Law on Simhath Torah. And brass mirrors and glass mirrors, mirrors within mirrors, the echo of happiness within echoes of happiness.

The tables in the café were so small and low that it would have been easy to purloin one of them unnoticed—for a woman, under her skirt, for instance. Such tables are not good to make big plans on. They are existentialist tables, *ad-hoc* tables, tables of eat and drink for tomorrow we die. I walked in between the tables and the voices. A woman said in English, "Listen, darling, listen to me." I heard a man talking Arabic. Near the railing of the gallery a number of girls' heads could be seen, hair dyed blue and eyelids green. Aside from their heads, I could see only their feet, sandaled, or spike-heeled like the spearheads on which buns were impaled. Their hair was done in various ways, pony tails and spit curls, ringlets and unkempt masses. College girls look like whores and whores look like housewives; provincial girls make up to look like aristocrats; and all of them look American. It occurred to me that they had all met here for the first time. I turned to the fish dashing madly in their tanks on the opposite wall.

I sat down and a waitress sporting a white flowered apron came up to me. But the apron would no longer protect her against stains. It reminded me of the shields and armor of the Renaissance period that were adorned with many decorations after they could no longer protect their wearers against bullets. I ordered mulberry wine. I affected a foreign accent so they should not guess I was a native. The waitress brought me a huge hemispherical beaker. Once it had been a complete sphere, and now it had parted in two, one half joy and the other half sorrow, and I didn't know which half I had received. She poured the wine, which was thick and dark as blood. A shoe fell near me. A brown-eyed, blue-lidded, oval-faced girl implored in a childish voice: *Bitte*, please toss the shoe back to me. I flung it to the gallery and she threw me a kiss. I grabbed the kiss and put it in my pocket. The girl in the gallery laughed and I knew that I was permitted to laugh with her, for she must have been no more than two or three years old when Ruth was burned.

A young priest came in and talked precise Italian. The fountain in the doorway belched its water, and opposite stood the manikins and waited against the painted airport. From where I sat, I now saw another show window displaying a Mediterranean beach. Only the yellow sand and some of the sea shells were genuine. Men and women in bathing suits (29 Marks) played with a colored beach ball (12 Marks). But I knew that they had no sex organs. They were neuters of the shores. There were also painted dolphins and one made of rubber (18 Marks). Yellow electric light pretended to be the Mediterranean sun. People walking in the tunnel alternately looked into the café and into the display windows. I recalled the property of Mr. Rosenbaum. I had not forgotten him. Tomorrow I would look into the business he had entrusted to me. I raised the beaker and sipped a few times; then I leaned back, as one does on the night of the Seder, but the back of the chair gave me no comfort. I again reached out for the beaker but misjudged the distance and clutched air. I felt warm and became filled with a sweetness more terrible than death. Only now did my feet become aware of how much they had walked. Only now did my thoughts realize how much they had thought. Some heavy weight tried to attain equilibrium within me. A heavy weight wandered all through my body.

Dead little Ruth sat opposite me and I invited her to drink the wine. The hemisphere of the beaker stood between us.

"You remember how we quarreled once when we played marbles? You said I was cheating."

"For two days I refused to see you."

"But I tried to see you. I passed by your father's study. He sat in his upholstered leather chair preparing one of his sermons. The maid brought him black coffee."

"I played the flute."

"You squeaked like an unmusical bird."

"How did you return? How could you return to this place?"

"It is impossible to return. Ruth, I have saved all your letters."

"I wrote nonsense."

"I can still see your careful and precise handwriting."

"I am still the same, careful and precise."

Then she left and I said to her all the farewells I could think of: "*Shalom, Servus, Gute Nacht*, Goodbye, Ruth." A man came and wanted to sit down where she had sat. Ruth walked off on her crutches and disappeared amid the people waiting in the airport in the display window. The man who came was the Indian from the train. I was glad to see him and shook his hand. "I am so happy," I said to him. He said that this was what he most liked about Europeans, that whenever they were a bit drunk and lonely they were wonderful. He ordered tomato juice. I informed him that he was a soldier in my army and that I relied on him. He smiled with his white teeth and assured me of his loyalty and that he would never betray me. I promoted him in rank and he told me that he came to Europe to do a study called *The Essence of Western Despair*. He visits all the churches and examines the pictures of the saints for signs of despair. Not suffering but despair is what he is after. Then he compares the facial expression of the pictures with the expressions on the faces of people in the street. He thinks Germany is the most suitable place for such a study. From the radio came a popular song with the refrain:

> Oh, Varus, Varus,
> Where are my legions?
> Here people eat and drink and court women.
> Oh, Varus, Varus,
> Give me back my legions.

Varus was a Roman general who had been sent to subdue
a revolt of the Teutonic tribes and returned without his
army. This song is set to a jazz rhythm. A commander who
loses his army is like a child who loses a toy. More or less
steadily, I walked to the men's room. Some men waited in
the corridor. One examined himself in the mirror before
staging a final assault on a stubborn girl. Another counted
some change. I came back and noticed that the Indian wore
narrow white trousers and a white shirt, as Indians usually
do. We began to converse:

"The inner world is turned outward.—The outer world is
turned inward.—The despair of action.—The despair of in-
action.—Buddha says that it is wonderful to observe
earthly creatures but terrible to be one of them.—Yoga and
synagogue.—The Jewish people is in permanent analysis. It
lies on the world's couch and tells its past.—Yoga and synagogue. The faith of Hasidim. Faith and confidence."

The girl who had dropped the shoe from the gallery got
up to go. I am told she is a student of jurisprudence. When
she becomes a judge, she will take off her shoe and pound on
the table: "Silence in the courtroom." Two young men followed her. All three stopped before the display window and
laughed and giggled. My conversation with the Indian continued:

"Something between yoga and synagogue. The redeeming
angel and the despairing angel.—The inner world turned
inside out like a glove that has been pulled off too rapidly.
—Despair compels action and prevents action.—A person
should live outside the balance sheet of action.—What
about justice? What about equality? What about inequality?
—And what about the castes that still exist in India?—
That's a different matter.—And what about the dead from
hunger?—That's a different matter."

> Oh, Varus, Varus,
> Where are my legions?

Then he told me that his father is buried on one of the hills of Jerusalem, since he was a sergeant in General Allenby's army. As Shakespeare says, "Despair and die." Despair exists. An entire installation of despair. A display window full of despair. Action undoes the cause of the action. Despair erases everything as from a blackboard. The Germans have a legend about a man who went out to learn fear.

Then I told him a little about what brought me here and about Henrietta and about the river and similar things. From time to time I raised the beaker but did not drink from it. The Indian assured me that vengeance like mine, which comes after some years, belongs in his book on despair. He thinks that the story of Orpheus is the embodiment of despair, for in descending to the nether world to reclaim his wife he knew that it was in vain. I said, "Here's to your health and to the health of your father, the sergeant in the Twenty-ninth Lancers Regiment which was attached to the Scottish regiment." He said, "Do you see this young man?" "Yes," I said. "He is the son of one of the most prominent Nazis in Weinburg. His father fled abroad and the son is dark-haired and nervous like a young Jewish intellectual. And as for Orpheus, how do you know that there is no nether world?"

We talked English. I wished I had a sweetheart to whom I could talk English. Maybe because most of the movies I saw in Israel were in English. I wished my friend Zeiger were here, for as a former member of the underground he could tell me how to begin my activities. I was like a school kid who begs his teacher, "At least start the composition for me and I'll do the rest." I paid for the wine. The Indian escorted me as far as the tunnel. I advised him that for the sake of his study on despair he should go to the bridge and look at the faces of the saints, and then he should go to the Home for

the Aged and talk to Mrs. Munster about her daughter
Clara. He advised me to begin my work of vengeance thus:
"Sit in the same place frequently. Come back to it at various
times during the day and night. This will give you a status in
the city. And regularly ride on the streetcars of Weinburg.
There are only nine streetcar lines."
I went back to the café, which was now nearly empty.
One girl remained and she was filling out a form. She was
disheveled and her hair hung about her face. I called her
Sun, and she called me Mediterranean Moon. I called her
sun girl from the washroom, and she called me drunken talking bear. I called her slut of outdated Socialism. She called
me helpless Be'el Zebub. I called her Astarte of Weinburg,
and she called me Moloch with trachoma, and digger after
aborted dreams. Nazi. Pitiful pursuer of the Gestapo. Four-
thighed beast. Circumcised Jew. Lame angel. Asian savage.
Ridiculous saint with a tin halo. Broken-down car after an
accident. Plague-ridden Egypt. Saint Magdalene. Jesus from
the land of the Jesuits.
She finished filling out her form. The radio and the lights
in the fish tanks were turned off. The streams of water subsided into the fountain.
Now she said out loud, "You imitate the local accent quite
well." I asked, "Are you closing up?" She said, "It's a long
business that takes at least an hour. You can't lock up and go
just like that."
I walked up the street of the Dome Cathedral. Some laborers were sweeping the street. Others were welding a
break in the streetcar tracks. The face of the welder was
protected by a metal shield like a medieval knight. Bright
sparks lit up the faces of the kneeling men. Tomorrow I will
be able to ride, since the tracks will be repaired. From side
alleys came the shouts of drunks. I walked along the tracks
and crossed the market square. The first trucks were begin-

ning to arrive. Then I crossed the square in front of the railway station. Saint K., who suffered martyrdom at the hands of pagans, blessed me and I came to the hotel entrance. The night watchman gave me a heavy key. Perhaps I, too, will be so heavy that I will tumble to action. A tumbling snow avalanche can also be said to act. I brushed my teeth. I was afraid of dreaming, for I knew I'd see Ruth in my dreams. I took a shower and shocked my body alternately with hot and cold water until it became full of warmth and my mouth cried out many names which I had not uttered for a long time.

I scrubbed myself with a towel until my skin became red and then I lay down on the bed on my back, but I did not fall asleep. Despair came in the form of insomnia. I tried to evoke memories but the images I brought up were not well masked. I mourned for little Ruth—for death and a young girl inhabiting the same body. If she had been able to dance, perhaps she might have escaped her fate. I looked at the wallpaper which was lit up by the changing beams of the traffic light near the hotel entrance: green, yellow, red, again and again. The traffic light worked to no purpose all night; only once did I hear a car stop for it, then start again. The bulkheads within me began giving way. Every person has bulkheads like a ship, so that if water pours into one compartment the others remain intact. It is the same with man, who is always in a state of drowning until he finally sinks for the last time. Many of my friends sail about like dead ships with all their lights on. Woe to the man whose bulkheads have broken down, for then love becomes confused with hate and dream overwhelms reality. Tomorrow I will take little Heinrele to the river; I will visit Henrietta; I will go to the place where the synagogue used to stand. I will visit Leonora. Not even a dream will have mercy on me. I went into the bathroom and urinated. I thought it was good that I was emptying myself and could now lift off like a balloon. Sometimes one sinks into sleep and other times one rises up into it. Sleep is everywhere, except within me. I also used to urinate before going into battle, so that I should be light and so that I shouldn't wet myself in case I was hit. Why is Company B late? Why is Company C lost? As a matter of fact, it was the fault of the other regiment that took part in this action. Little Ruth would have been proud of me had she known that I was a soldier in the Holy Land fighting for our people and our Land. Thoughts of the battle calmed me and I finally fell asleep.

24

I am beginning to resemble my father, Joel thought. When I was born, I resembled him, people said. Later I went my own way and I didn't know that a long rope kept us tied together, and the more I ran around in circles, the closer I came to him and the more I resembled him.

Joel came alone to Einat's party. Neither Ruth nor Pat was with him, a suggestion of things to come. Einat tried to make the party especially original. The books were removed from the library and the guests lay on their backs on the floor. Then they recited passages from Job. Somebody suggested, "Let's all get undressed." (Are you mad?) And the poet Imron bleated like a goat. (Let's play resurrection. How?) Then they behaved like kids on an outing. The lights were turned off and they smeared one another with lipstick. Somebody cried out, "Let's go home." Then they ate *humus* and fried chicken in the kitchen, which was too small to hold all of them. But the bathroom was huge and the toilet seat was immense. On the walls were many pictures and drawings of devils and monsters, copies of pictures from the Notre Dame Cathedral. Somebody came in and said, "I heard that Minister S—— died." The poet Imron walked on all fours and barked like a dog.

Dr. Manheim took off his phylacteries. On summer mornings like this one, their leather straps are warm. He was seated in a chair on the balcony. He discerns only indistinct images. Black is the only color that he is conscious of. He knows only three persons: the doctor, who occasionally walks by and asks him how he had spent the night; Yona, the nurse; and Dr. Itzhak, with whom he sometimes converses. Dr. Itzhak will come later to arrange the straps of the phylacteries, for the old man's hands tremble too much. Many times in the past, he has taught boys how to wind the straps of the phylacteries after morning prayer. The strap of the phylactery of the arm is wound about its base so that it finally looks like a tractor. Thus he would explain the process to boys. It was terrible that he made such comparisons. Dr. Manheim did not tutor Joel for his Bar Mitzvah for Joel had already gone to Palestine, but he had prepared his Bar Mitzvah speech. Why didn't Joel come to visit him more often, he wanted to know. It was necessary to discuss the speech, and also the other speeches that had been left behind in Weinburg. Perhaps it would be possible to recover them.

Joel entered the parliament building and joined the silent line of mourners who passed by the bier of the dead Minister. He covered his head. Some men stood and recited Psalms in a low voice, in this building which was accustomed to loud shouting and the banging of the chairman's gavel. Mr. Sand, the newsdealer, passed behind him and whispered, "See that man? He was the Minister's enemy, and

that other one, over there, was his secret supporter." Mr.
Sand knows all the people here, for they come to him to buy
papers in which they read their own speeches. They are so
proud of their own sage remarks. Mr. Sand was wearing
broad shorts on his skinny hairy legs. He brought the shorts
when he returned from serving in the British Army. An original man, Mr. Sand. Nights he writes his autobiography, but
he makes slow progress, hardly faster than the monument
maker, who has the shop next door, with his inscriptions.
The smell of the pine branches in the room aroused a pleasant sensation in Joel and reminded him of the fine *sukkah*
his father used to build in Weinburg. The day after it was
finished, the *sukkah* would begin to smell of pine and fir.
Once, as a child, Joel was photographed at the entrance to
the *sukkah* holding the *lulab*, a tense and artificial smile
on his face. (Pat says, "Your smile rips my heart to pieces.
I can never be driven away from you.") When Hitler
came to power, an S.S. man threw a flowerpot on the *sukkah*,
and after that until his father took them to Palestine it was
built in the yard of the Home for the Aged. On the day of
vengeance, the flowerpots became bombs and Weinburg was
destroyed. The smell of the freshly cut branches intoxicated
Joel and raised alternate waves of elation and depression
within him.

25

I awoke and knew at once who and what I was, where I
came from and the place I was in now. (Go slow. Don't
move. Lie on your back. Walk down ramp No. 6.) I recall
that during the war when I also slept little, I'd awake in an

open field just before an attack and know at once what I was about—a trench and a cold rifle, and soon we'd assault the dreaded fate. But when I am in an unfamiliar environment, I don't always know when I awake where I am and whose head is next to mine. I then have to fall back on objects to orient myself—a window, a dresser, a curtain.

Now I lay on my back, my hands crossed on my chest like some ancient dead Egyptian king. I recognized the wallpaper. I also realized that it was raining outside. Which direction does rain come from here? What wind brings it? In Israel, which is rimmed by the green sea, the clouds come from the west. They pass over sand dunes and lowlands and slopes and hills until they reach Jerusalem. I lay awake and the traffic signal continued to cast its lights on the wall like a series of directives: permitted, forbidden, permitted, forbidden. Beloved, the traffic signal stands between us, I thought, but I did not know whom I was addressing. I tried to remember many things, and felt remembrance like an ailment. The rain fell, thin and sad. This wasn't the kind of rain that causes big trees or great deeds to grow. All my deeds are deeds of love. My biography is the story of things that aroused love within me. Henrietta caused me pleasure by caressing and tickling me when I was a child, and she entered into my biography. My biography also contains the opposite of things that cause pleasure and love—in other words, pain and those who cause it, both of which I try to avoid. The problem that preoccupied me this morning was how to get to the point of action. Whether this would entail hardening and armoring my heart or ignoring it altogether. Thus I lay on my back with hands crossed on my chest like some Rameses or Thutmose or other embalmed figure and listened to the sounds. I wondered, Is there also a no man's land between what one must do and what one must not do? I heard the subdued noise of a truck and of people far away in the rain. It seemed to me that I also heard brisk commands. I, too, awoke to action. I dressed and went out into the hall. A weak light had been on all night. Shoes stood at the doors, shining and sparkling. At both ends of the hall were mirrors which showed me to myself as I walked rapidly. It was 4:30 A.M. Soon it would be light. The night watchman was asleep and did not wake when I walked by him on the carpet. It was still raining. I waited at the intersection for the traffic light to turn green. A milk truck passed. Then I crossed the square and the splashing of Saint K.'s fountain. The rain turned into thin mist. At the entrance to the station two gates of honor had been set up. One said: "WELCOME CONGRESS OF APIARISTS!" The other: "WELCOME INTERNATIONAL SKATING TOURNAMENT!" The morning papers were brought. I could still get away, should it become necessary.

I walked in the direction from which the noise came. Yesterday I had noticed that a side annex of the railway station remained as I remembered it, built of bricks blackened by soot and rain. I walked into Pestalozzi Park and saw a small crowd of people, their heads bent, carrying decrepit suitcases and all sorts of bundles. A man wearing a black S.S. uniform came up to me and said, "Sorry, sir, you can't pass here." Light from a lantern was reflected from his shiny visor and his boots. I moved aside. "Caution! Electric Wires!" I stepped over some thick cables. Another man came up to me and said angrily, "We had decided to start promptly at four! Why are you late? Hurry up and join the others!" I found myself in the midst of some people who stood crouching in the rain. I didn't know any of them but all were unshaven like me. I saw a girl of about eleven with black braids dragging a doll. (Ruth never played with dolls.) I helped her carry a heavy bundle. Somebody laughed. Someone else shouted, "You crazy? We won't pay you a cent if you laugh."

The laughter stopped. I turned to the girl and took her hand in mine. She burst out crying. I said, "Don't cry. This will all end." Her hand was hot and dry. "Yes," she said, and cried still louder. A voice from the direction of the park shouted, "Very good! Very good! Keep it up, little girl; go on crying." She clung to me fearfully, and the voice from among the trees said, "Very good, there." Then it said, "Cut!" At once most of the powerful lights went out and someone lit a cigarette. "No smoking! We are still taking pictures." The crowd began pushing toward the old station. A number of black-uniformed S.S. appeared and shouted, "Forward! Quick! Jew sows!" A man in a bright-colored shirt and wearing a little cap with an upturned visor shouted, with an American accent, "Not like that!" He grabbed the whip from the hand of one of the S.S. men and began cracking it over the people near him. The other S.S. men took their whips and followed his example. The people tried to avoid the blows and shoved one another to get to the center of the crowd, shoved and shouted in great confusion and cursed aloud. I picked up a stone and threw it at one of the whippers. A little man ran up to me, clutching at his head. "What are you doing? Are you crazy? That is not in the script." But the loud voice from the park exclaimed, "Wonderful! That's the spirit! To hell with old-style theater. This is a new-wave film. Free expression." The S.S. man said, "I don't give a damn about old wave or new wave. I don't want rocks thrown at me. It's a breach of contract." "You are insured like all the rest," a man with a label, "Windmeyer," on his jacket said to him in German. And to me: "Take it easy; don't get too excited. But in general you are doing just fine. How you seized the little girl!" Someone from the crowd said, "*Then* they didn't throw rocks. You would have been liquidated at once." A coffee break of ten minutes was announced. "You can leave your suitcases and bundles here."

We sat in the little park and sipped hot coffee from paper cups and ate delicious little sandwiches. The man with the Windmeyer label on his chest sat down near me. "This fog, it's wonderful," he said. "Smoke from trains and the people in the fog and rain. Wonderful. *Wunderbar!* You new here? I didn't see you during the previous filming. What's your name?" "Earl Winter," I said. "Where from?" he asked. "From Munich," I said. "Here for the apiarists' convention." "You are an apiarist? Must be a philosophical occupation. Like Virgil. Eh?"

"Yes, like Virgil."

"You should have been an actor."

He left. A woman near me said, "You can ask for a raise. These Americans are stuffed with money."

Herr Windmeyer returned and made a little speech. "Now it is getting serious. Remember, most of you know that you are going to the crematoria. I want to see you show that you know you are facing death. I want to hear moaning and weeping. Have you no feelings? You are going to die. Remember this. And we are paying you good money. If somebody laughs, the laughter has to be hysterical, laughter that turns to screaming and weeping."

As he made his little speech, he acted it out and waved his arms. The American near him was silent. I became aware that I was sitting on the base of Pestalozzi's statue. When I was a child, we sometimes played here and the name Pestalozzi made us laugh. ("You Pestalozzi, you.") I got up off the lap of the gentle educator whose stone eyes saw all and returned to the crowd. A diesel motor increased its pitch and many electricians and mechanics were busy overhead. The little girl said, "Mister, let's play together again." I gladly agreed. This time the S.S. men played their role with suitable ferocity, but suddenly the church bells began ringing. "Damn the bells!" the American cried. The man who had been present during the real deportations said, "The bells rang that time, too, and the good Christians prayed for their souls and praised God." I whispered to him in Hebrew, "A Jew?" But he moved away. The girl began to cry, the S.S. cursed and cracked their whips, and we were herded in the direction of the old wing of the station. Fog and smoke mingled in the beams of the floodlights. Then we stood in the freight station. A number of German soldiers returning to the Eastern Front stood there bidding farewell to their wives. They photographed some of these couples and left us alone for a while. "No smoking! Absolutely no smoking!" Then the terrible light was again focused on us.

Some freight cars glided eerily into the station and the S.S. men began to herd us into them; others separated children from their parents and anguished cries rent the air. The girl clung to me and ripped the lapel of my jacket. Then the light was focused on the door of the warehouse, and a woman like an evil angel mounted on a black charger emerged from the door, her loose blond hair falling about her shoulders. "Leonora! Leonora!" I cried, but she did not hear me. The horse advanced slowly and the woman looked with scornful curiosity on the mass of unfortunates. I waved my fist and approached her, dragging the girl with me. Behind her was written: "Odol Cleans Teeth. Fersil Cleans All." The S.S. commander came up and kissed her white hand. Her pretty nose expressed aversion for the scene. Then she bent down to the commander, whose uniform was covered with badges of high rank, and whispered something to him which made him laugh coarsely. She cracked her whip over those nearest her, and they raised their hands to protect their faces. Finally she moved out of the terrible light, which was the light of the end of the world. Again the uniformed men fell upon us. The sound of blows and the ripping of garments was heard. Faces were distorted and genuine crying rent the fog. The girl hid her face in my bosom. A man came up and tried to tear her away from me and I did not let him. The girl cried, "No! No! Don't let them!" Her entire body shook. "Stop it! Stop it!" I cried. "She will get sick! You can't do that!" But my voice was drowned in the noise. Two S.S. men came and knocked me to the ground. I saw one of them grab the girl as she kicked in a frenzy; then I saw her being forced into a freight car. "Ruth! Ruth! Ruth!" I cried. Tears choked me and I tried to force my way to the car. At once they grabbed me and shoved me into another car where many had been crowded before. We stood jammed together. Somebody said, "Don't smoke now; it's crowded." The train began moving and my hands still shook from the excitement. I thought of little Ruth who rode this way. In a short time the train stopped and the heavy car doors were opened. We all pushed out. We were not far from the station. Everybody was excited and chattered gaily: "Let's have a cigarette. Got a match? This time it was successful. We finished ahead of time." Odol cleans, Fersil cleans, and on the billboard a big woman stood, her arms up to her elbows in white foam. The fog dissolved and a mild summer sun shone to one side. Herr Windmeyer came to me with cries of enthusiasm and praised me for my acting and invited me to participate in the next filming. "You must come. The synagogue will be burned and the local rabbi comes poking around in the ruins. How about playing the role of the rabbi? The man we engaged might turn up sick."

The girl came up and curtsied before me. I was surprised that it was still being done. Then she looked up to me with her brown eyes and asked, "Why did you call me Ruth? My name isn't Ruth." I did not answer, and put my hand on her dark hair. The girl ran away and I saw that just outside the park a woman waited for her and embraced her. Then the two disappeared in the thinning fog. The people dispersed and the mechanics began winding up wires and folding their long-legged equipment. The S.S. men disappeared into a station wagon; then two of them emerged wearing American military uniforms. I was told that the director had asked the American troops stationed nearby, one of whose duties was to re-educate the Germans, to assist him in the filming. He could find no Germans willing to play the roles of S.S. men. Again I sat down on Pestalozzi's lap.

Herr Windmeyer came and showed me an official document. "We are doing everything according to authentic historical documentation," he said.

It was an official letter regarding operation *Heimat*—the deportation to the camps of the last remaining Jews of Weinburg. The order included instructions to Police Superintendent Kleinrot to send nine policemen and five supernumeraries to preserve order. Also instructions to the district court to assign three court officers to this operation and one judge to inform the deportees officially that they were being deprived of German citizenship. The presence of this judge was essential, for without him the operation could not be made legal and thus could not be carried out. Also instructions to the municipal health and sanitation department to send three men and two women to clean up after the deportation. All were to report at 4:30 in the Pestalozzi Park. There were three signatures on the document: Von Zeitlus, Dieters, and Schmieters.

Then he showed me another document, which was extremely faded and looked as if it had been forgotten in the pocket of some garment that had been through the laundry. This order, which was marked "Urgent," instructed the railroad administration of Weinburg (copies to Gestapo, Central Railroad Administration, Ministry of Transportation) to transfer one cattle car from train B-764 to train L-647 and to provide rations for the guard accompanying the train, who would report to the station at 11:37.

Then there was a final document. This was the report of the guard in which he demanded compensation for two nights in a hotel, four meals in a restaurant, and a special allotment for extra coffee. This claim was endorsed by the guard's supervisor "in consideration of his difficult and nerve-racking assignment." This man is now assistant station-master.

The day was coming to life. Trains began to arrive and depart. I heard them pass behind the brown wall. A single film technician was still laboring over some sections of equipment that refused to come apart. Bicycle bells rang; pedestrians going to work chatted. Traffic was getting heavy and the traffic light was kept usefully busy, instead of wasting its light on hotel wallpaper as it did at night. Cars stopped and pawed impatiently for the light to change, and when they saw green they leaped forward with a roar as if they felt insulted at having been halted for the sake of a single pedestrian.

"You are leaving already?" they asked at the hotel desk, and at once called a bellboy to take my suitcase to the station. So many travelers. Now a congress is in session and in a week another convention will be held. The bellboy and I crossed the square. "Two weeks from now there will be a congress of the Alliance of Catholic Women," he said, and laughed. We passed under the welcoming gates for the apiarists and the skaters, and he put my suitcase on the counter of the checkroom. I gave him a tip. Immediately he bought a book at the news counter, *The Essence of Existentialism*. I waved goodbye to him. He waved the book back at me. A man stood on a tall ladder fixing the huge clock in the station. I asked him where the office of the assistant station-master was, and he pointed to a broad flight of stairs to the left. I came to a door with a sign: "ENTRANCE THROUGH THE

OFFICE ONLY." I went to the office. A young woman with black cuffs up to her elbows asked what I wanted. "Is Herr Weberlin in?" "What do you wish to see him about?" I didn't know what to say, so I said I was from the film company. Her face lit up. "One moment, please," and she disappeared into the neighboring room. A moment later she returned and said, "Come in, please." I went in.

"Sit down, please. Cigar? Cigarette?"

"Thank you, no."

"Please excuse my secretary's rudeness. She is only a substitute. My regular secretary is on vacation. She is a sharp one, like your American secretaries." I tried to give my German speech an American accent by a movement of the chin. The assistant stationmaster told me more about his regular secretary—that she had a strapless bra. When I failed to be impressed, his kind face showed concern. I told him that I came to get particulars about the last deportation of the Jews. He turned pale. I said, "We lack authentic witnesses, and without them we have difficulty completing the film. I heard that you participated in the last deportation." He at once assured me that he had only been an official with the railway administration, and that the railroads belonged to the government, and that in fact he wasn't involved, beg pardon; he didn't know what was being transported in the trains. The door opened and the head of the substitute secretary asked, "Yes?" "I didn't call." "The bell rang." Herr Weberlin at once began to sing the children's ditty "The bell is ringing, the bell is ringing, bim, bam, bom." And he laughed. Then he grew serious. "What will you drink, tea or coffee?" I said, "Coffee or tea." The secretary became angry: "Gentlemen, make up your minds; what will it be, tea or coffee?" My host rose and opened a curtain that covered the entire opposite wall. "See, here is a map of the railroad station and the yard and all the subsidiary stations and junctions. Though Weinburg is not one of the biggest cities—speaking in railroad terms, that is—in terms of engines and tracks and international connections this station is an important junction. Many roads branch off here, and one who is not a specialist cannot know what comes here and what goes out, where it comes from and where it goes to."

Then my host opened the window and we looked out upon a maze of tracks. My childhood ambition to be a train engineer revived in me, to know all about brakes and semaphores and tracks and signals, to be able to press a button and make trains glide smoothly from one track to another. I was also shown the complex apparatus in the dispatching room, boards where lights went on and off like the Urim and Thummim on the vestments of the High Priest. I heard the clatter of dishes. The secretary brought a tray with four cups, two of tea, two of coffee. Below, loudspeakers announced the arrival and departure of trains and the delay of others. I saw a platform with two trains on either side of it. They began to move simultaneously in opposite directions. With light tugs on the couplings and with almost an imperceptible gliding, as if separating after being joined in love, the two trains slipped away from each other. We drank tea or coffee, and I asked him whether at the time of the deportation there were also soldiers and police present, or only S.S. men. The cup shook in his hand and a little tea or coffee spilled. "What is this game? You came to question me, and not to get information for the film. Some weeks ago that blond actress, the one who plays the wife of the S.S. officer, also came to quiz me. I told you already that I was only a minor railroad official." With these words he sank into his upholstered chair and fainted. The secretary at once came in carrying an instrument that looked like a fire extinguisher or an appliance for administering enemas and sprayed him with a strong-smelling liquid. "This happens sometimes," she said, "and the regular secretary instructed me to use this instrument." Since he failed to regain consciousness, she quickly unbuttoned some of his buttons and began tickling his belly. He revived and she returned to her room and we again heard the clacking of her typewriter. "She isn't fooling me," he said. "She isn't really typing; she is eavesdropping and spying on me." I took out the snapshot which showed a number of deportees being shoved into the cars while some station officials stood to one side, as in the pictures of the crucifixion of Jesus people and animals stand to one side without being involved in what is going on. Sweat covered his brow. I rejoiced. The wretch was breaking before my eyes—like the evil king in *Hamlet*. Then I was angry with myself that I could think only literary thoughts. I laughed, and Herr Weberlin seemed to faint again. I picked up the extinguisher, but he shook his hand and said, "No need. And as for the snapshot, you won't find me among the railroad workers, for I was in the toilet when the picture was taken. And my brother was killed in the snows of Russia. Don't think that we had it all nice and easy either."

My maternal uncle also died amid snow-covered mountains, during World War I, and his name was published on the list of war casualties which the Jewish front-line veterans issued and to which Field Marshal von Hindenburg wrote an introduction. My uncle's picture, in an oval frame, hangs on the wall in my mother's room near the window which faces on the eucalyptus tree whose branches always sway. My parents used to tell me that I resembled him. Each time my mother has the wall whitewashed, the picture is taken down and she looks into his dark eyes. My host went on: "Our Lord Jesus already visited justice upon us. Weinburg was like a fiery Venice with rivers of fire." He crossed himself and breathed heavily. The secretary stuck her head in the door but said nothing. "That's on account of my hair," he said. "It grows in my nose and in my ears and it simply chokes me. My legs and my back and my belly are covered with it and it gets all tangled so that in the end it will choke me. Entire rows of houses collapsed on that day of wrath into a sea of flames. Big houses went down like so many cattle in a slaughterhouse. The mills of the gods grind slowly and thoroughly and we are the flour—fine flour ground in the mills of the gods, as the maxim says. And now they make from us loaves and rolls and cakes. Flour, flour, flour from the mills of the gods. You in New York have skyscrapers. We here have abyss-scrapers. I could have been a minister. At that time I handed in a bill for expenses. I stayed in a hotel and I had to take my meals because the empty cars were detained in order to bring back a shipment of burned bricks. They laughed at me and said, 'You pitiful little clerk.' But I insisted and got what was coming to me, to the last pfennig. Some weeks after I returned, the city was destroyed and the cars which carried the deportees were pushed by the force of the explosion as far as Schwinefeld. After you Americans came, I worked in the restoration of the railroad system."

I asked him if he remembered seeing a little Jewish girl with an artificial leg. No, he didn't remember, but he did recall a big girl with one leg, hobbling on crutches. I had forgotten that Ruth was grown up by then. Apparently they took her artificial leg before she was sent away. Mr. Rosenbaum had told me that they collected artificial limbs in big heaps. I recalled that I had to look into the matter of Rosenbaum's city lot. But I will first look for the artificial leg. Hadn't this Esau choking on his hair told me that the leg had remained here?

I went into the main concourse and found that the men who had worked on the clock were folding their giant ladder. At the book counter a new volume, *They Walked in the Dark*, replaced the one which the bellboy had bought. The concourse was painted in pastel shades and the loudspeaker was intelligible and not too loud. Here a person starting out on a journey is made to feel relaxed. In Israel, when a person takes even such a short trip as between Jerusalem and Rehovoth, he is given an immense send-off, for there is no security. His well-wishers come to bid their farewells on the hot and ugly square near the public toilets. The sun peels the skin off the people with brutal fingers. Thorns and thistles grow amid greasy spots of spilled black oil. The cries of the peddlers sound ominous. When I return to Jerusalem, I will walk through woods that have been partly burned. The trees had been planted to commemorate our burned brothers, and now everything is burned, man and animal and the trees that were supposed to perpetuate memory.

A little child came up and tugged at my sleeve and said, "Pappa." Some adults came and laughingly took him away. "This isn't Pappa, this is Uncle."

I will go to the Home for the Aged; I will talk to Henrietta; I will look for Ruth's artificial leg; I will attend to the matter of Rosenbaum's real estate; I will ride on all the streetcars as my Indian friend advised. I will go down to the river to watch Leonora rehearse—Leonora the waif, Leonora the actress and dancer from the kibbutz, Leonora the model with the trembling nostrils. I stopped at a streetcar station to wait. A trolley came and on its side was inscribed "Osram is the best . . ." To see the rest of the inscription, I would have had to walk around it. The dispatcher said, "Please step forward." Without words I said to him, "When you shoved Ruth and her brother into the freight car, you probably yelled, 'Step lively, dirty Jews!' " The conductor clanged his bell and the streetcar moved forward smoothly like a rowboat. A young man stood near me and a transistor radio swayed from his shoulder in rhythm with the motion of the streetcar. If little Ruth had had a transistor, she might have been able to hide it in her artificial leg. What would she have heard? Hitler's voice, and maybe the beating of my heart. Sick thoughts. Suddenly the streetcar came to a halt. The passengers complained, "There is no stop here." Somebody grumbled, "On account of the film. It's all on account of the film. Wish they'd go away." But another man remarked about the economic advantage to the city in the making of the film. A third one merely said, "The economic miracle," and winked at me. The streetcar started again and passed Kings Street and a street named after some prince. A new and shining bank stood near a ruin. Then the streetcar passed the heap of rubble under which was the café where I had been the night before. The tracks had been repaired, and we proceeded safely.

I got off. The rain began falling again and I sought shelter in the recess of an old house. People walked by rapidly without noticing me. Another streetcar passed, and because of the heavy drizzle its lights were turned on. Grass sprouted from the wall of the house.

In this house I was born, and now all that is left of it is a wall sprouting grass and behind it a new building rises. I was born at home and not in a hospital. Even then the house was old. Because of the housing shortage during the inflation that followed World War I, my parents shared an apartment with Henrietta and her old aunt. The aunt used to wear a brown wig, and when she became old the wig appeared bigger than her head and wrinkled face. Every wrinkle on her face was like a smile, a crosshatching of smiles on which the light glided as on tracks. And all the wrinkles finally led to her heart. Much delight was caused me by these two women in their small apartment in the midst of their great loneliness. *Ach, du Lieber Augustin,* now all is over and lost. It is not the house I remembered so much as the ugliness of its narrow dark corridors. I also remembered the smells from the grocery store which Henrietta and her aunt operated, the aroma of sugar and cinnamon, the odor of wrapping paper, new sacks, and wooden boxes. And, above all, the smell of soap. Some years later we moved to the new quarter and the two women rented an apartment in the old quarter near the river. Not far from here should be Mushler's bakery and confectionery, where I used to be sent to buy fresh rolls. The rain continued to fall. I came to take revenge, and I hide from the rain and recall the aroma of fresh rolls. Rapid steps passed by me. The sound of steps is enough for me; I do not have to see the people. "Who can bear reality?" Rilke said.

I looked down St. Augustine Street to its end. There was a cloud, like a man ready to extend welcome. The rain had stopped, but I knew that this cloud would not bring rain. In a side alley some people were moving from one apartment to another. Furniture was piled on the sidewalk. I saw myself in a dresser mirror. One eye was alert, the other indifferent. I went to the post office. People were sticking stamps on letters; some licked them with their tongues, others moistened them with wet fingertips. I will choose my army—like Gideon—from among the stamp lickers. Who is with me? Who? At General Delivery I asked for my mail. This time I used a French accent and the man answered me in French, which I did not understand, but I nodded assent. The hall of the post office is modern and full of light. I leaned against a mailbox and pressed my ear to the slot. It seemed to me I heard the sound of rushing waters, as in a sea shell. Suddenly I was overcome with an unbearable tenderness, like falling in love, on account of this place which establishes contact between people. I thought of little Ruth's letters, which she wrote in a neat and precise hand. Once, she wrote, "If you don't want to correspond with me, let us stop." She was always so anxious to force things to a conclusion, though she was still a child and I was a boy playing in the streets of Jerusalem and the summer stars pierced my sleep at night.

I wrote a card to my wife to the effect that I was alive and well, that I was calm, but that my heart was crying out in despair. In the end, the vengeance will be turned against myself with teeth and nails and sharp little knives. Then I went to the Dome Cathedral, which is built of reddish sandstone in terrifying early-Gothic style. The Cathedral was destroyed during the bombardment and has been restored in its original style, and pigeons have not yet soiled it with their droppings. In all cathedrals there are many pigeons, like angels, only angels do not cast their droppings in the houses of God. There are no pigeons in synagogues because there are no niches and statues, but there are many flies.

I saw a number of young people go through the ancient city gate and I followed them. They were lightly dressed in summer clothes and the girls' hair waved in the breeze. I deceived myself and felt at ease as if after the revenge. On the gatepost was a plaque which read, "Here the Knight Von Tuchtolz Fell." I recalled this knight and the story of his death. As school children, we were taken on trips to get to know the city. I passed through the gate and followed an alley till I came to the sign "Here the Second Arrow Struck the Knight Von Tuchtolz." All the alleys of the ancient part of Weinburg have plaques describing the condition of this knight. Were I to follow the alleys in reverse direction, I could read history backward, from his death to the day when he first raised his sword in the peasants' rebellion. Were I to follow the story of my search for vengeance backward, it would lead me back to my previous life in Jerusalem, whose stones lie heavy on my heart. Some maintain that the stones of Jerusalem have healing power, like cotton that stems the flow of blood, but they press and become heavier until even a man like me is driven to action.

The Knight Von Tuchtolz rides on. Little Ruth, who was a diligent pupil, knew his history in great detail: how he led bands of rebellious peasants brandishing scythes and sickles and pitchforks and threshing rods. He alone had a big sword, which could only be swung with both hands. And he was all goodness and all covered with steel, and even his scrotum was enclosed in a case of woven steel threads. Why did he lead peasants rebelling against his feudal colleagues? Maybe he, too, was moved by personal vengeance. I returned to the gate where he fell from his horse and where the young people, descendants of the peasants, had passed. Near me stood a living man in uniform. I asked him where the men's room was.

26

What goes on in an untenanted house? A drop of water collects at the lip of the faucet. It grows and stretches until it falls of its own weight. The drop of water bulges and stretches until it hangs waiting for the verdict that it should fall. For judges earnestly weigh their verdict about each falling drop, and never invoke the precedent of other drops that were also sentenced to fall. Every fall requires a new verdict, as if the matter had never been discussed before. And there is no appealing the judgment that drops should fall, any more than there is appealing against love, or the breakdown of love. Yet some people insist that love is not subject to this law, that it is ruled by freedom of choice. For lovers are by the nature of things conservative. Such were Joel's thoughts.

And Pat, standing alone in her room, loved to think that she belonged to generations past, to the end of the nineteenth century, as some of her clothes suggested, like that long-sleeved blouse that closed with snaps over her wrists enclosing her arms in soft ivory-colored lace. The blouse did not reveal her back or disclose her armpits, and fully covered her shoulders when she buttoned its glass buttons to the nape of her neck. She had not yet put on a skirt, and the blouse descended to her hips, disclosing simple white panties that held her buttocks firmly, lightly cutting into them at the edge. The suns of all the seas and oceans on whose beaches she had lain tanned her legs—the Pacific and the Atlantic and the Mediterranean. And who knows on what shores her forebears walked, in Mexico, and Ireland, in Scotland, and California? She was barefoot now, and the sound of her steps was like the steps of a child or an animal as she walked to the bathroom to subdue the rebelliousness of her heavy hair. Joel had once told her that her lips were as riotous as her hair, but that at least she could comb and rein in and discipline her hair. And she had said, "My lips are cursed. Don't you see that they are too large and that they tremble? A mouth should be a good likeness of the heart. My mouth tells whatever is in my heart. It represents my heart as the Pope represents God."

What does a homeless man do? He goes, for instance, to open a congress of archeologists, and perhaps even delivers a short address. What happens to an untenanted house? Sounds flow into it like water into an abandoned ship, sounds made by children and by cars shifting gears, the sounds of dogs and of radios, all penetrating and filling the house though there is no one to hear them.

In its loneliness an empty house imitates the sounds of the people who were once in it. A table creaks as it expands or contracts, just as we learned as children in physics when we heated a metal ball and it could no longer be passed through a ring. A house imitates the sounds of its people, the squeaking of a dresser and the humming in the water pipes and a groan as of one awaking suddenly. The drop of water falls into the sink with a gay splash, and the ceiling sheds a bit of plaster. A house imitates the sounds of people because it doesn't know any others. But the sea knows, and so does the desert. And all things within the house—book and bottle, cup and pencil, plate and cake of soap—become alike since they are not used. Joel's wife, Ruth, had gone back to her parents and brothers as women in olden times used to return to their fathers' houses.

Pat is still barefoot, though she has put on a skirt. She zipped it over her belly and now she is turning it around so that the zipper should be behind. Before dressing she had washed herself thoroughly all over to be rid of the hospital odors. She shampooed her hair and put some of the foam on her eyebrows and on the tip of her nose and looked into the mirror and beheld the face of a clown.

Pat's footsteps slap softly on the floor. Her feet are still wet. A puddle still stands in the bathtub. She dashes around, holding some hairpins between her teeth. Are the flowers in place? The records? The curtain is washed and starched. With her bare feet she kicks her sandals under the couch.

Through the window the hills of Jerusalem are visible, and on one of the hills, in the university amphitheater, the opening session of the Congress of Archeologists is coming to its end. Joel has left the meeting. He left the stage unobtrusively and went to meet the night. Mina sits between her husband, Itzhak, and Major Patterson. The sun is about to set. Itzhak is like the captain of a ship and towers silently at the prow. Mina floats in the ship of her imagination. So does the Major. Only his military cap indicates that he is a soldier. His uniform is bedecked with numerous gay and colorful badges and ribbons and stripes.

Driven by his heartbeat, Joel rejected the thought of a taxi or even of a paved road and cut across two hills and a valley along ancient paths. He passed by the monastery and ascended the slope to Rehavia. He fled past Dr. Manheim, who did not see him from where he was seated on a bench near his nurse, all in white—she has looked after him since he was released from the hospital.

He found Pat sitting on the steps near the entrance to the house. She was impatient and her breath came heavily. She wore the lace blouse which she had received from her grandmother, a blouse severe around the neck and arms but carelessly soft on her bosom. She saw him coming down the narrow lane and her legs became too weak for her to rise, and she laughed at herself: What is the matter with me? I am behaving like a silly schoolgirl. And, thinking so, she smiled.

27

I walked into the shop and there was no one there. I coughed, but no one came. I sat down in a chair in the light that was weak though it was the morning of a summer day. On the shelves and in the wall cabinets were artificial limbs, arms and legs, and hernia belts and crutches of all sorts. I heard a sound as of a woodpecker in this forest of artificial limbs. I felt as though I were being observed but I did not know by whom. Some of the legs were bent as if running. A voice from a distance suddenly said, "One moment, I am coming." I answered weakly, "It's all right; I have time." I heard the subdued sound of the humming of a machine in the distance. The humming stopped and gave way to the sound of feet descending wooden steps.

At first, after Ruth came out of the hospital, I used to carry her books to and from school. Later, when she got the artificial leg, it became like some growing tree and lent her strength. One day in the Palace Park, near the lagoon where a stone nymph poured water into a marble basin, Ruth asked me, "How will things be in the future, do you think?" I was frightened. To this day I am frightened when I am asked such a question. Even the present is an almost unbearably terrifying vision, let alone true prophecies.

I said to Ruth what I had heard from the adults, that nowadays a physical disability is not a problem and that in the twentieth century a person without a leg could easily make a place of honor in the world for himself. And I added a list of professions which she could attain, such as being a lawyer or a linguist. Yes, studying languages, that was it. She heard me out and her voice was calm as the waters of the lagoon when she said, "Of course. It's no problem at all. I am surprised I asked you such a question." She was twelve then. We got up and I helped her walk to the black cast-iron gate of the park. From that day on she never talked about her disability, and I dimly felt that something new had arisen between us. My father began to liquidate his affairs and to dispose of his stock of buttons and thread and pins until his store closed. The nymph continued to pour her waters. After a while not even Ruth was allowed into the park, because she was Jewish. Now I am again free to sit in this park, but I haven't gone there yet. Only dead Ruth goes about freely everywhere.

I heard the sound of firm steps and a man appeared from amid the limbs. His hair was long, like that of an artist. Later I learned that in his free time he made violins. He moved his glasses to the tip of his nose and apologized. One of his assistants, he said, was on vacation, and another was attending an international conference of artificial-limb manufacturers, and his apprentice wasn't experienced enough, and he himself was being kept very busy, for the wounds of the war were still numerous. I told him my request: an artificial limb for a girl about sixteen years old. "Where is she?" he asked. I said she'd come after we had agreed on the price. He handed me a number of illustrated booklets showing happy people. "I am like everyone else," someone in a picture declared. When the man saw that I was not enthusiastic, he suggested a cheaper kind of limb. I remained silent, and he thought that I was a shy and proud beggar and said, "Perhaps something secondhand?" I nodded enthusiastic consent. He disappeared and I heard him puttering in the stockroom. Some heavy objects fell. In a little while he returned lugging a number of artificial legs. One of them was slung over his shoulder like a lamb over the shoulder of a shepherd. I helped him distribute his burden, and when he finished he said with a sigh, "All these are prewar, but there are no new patents. Now, this is a firm leg made of good materials. I'll fix a good leg for your daughter." And he placed before me one of the limbs and praised its wood and buckles and bolts and hinges. He also pointed out that it was made in 1935. "All right, I'll take it," I said. He was surprised. "What do you mean? The girl has to come here and be fitted." I said, "I want to show it to her first." He shrugged and wrapped the leg in some newspapers that carried reports of peace conferences and disarmament conferences. I asked him if he had a record of whom the leg had belonged to, so that I could ask its former owner whether it had been comfortable. He took out a card file and read from it, "No. 22704. Nickel, Grade B." Its last owner was one Joseph Kalter. The boy was wounded (poor Joseph) during the great bombardment. At the age of eighteen, he changed this limb for another one. The man wrapped some sheets from a literary paper about the limb, and finally some brown paper, and tied the whole bundle with string. Now I would go to Caroline Alley and there the riddle would be solved.

I did not take a streetcar. Instead I walked through alleys until I came to the place of the former fish market. But now there were no fish or fishmongers in rubber aprons. A young man sitting on a motorcycle laughed as I passed. I waved the leg at him, and he fled amid a great sputtering. I walked by a fashion shop, and a woman said, "They are delivering the leg." I explained to her that she was mistaken. She had been expecting an artificial leg for a display in her show window. It's the new style, not to put up complete manikins but only parts of them, an arm carrying an elegant pocketbook, a leg in a silk stocking, a hand in a glove. I asked how to get to Caroline Alley, and they told me to retrace my steps through the fish market. I recalled how Herr Messner, the fishmonger, used to kill fish with a wooden mallet, like the ones used to drive tent stakes into the ground in the desert. Then he would wrap the fish in newspaper, like Ruth's leg which I was now carrying. I followed an alley and suddenly saw the Square of the Four Cisterns from a new angle. Because so many houses had been destroyed, distances became foreshortened in Weinburg. An old woman said, "Once, the square could not be seen from here." I told her that it was necessary to destroy many houses to get beautiful landscapes. I stopped and leaned on the leg. What should I do with it? Out of habit I referred to it as Ruth's leg. The old woman said, "You can follow me. You are probably going to Joseph, the musician. The river is not far from here."

The old woman led me down the alley and through a court where stood a tailor's dummy with a hole ripped in it and dried seaweed spilling out of it. She asked me if I was a refugee from the East. A cat rubbed itself against a fence. A small plaster angel lay on its back and looked at the sky. Its wings were broken, and also one hand from which a thick wire protruded. I heard someone playing a clarinet. The old woman said, "Do you hear? This is Joseph. You must be either a refugee or a returned war prisoner. Most of them have already returned, except for those who are dead." I told her that I had returned from among the dead and that I had seen that smoke. She said, "Smoke hurts the eyes, and not only the eyes. Here is Joseph's door." I knocked on the door with the leg. Joseph opened the door but it was dark in the corridor and I could not see him. I leaned the leg against a closet. "Sit down, please. I will be with you in a moment," Joseph said, waving his clarinet. I sat down to wait for him and suddenly realized that this was the apartment where Henrietta and her aunt had once lived. But before I could assimilate this realization, the cripple returned. I told him I came on strange business, and I picked up the leg and unwrapped it. I put it on a table and he put down his clarinet. I explained to him that I came to inquire how good the leg was. He picked it up and examined it and then began weeping. I knew that this had been Henrietta's apartment. In the corridor, there used to be a stand with many wooden hooks and a large mirror inscribed: "Begin with God and end with God—this is your way in the world." There were flowers in pots hanging on the wall, and creepers which in Israel are called the wandering Jew, though they have roots. The small window was hidden behind lace curtains embroidered with fat little angels. Another long-legged stand held a large, spherical goldfish tank. The room where the crippled Joseph and I now sat used to be the living room, and the window was set back in a niche where Henrietta used to sit and knit and tell me stories. From time to time she would tickle me with the long knitting needle. The cold needle against my skin under my shirt would cause me great pleasure. It is from that time that I know the world by the degree of pleasure it causes me. The shelves and dark closets held antiquated pottery and glasswork cracked like the skin of an old woman. Also dull pewter dishes. In this house the light was always dimmed, a permanently pleasurable twilight. A traditional Sabbath lamp shaped like a five-pointed star hung from the ceiling and it could be raised or lowered at will. But it was never lit.

The two women used to sleep in the adjoining small room on beds that rose like feather mounds. It was a delight to tumble around in the pillows and quilts. In my imagination they were monsters and giants blocking my way and challenging me to battle. With tearful eyes the princess awaited the outcome of the battle. At first they would come upon me and knock me down and smother me, and I would kick my arms and legs like an overturned beetle. But at the right moment I would make a desperate effort and mount the pillows and seize them with arms and legs in terrible holds from which they could not escape, and complete the struggle by pounding them with my fists while the princess smiled at me.

In the small kitchen was an oven of red bricks and a bucket of coal. The small kitchen window opened on a minute court where no one except the cat was allowed. I never took Ruth to Henrietta and her aunt. Despite the love between us, I wanted to keep this corner of pleasure all to myself.

Joseph wept, then played his clarinet, then wept again. Only some time after he left did I become aware of his departure, and also realized that he was not crippled at all but had two sound legs.

28

Patricia's apartment was empty just then. She was remote, in a dream. At the entrance to the house dry leaves had been swirled by the wind into a pile, and suddenly they were blown into the hallway. Patricia's apartment begins with the raucous bell on the door. Then comes the square foyer. Now, in the evening, the entire house was suddenly filled with a maddening smell of jasmine. On the door is an inscription: "Klein." In the foyer there is a closet, and from the key inserted in its door hang two brass pokers to stir the fire in the fireplace. There is no fireplace in Klein's apartment. As a matter of fact, it has central heating. Every time the closet is opened, the brass pokers jangle. It is best not to open this closet, for it is filled to overflowing with bundles of newspapers and letters which are likely to spill out and fill the foyer. "This night I have promised you," she had said, and her eyes filmed over with the moistness of excitement and passion. Some of her personal belongings are also in this closet, some crumpled clothing and a rubber bathing cap. All the things crammed into the closet leaned on one another and supported each other, boxes and bundles of letters and a sweater smelling of naphthalene; everything was casual and provisional and about to collapse in a heap and to be picked up and carried away by the wind like the dry leaves at the entrance.

In the bedroom, too, there was a big closet filled with things prepared for a quick getaway. Linen and sweaters in plastic bags and clothing neatly folded and many hats which she had never worn. And here, too, were many letters which she had read with trembling lips, and letters which she had held in her ancient hands and whose contents had sunk deep into her soul like rain into underground springs.

On the window sill over the bed lay a rock containing an ancient petrified leaf, a brother to Pat's own hands. Late in the winter, the window looks out on a tree with violet flowers. In the summer, one sees the rocky slope of a hill. That is the direction from which the clouds come. They pass over Pat's house and halt there for a moment, adding a note of expectation.

Still other letters lie about, like the one from Klein in which he inquires whether everything is in order and whether his friend, his agent, is taking care of things satisfactorily.

When darkness falls and Pat is not at home and the windows are open, a light goes on near the head of the stairs and the screen in the window casts its shadow on the opposite wall. The yellow light gilds everything it touches, leaving all else in darkness and anticipation.

When winter comes, where will Pat be then? How many ages will pass before winter comes? They cannot return to the past winter, for then they didn't know each other, and the next one is far away. No doubt it will be good to love also in winter and not only on the one promised night. After the cool evening breezes, the night will fade away and sink into the heated rocks.

29

I thought that it was time to check the artificial leg at the railroad station, and I got on streetcar No. 6. Near the statue of Saint K. a band played in honor of the many arrivals for the tournament. I winked a greeting to the Saint as I watched the newcomers march past. The standard bearers of the different countries marched in front. I saw Leonora pass by at the end of the procession among the other stateless participants ("reckless and frivolous people"—Judges). I waved the leg in greeting to her. She noticed me and motioned for me to wait for her. I waited and we went into the station dining room. She invited me to the tournament. "You must come."

"I will come if you will win."

"You must come so that I will win."

"I can't on account of this leg."

She took the leg and hung one of the skates on it. "I am tired," she said.

"I see that you are tired; that's bad before the tournament. Smile, Leonora. Don't be so serious."

She was moving the leg with the skate on it back and forth, and suddenly burst into a rage and cried, "God damn you!"

"What's the matter? Why all of a sudden?"

"You are spying on me. You are following me. You are trying to get into my soul, you and that Hindu you have hired."

"He is doing a research job; leave him out of this. Go back to Israel."

"I have nothing there. I like it here."

"Among the saints on the bridge?"

"Here I can ride horses."

"There are horses there, too."

She laughed like a child. "Only the President's guards in Jerusalem have horses." Now we both laughed, recalling the commander of the Presidential guard, a middle-aged beefy man who made his mount look small and pitiful.

"When are you going back?" she asked.

"When I finish."

"I, too, will return when I finish."

I left Leonora and walked down Kings Street and across empty lots that once were alleys. I walked to the café where I had been the night before. The Indian was not there, yet it was important that I discuss the problem of how people establish relations. Every man, like a country, has his private territorial waters which no one else may enter.

I sat down at a table and suddenly became aware that I did not have the leg with me. It was stolen from me, or I absent-mindedly left it somewhere. Ruth's leg. Where is she?

Sometimes I wait for my Indian friend, and sometimes he waits for me. We need each other. We use each other. I serve him as an invaluable mine of cases of despair, a laboratory for the cultivation of a culture of despair. He serves as a camouflage for my revenge and for my spying activities. He provides me with valuable information about the movements of Leonora, and the inn where the assistant stationmaster Weberlin drinks his daily beer. He also supplied me with some documents and interesting information about Professor Kunz, whose private seminar he attends. Likewise he advised me to insert an ad in the papers about the lost artificial leg. Sometimes we sit opposite each other, shamelessly holding pencil and notebook, prepared to write down whatever each thinks important about the other. In the introduction to his book, he will probably make grateful acknowledgment to me for the valuable assistance I gave him in collecting his material. He brings me some document or other, a certificate of deportation, or a last letter from one of the Jews of Weinburg, and observes how the reading of such a document of despair changes the expression on my face, and sometimes he even photographs my expression with his spy's camera. When my head is filled with heavy sadness, or the fumes of St. Johann's wine, and it rests on my fist, the Indian sits faithfully before me. When at times I doze off, he remains near me and notes down the casual words that escape from the web of my dreams. Finally he says that I am a case of despair within despair, for, he says, I despair over what has happened here and I also despair of myself because I came too late and nothing remains to be done.

Then he consoles me. He teaches me to breathe long and deeply. In time he might even teach me yoga, though he is no great expert at it. Since everybody expects him to be a yoga expert, he has no choice but to pretend to be a yoga expert. He does not wish to lose people's confidence.

I now stay at the hotel near the market square. From my window I can see St. Mary's Cathedral, of which only the shell remains—inside it is all burned. Many little shops cluster against its wall, as in the Middle Ages. I am on an upper floor. Sometimes I open the window to look out on the square; other times I hesitate. On the ground floor of the hotel, in the barroom, people drink foaming beer and eat pale sausages and smoke constantly.

I asked at the room clerk's desk whether there was any mail for me and he gave me a couple of letters. One was from my friend Klein, who trots about the world; no gravity can tie him to a single place. In his letter he informed me about the blood bath that would soon engulf the world, and that all mankind could do was to postpone it. He also announced that he was no longer living with his wife; they did not stay in the same hotels or travel in the same car. The second letter was one of many I had received in response to my advertisement about the missing artificial leg. A joker wrote this one and suggested that I look among the participants in the skating tournament; one of them might have wanted a third leg to help him win.

I went out to buy shoes. Up to this time, I avoided buying anything in Weinburg except food. The saleslady brought me a number of styles. I sat in a soft chair and could not make up my mind. The moment I buy some item of clothing in Weinburg, I will become part of the city and will forfeit my right to revenge. This is a special version of the Bedouin law of the desert which I made up for myself. Don't spit into a well from which you drink. I knew that these were silly thoughts and that I needed shoes, for I had walked a lot. Finally I bought a pair of ash-gray shoes, suitable for camouflage. Near me a little boy cried. His mother tried to comfort him and said, "See, Uncle is also buying shoes and he is not crying." The child looked at me and saw what was in my eyes and said, "That's not right. He is crying, too." From where I sat I could see, through all the shoes on display, the Square of the Four Cisterns and the tower of the ancient City Hall. A truck stood near the tower, and barrels of beer were being rolled from it into a cellar where there was a famous beer hall. People were coming out of it, as if the barrels had crowded them out. My eyes dimmed and I saw my teacher of many years ago as he used to come out of the cellar, arm in arm with his drinking companions, the piano teacher in the conservatory and the high school teacher. I beheld my teacher, his belly protruding before him, and on it a swaying golden chain which supported a watch. He used to put this watch on the flat of his hand and snap it open with his thumbnail. He was my teacher in the third grade and his favorite word was "symbolic." Whatever he taught us was "symbolic." To flatter him we would use the word in our answers, though we did not know what it meant. In time we used it as a swearword: "Hey, you symbol," or, "I'll symbol you as you've never been symboled before." My teacher, too, died—died and was burned, and his smoke was borne by the wind wherever it is that smoke is borne to. He loved little Ruth. What was it she used to say about my buying shoes? For a man who is not practical, even buying a pair of shoes becomes a deed.

The saleslady asked me if I wanted to carry the new shoes with me. I told her I'd wear them, and the old shoes were put in a box. I walked out and stood before the heap of rubble that had once been Mr. Rosenbaum's house. His father, the butcher, used to stand here cutting meat, weighing it, wrapping it; sometimes he would give me a thin slice of salami. I loved the smell of the butcher shop—unlike the Indian, who does not eat meat but loves to observe the despair of flesh and blood. There are times when I cannot stand the Indian spying on every expression on my face, every twitch and movement. Lately he has added a new department to his researches: action beyond despair, instances of back-to-the-wall resistance, mice against cats, early Christians against lions in the arena.

I finally entered the café. The Indian was already there playing chess by himself. I grabbed all the black pieces and he stopped playing. We talked freely. It was quiet around us. The day was still young and the fish swam in their aquariums in the walls. Only the click-clack of the chess pieces as they were being thrown into the box disturbed the silence.

Then the board was cleared and the pieces lay scrambled in the box, a knight near a queen and a pawn upside down near a castle. "As in the freight cars when they were being sent *there*," I said. "Not again, not again," the Indian said. I told him of a discovery I had made, that in German the word for despair was feminine while in Hebrew it was masculine. He took up the idea and delivered a pretty speech about despair which leads to love and lust. Some young people came in and asked the café owner to turn on the TV. A man's head appeared and announced that we would be shown a telecast of the last quarter of the skating tournament. A march was played and the television screen was convulsed with a shudder like that which passes over the hide of a cow. Then we saw the crowd of spectators and heard them cheering. I continued talking to the Indian.

"I am homesick for Jerusalem."

"My father is buried there."

"I know. He is buried on the way to Bethlehem, under some tall pines."

"Someday I will go there."

"You must come. From the military cemetery the dead soldiers can see the part of Jerusalem that is on the hills. Jerusalem always holds its breath; it always keeps itself under control, always turns inward, always practices yoga."

"Will you go back there?"

"You doubt it?"

The screen showed the male participants in the tournament. One fell and was carried out of the arena. The remaining two continued circling. I also saw the river and felt homesick for it. An interlude was announced and I drank a cup of coffee. The young people sat quietly. They were rehearsing how to be calm. The Indian continued to develop his ideas on despair and love. "The only pure action is delayed revenge, when all excitement has died down. Love is not action. In love there is only passivity. Both the lover and the loved one are merely tolerant, and do not engage in pure action. In love, whether one is above or beneath, one merely moves without direction. In delayed revenge one is detached from the object of the vengeance."

The competition of the women began. Five girls dressed in tights toed the starting line. Leonora, too, stood quietly and waited for the signal.

30

"Arise! Arise!" Joel said in Biblical fashion, and stretched out his arms to her. She grasped them and raised herself, smiling at her seeming effort. Now she stood facing him but was remote and strange. He put his hands on her shoulders, but she removed them and whispered, "Not yet." He did not understand and saw only that her eyes shone with a dark glimmer. She smoothed her tight skirt and asked, "Do you like my clothes?" He looked at her lace blouse and his fingers touched the glass buttons on her back. He looked into her wide face that now contained all his life and the broad distances which had opened before him during the last days. Her hair was arranged in braids on her head. She raised her hand and adjusted the barrette that held a braid in place. Her skin was brown and her heavy lips moved as if in constant prayer or intoxication. He took her hand and they walked together. She said, "Don't you think that this blouse is old-fashioned? I am myself a bit of that time and of that place."

When they walked down the street and passed by the olive grove, she said, "I am yours." She said this calmly, as if defining a fact, and added, "I love you," in the same quiet tone, like a doctor diagnosing symptoms of a disease. The rest of her speech was lost in a breeze that blew from the Old City. And so they walked together until they came to the plot where stone monuments were carved. The mason was still at work by the light of a lamp, completing three marble plaques in honor of donors of trees to a forest of the Jewish National Fund. Joel described to Pat the monuments that are set up over graves of *Kohanim* on which are carved two hands with fingers parted in blessing, and he also told her about his Uncle Moritz, who had been a *Kohen* and blessed the congregation and was finally buried in a provisional cemetery in Sheikh Badr. It turned out that she, too, had an Uncle Morris, in the French branch of the family, ruddy-faced and a gay lover of drink.

"You start telling me stories and you never finish them," she complained.

And all of a sudden Joel was overcome with a feeling that the end had come, the end of his love and the end of this summer. When he told Pat, she said she was accustomed to such sensations, which come to her often; at times they are strong enough to cut her breath short, like an impetuous lover alongside her. Again they turned toward Pat's house and a flush of great heat passed through Joel, not only because of Pat but also because of the entire city and all those who were his friends. All, all of them, may the good God preserve them wherever they are (as Dr. Manheim might say in one of his sermons), all who act courageously, not only the guardians of the borders, or only his beloved Pat, but all, all who act faithfully and even those who don't, and all those who gather this night to plan the future, or to resurrect the past, and all those who know that there is no escaping evil just as there is no avoiding the good, all, all, his friends who are now big wheels in the government, and the

Romans of that evening of the party, all his friends who fell in the war, and those who are buried alive in their fancy apartments, and all those who are marching upward and onward, from one success to another, from one assignment to another, up the ladder of values and of ranks and of social status.

Thus Joel blessed them in his heart.

And still the speech unreeled in his mind as he went on his way to the night of his love with Patricia:

... and all those who go on living with the courage of men who begin building a bridge from the bank of a river without measuring the width of the river—Itzhak, Mina's husband; and Yoske, who returned to his kibbutz after the old house on Jaffa Street that he lived in was torn down; and Zeiger, who had known the dark byways of the underground and its tunnels—all those who still refuse to concede that it is all the same in the end and that after the revolution and after the liberation comes the time of "ivory couches" and of corruption and bribery and injustice and scheming and falsehood, all, all, the living and the dead, those who are covered with the yellow loess dust of the Negev and have seeds of thistles and thorns caught in their hair, those who know their courage and those who don't know it, those who wander in the tunnels of defeat and those who are caught in the terrible labyrinth of success, all his friends and comrades, those whose sun is setting and those whose sun is rising, those who dance and those who sit on the sidelines; they part from one another yet hold hands in their falling and in their rising, their courage remains undaunted, and they grind their teeth even when they lie stretched out on their ivory couches. Thus, no doubt, Dr. Manheim would have said it: "O ye drunkards of Ephraim on your couches of ivory."

They nearly stumbled on a branch that lay in their way.

The electric company trims the branches that get too long to prevent their touching the high-tension wires.

"Pat, you hear me? I will never abandon any of them."

"Why do you say this in anger? You shouldn't be angry with me. It wasn't I who came to you. You came to me. You have confused my life as one shuffles a pack of cards. Now I have nothing left but you."

"And why do you give me only one night?"

She did not answer. They stood near a tree. Had it rained suddenly, they could have found shelter under it. In the end Pat would take him away from this city. Her bosom is infinitely broad. Nearby in a house someone was beating an egg and the sound of the fork against the dish was heard plainly.

"Pat! Pat! Your arms . . . Your thighs . . ."

"Forget my silly thighs. What's so special about them?"

He pressed her powerfully against the trunk of the tree until she began to breathe heavily and whispered, "Come, let's go home, quick."

"Pat . . ."

"Listen. Always call me Patrice—not Pat or Patricia but Patrice, with the French ending."

A newsboy crying a late edition approached them. They passed by the butcher shop in which a big refrigerator hummed a lullaby to the slaughtered animal within it.

"We are getting close, Patrice."

"Yes."

A street lamp hung over them like God, shedding light but providing no protection.

He looked at her and her face glowed under the lamp like the face of one who is departing late at night in a huge, empty, and resounding station. And since they were already at her doorstep, she said, "Be calm, be calm." She, too, had reached the end of her circular thoughts.

Klein's apartment house was an aggregate of cubes. Most

of its windows were still lit up at this hour. From time to time a light went out in one window and passed on to the next, from bathroom to bedroom, from kitchen to living room, and the effect was of runners passing a torch.

The lamp suspended over the door rocked slowly and cast shadows that waved in the breeze. They entered the hallway. From outside, the aroma of a summer night in the hills of Jerusalem wafted in, the almost painful odor of summer plants, of sage, of faraway burning grass and thorns—all the smells of a Jerusalem night, of quiet constant despair, of water measured by the teaspoon. And these were mixed with the smell of rock cooling slowly, of dust-covered pine trees, of the ascetic soil of Jerusalem lacerating itself in the long summer. Against this Patricia was abundance and fullness and splendor, all the islands and swift rivers and waterfalls and dark forests of her native land.

Out of habit she opened her mailbox, and Joel barely noticed that she took out a note and that her breath caught as she read it. Because he was wound tight to the point of despair, he thought that they would never reach this night of theirs, for the gods were jealous of them and would not allow them to be by themselves, alone with each other between walls.

At the entrance to the apartment they found two bouquets, carnations and roses. She asked him to open the door, which he did, and she went in and disappeared into the bathroom. Joel was still standing at the door when he heard the sound of footsteps. He put out his head to see who was coming and at once became involved in a farewell to Yosel, who had come to bid him goodbye.

"I'm leaving." "Where to?" "You know, I have offers to play in orchestras." "Come in, come in." "No, Einat is waiting for me downstairs."

Einat was indeed standing on the lower landing, and

every time the automatic light in the hall went out she pressed the button and turned it on again.

From within, Pat's bare footsteps were heard. Joel and Yosel stood on the landing, and Einat, who was weeping quietly, stood below and kept turning on the light.

"Well, goodbye, Yosel. You will return. You will return." Yosel's footsteps receded till they were lost in the night, and Pat came and pulled Joel inside and closed the door and pressed against him like a huge sea, so that his passions rose within him. The light had not been turned on, and in the darkness he touched her face and the protruding bones of her hips. "I am hard here," she whispered and he bent to touch her, but she seized his hair and raised his face against her own, as against a lamp, to see him in thé weak light that came into the room through the shutters. Together they walked from the foyer and in the dark they stumbled against the door of the closet, which opened, and, as if from behind a dam, a flood of objects tumbled out: packages and letters and books and sweaters smelling faintly of naphthalene. She laughed against his chest and said strange things in her American language. Were they lines from poems or words of her own? Gently he tried to guide her into the room but she suddenly became taut and resisting, and she whispered, "You are killing me, you are enslaving me." Thus she spoke and her whisper was followed by another deluge from the closet, like a final sob from the deepest depths—objects from different countries, picture postcards, castanets, little Greek jars, a miniature Eiffel Tower, and still another sweater, bringing memories of a winter in the French Alps. Suddenly it seemed to him that there was a ring of the doorbell, but he felt the flatness of her belly and knew that he had heard nothing. In any case they wouldn't open the door. But there was another ring and Patricia broke away crying, "I am coming, right away!" With terror and trembling lips she cried this as she pushed Joel into the room and turned on the light. And to him a quick "Straighten your shirt; fix your hair," and then he heard the click of her heels in the hall. He put his hands on his forehead to calm himself and invoked all kinds of thoughts and images to subdue his passion, to forget it: he made himself think of the sorrow of his wife Ruth, who had returned to the kibbutz and whose weeping face he last saw through the window of a bus; of little Ruth in an extermination camp; of his mother, who refused to see him; of Dr. Manheim, who sat on a bench leaning toward death like a ship that is keeling over to sink. These thoughts he invoked feverishly and they calmed him, so that he felt under control when he heard the bell ring again and the door open and Patricia's voice and a masculine voice that talked with an American accent. Then the door of the room opened, and he saw Patricia's face and her eyes glittering with fear and her mouth imploring Joel to be patient with her, to be patient, that despite all she was his.

31

There are so many things I must do: visit the Home for the Aged again, visit the sick nun and hear from her about little Ruth, look for the artificial leg, look for Leonora. Since she failed in the tournament, Leonora disappears frequently. Now she is here and the next moment she has vanished. But I heard that she is very successful in her work on the film. Recently she has been filmed making love to a Gestapo commander while beyond the wall a Jew was being tortured. This was done very simply. Windmeyer, who is substituting for the American director, explained it to me. They took a chunk of meat from a slaughtered old horse (later I heard that it was from the mare Falada, the good old mare from Kleiman's stable) and they whipped it with a strap. After each blow a man moaned and groaned. Both sets of sounds were recorded and then synchronized. Several attempts were made before complete success was attained. This recording was played behind the wall of the room where Leonora lay on a sofa. She wept because of her failure in the skating tournament. It is true that most of her tears over the failure had been absorbed in my shirt, but new tears were ever ready. The assistant casting director said that these tears would do. They could just as well serve as tears of passion or lust or laughter, and it would not be necessary to induce her tears artificially. Thus Leonora lay on a red sofa and a man whose black shirt lay crumpled on a chair held her head. The director called, "Two—six—four," and the man bent over to kiss her, but she slapped his face and began crying. "Two—six—four" had to be repeated. Then the director called, "Two—six—five," and the door to the adjoining room opened and two husky S.S. men brought in a man half of whose clothes had been ripped off and whose mouth oozed blood. The director cried out in anger, "Where is the make-up man? You call this blood? It looks more like he had eaten jam and hadn't wiped his mouth properly. Is that how a man who has been beaten half to death looks? New make-up! At once!" Someone else told me that Leonora could have a great career in films and on TV but that she is stubborn and wastes her talents on skating events. "Look at her blue eyes, and at the wonderful way her nostrils flare." But Leonora had retorted, "I've already been praised for my blue eyes and fair hair when a German officer saved me from death, afraid of killing such a Nordic-looking child together with the other Jews." How old was she then? About six. The assistant director declared that at times he was himself frightened by the horrible film he was making, but that it was his employer, the American director, who had conceived the idea of the film. And he also said that I must meet this man, a unique character; something was bothering him, some memory that grew from year to year. And meantime the beaten man was brought in again, and this time the make-up man had done his job to perfection. The welts from the lashing on his back showed perfectly, blood covered his face, and his eyes cried out accusingly, so that one of the S.S. men said in American, "Like Jesus! By God, just like Jesus!" He was of Italian descent and a Catholic.

Again they called out, "Two—six—four, two—six—five," and the filming resumed. Leonora drew to herself her beloved S.S. commander and he shouted to his men, "Take away this filth!" And the man of sorrows was led off. A heavy door slammed shut and the sound of the beating in the adjoining room resumed.

The city was deep in sleep. Frequently I had visualized the destruction of the city: all the houses splitting open and devils and evil spirits fleeing from them. In Shakespeare's plays ghosts of the murdered and evil spirits frighten the wicked ones. What should I do, since I am neither a ghost nor an evil spirit?

There was light in two windows of a house where my violin teacher used to live. The sweet smell of violin wood still hovered in the doorway, together with the odor of milk. I rang the doorbell but no one answered. I rang a second time and noticed a small sign: "YOGA INSTITUTE, WEINBURG." I opened the door and went in. In the room where I used to practice as a child, half-naked men sat or lay on their backs. The piano still stood in its usual place. No one paid any attention to me. A dim light illuminated their faces. From an adjoining room came an indistinct hum. An indistinct hum always seems to come from adjoining rooms. I crawled on all fours to see if I could recognize anyone among those lying on the floor. I recognized the head of the Indian. I lay down near him and we talked, head to head, like heads floating on the water.

My head said to the Indian's head, "Here Mrs. Lewison used to give me violin lessons." The Indian declared that everything persists in its own place. I told him that she was burned, and that her violin was broken the same day the windows in Dr. Manheim's house were broken and slivers of glass covered little Ruth as she slept. Nonetheless everything persists, he said. Who said that it was out of the question for dead things to be in many places at the same time? They are free. Even living people can carry on simultaneously in more than one place, especially people who cannot make up their minds. My Indian friend added, "Yoga means control and unity, but you try to introduce division. You are both here and there." I said that this was indeed so in dreams. But he insisted: "No, no, real people can be both here and there." As he talked, he stood on his head and had some difficulty speaking.

I crawled among the physical culturists. The assistant stationmaster did not recognize me. The room smelled of male perspiration. The Indian clapped his hands, and the men sat down cross-legged and stuck out their tongues and practiced all kinds of breathing. I imitated their breathing so that they should not realize I was not one of their group. It occurred to me that I had made a big haul, for all of them were forty or over, all were enemies, a veritable lions' den. The Indian told me in a whisper to pay particular attention to the fat man; he had something tattooed on his lower belly and must have belonged to an important Nazi organization. He had noticed it in the shower room, the Indian added, and showed me where the showers were. I went in and the humming stopped. Four shower stalls were built into the wall, like confession booths. I stripped and showered. Soon the others came. They maintained a terrible silence, unlike ordinary people who chatter loudly when they are about to take a shower. The Indian told me that they all take the yoga courses to find mental peace. Among them were two lawyers, three judges, and five professors who teach classical philosophy and neurology. The university buildings had not been seriously damaged during the bombardment, and they continued their courses even when there were no students and refugees were moved into the lecture halls. That year all of Europe consisted of refugees. As for me, I have been a refugee since birth. Leonora remained a refugee ever since Henrietta and Mrs. Munster picked her up.

The water flowed quietly over the bodies of the showering males. I washed again and again, waiting for the suspicious fat man to shower. I looked at the tattoo above his pubic hair. When he noticed that I was watching him, he covered his belly with a towel even though he was soaped. His gentle canine eyes were terror-stricken. The others had already gone and scattered in the night. I leaped on him and we wrestled on the floor of the shower room. It was hard to seize him for he was soaped and slippery, but I was dry from wiping myself several times while I was trying to gain time. He got on top of me and, breathing heavily, tried to knee me in the groin. I called upon Saint Ruth and experienced a great access of strength and seized him between my legs. He groaned and his face assumed the well-known expression of Laocoön trying to free himself from the coils of the snakes. I sensed that his strength was ebbing, so I turned him over on his back and bent over him to look closely at the tattoo design. He struggled and kicked. I allowed him to waste his remaining strength. He kicked against the walls and overturned a number of chairs as he struggled. I struck him in the belly and he stopped kicking. Now I could see the tattoo above the curly hair. A mermaid! Like the mermaid on Yosel's arm. What was it concealing? He leaped up suddenly and fled outside naked. There he mounted his bicycle and drove off into the night, his fat white body glistening.

32

Now there were three of them: Patricia, the man she brought into the room, and Joel. Her earrings, which were shaped like small bird cages, rocked as she got up. Joel smelled of the plants of this dry land. The man, who was Pat's husband, gave off the aroma of carnations. There was a pool of darkness under the table; there was darkness under the sofa. Each thought his own thoughts. Joel looked at the man's face, which like the moon was alternately visible and concealed; sometimes he discerned only a single feature, the curve of the cheek, the mouth, the glint of his glasses. It seemed they had been sitting there a long while. Joel's hair would turn white; he would be buried in Patrice's apartment. Then they got up and moved around the room as if it were a big hall. The man said something and Patricia walked out, and when she returned there were tears in her eyes. "Don't let her drink too much," the man said to Joel. His face was handsome, like that of a Greek, and there was the mark of sorrow on it. His face showed that he had been a soldier; now he was a man of suffering. He put down his glass with a bang. Patricia went out of the room again and passed near Joel and lightly touched him, and his distress dissolved. Patricia compared the two men, as if it were possible to compare the past with the present, as if it were possible to choose between the past and the present. Why can't she go on living with him? Why can't she free herself of him? (Something is eating him. Something in his life is gnawing away at him. One could almost hear the sound of the slow chewing; one could almost see the dark throat that swallowed all of them.) Patricia went in and out, to cry, to look in the mirror, in her confusion to bring candy, to sip from her drink. Her lips were large and tremulous. ("Isn't she beautiful?" "Like Death.") She dreaded coming into the room where the two men sat. If they had at least stayed in one place, she might have become used to it, but they kept changing places. Joel grasps at the curtain; her husband turns the pages of a book; Joel moves to the chair; her husband walks over to the record player. They pass by each other like sentries and Patricia closes her eyes not to see them. Her lust has not subsided. Joel, on the other hand, has given up. It might have been possible to love this man. Like Orpheus he came to reclaim his wife, his pale and trembling loss. An Orpheus in reverse, dead himself, who came to take Patricia to the land of the dead. Her eyes were beautiful with terror. Now the three sat quietly and looked at each other, and because they were three their heads would turn almost imperceptibly from time to time. Each would fix his glance on the other the way one moves a chessman. One raises one's eyes with concentrated yet dreamy effort and one lowers them again hesitantly or firmly decisive. Joel sat sunk into the soft chair, which had broken springs. Patricia came up and lightly touched his hand and whispered, "Have faith in me. Please be patient with me." Her husband, who had stepped out of the room, returned. Who is he? What will be his next move? When will Joel face him squarely? A pity that he met him here. Under other circumstances they could have been close friends. This he knew. Orpheus rose and took his invisible lyre. Patricia stood holding the doorknob. He went out and they heard the slamming of the outer door. Her knees shook and she felt spent. "The door," she said. The word told everything. When people can't talk, inanimate objects begin to talk. A door, a window, a closet, water in a pipe.

When she returned, there was still terror on her face.

And then she knew that she did not have to explain anything. And she also knew that this love was real because it was not necessary to explain. All her life she had felt compelled to explain and rationalize everything she felt and did. Now Joel was accepting her without question. Cars passed in the street. Tenants in the house went to sleep. Sofas were moved and became beds. Sheets were unfolded and shaken before being spread on sofas.

They turned out the lights so that no more visitors would come. And when they stood in the dark, they said almost simultaneously, "Let's play at war!" For they did not know how to come together after Orpheus had put in his appearance. Joel crouched and, putting his hands alongside his temples like the horns of a bull, butted her in the stomach. She laughed and cried out, "*Toro! Toro!*" And skipped aside in the dark and called out, "*Olé! Olé!*" Joel hid behind the broken-down soft chair. She saw him and laughed nervously. Then they became two rampaging children; they were so confused that they could not do anything else. "*Toro! Toro!*" she cried, and took off her skirt and held it the way toreadors hold their red capes. This also released her sturdy legs for the battle. The bull snorted and laughed, which filled the brave toreador with joy and fear. Nimbly she jumped aside and the next lunge of the bull caused his horns to get stuck in Kant's *Critique of Pure Reason* in the bookshelf.

"You won't win," Patricia cried, not knowing what she was saying. But Joel, the bull, laughed. They cursed each other like David and Goliath, and encouraged each other like a crowd of spectators in a coliseum, and then they rested, observing each other from their corners, like a couple of wild beasts. As they became accustomed to the darkness, they dimly saw each other's faces and the outline of the furniture. Joel was red within and white outside; Patricia was golden within and white outside.

They approached each other in terrible silence and collided again, but his hands forgot that they were supposed to be horns and he embraced her knees and they fell and became one mass of bodies and limbs, and madness resumed and they seized each other. And now and then their heads met in calm love, like people meeting in a deep forest, and she submitted and ceased breathing and a great peace came upon them; and then they rose and sat near each other. He wiped the perspiration from her forehead, and their breath returned and they came back to each other and were silent, one alongside the other, exhausted and happy. And she brought out a box of Kleenex which she always had ready at hand. They laughed and he called her "terrible desert beast" and he smelled of anise, the plant that grows even in the deserts of the Negev, and its odor is sharp and dry and it aroused her, and she strained toward him to put her face against the hair on his chest.

Then her lace blouse, the family heirloom, ripped with a loud sound, not the sound of mourning but the tearing of impatient joy of life.

"My blouse, my good blouse, the grandma of all my blouses," she exclaimed, and laughed and cried. "But I have others. I'll show you all of them. Do you want to see them? I have one that is low-cut and another that is tight-fitting and a black one without sleeves."

They sat together on the soft chair with the broken springs. Joel's hand rested on her stomach. What was there to say? She caressed his curly hair and his shoulders. And she pulled a box of Kleenex out from under the chair, for she was crying again. She touched his chest; then she got up and brought some jam made of fruit picked before dawn. She stood by the refrigerator and was lit up by its light and its coolness, and she took out some apples and they ate. The taste of apples was still on their lips and they came together, mouth to mouth, and her lips became soft and wide so that all his life sank within them.

Later she said, "I have no husband, darling. No more. I am finished with him. He is only a melodramatic backdrop, a decoration, a lighting effect. Do you hear me? I am yours forever." She brought a crisp folded sheet and spread it on the sofa. "Look, we are still half dressed," she said. He ripped the remainder of her torn blouse off her and pulled off her panties and threw them on the floor and she stepped on them and trampled them, and their clothes lay about the sofa in a semicircle. Then they came to each other peacefully, skin to skin, eye to eye, thigh to thigh. And she opened to him gently and he entered her in regal pride. Thus it was again and again, he arched above her, her black hair spread on the white sheet, her arms outstretched above her head as if seeking some firm hold.

A radio was turned on somewhere in the house, and then some others began to blare. They could not distinguish the words, but the announcers seemed to prepare their audience for important news. Joel rested his chin on the window sill and looked out into the night. A sheet of paper caught against the wire fence about the house and fluttered as if trying to free itself. Scraps of paper cement bags, a rag, and an old newspaper were also driven against the fence by the night breeze.

Professor Oren's name came over the radio distinctly, but it all seemed remote from Joel and he was no longer interested. He placed his palms on her small breasts, then moved them over her stomach and hips which were full and mature. She lightly touched his heavy eyebrows and breathed quietly, about to fall asleep. Outside, the entire world pressed against the fence trying to get in. In an adjoining empty lot where a new building was going up, the night watchman squatted near his bonfire, his arms hanging limply. Boards were stacked in even piles. Iron rods lay among the rocks and barrels of lime and a concrete mixer. Doors, too, lay stacked in orderly piles, doors that will open and shut, doors to slam and doors of returning.

"Listen," Pat said. She sat up and seemed about to make a speech. "Listen, we will be committing a sin if we don't remain together forever, a terrible sin."

"You are preaching again, Patrice—now, in the middle of the night. The Reverend Patricia, a preacher, like Rabbi Dr. Manheim. I love you."

"You see, now I have this great love and I don't know what to do with it. Tell me, tell me, darling, what should I do?"

Instead of answering he kissed her bosom, but she went on: "No, no, you must listen to me. I want to ask something."

"What?"

"Why did you curse me when you came into me the first time?"

"Did I curse?"

"Yes, you were so wrathful, as if you were taking vengeance. Why?"

"I didn't know I cursed."

"What are you doing to me? You know that I will never love again, that I never loved like this before. What are you doing to me?"

She lay down beside him, and the voice of the radio announcing important events to come intruded on them. Then, restlessly, she sat up again.

"My husband, Melvin, says that I am destructive, that everything I touch is destroyed. He also says I am childish. Poor Mel. Darling, I am not destructive. Sometimes I see people in the street, and in their eyes there is a cry for help. They plead with their eyes, and my eyes are probably like that, too. Don't be mad at the people who come to me. They come of themselves, because they need me. I am not destructive, and I am not childish, and I never loved the way I love now."

He did not let her go on and he pulled her to himself, but she sat up and her dark hair almost touched his face. Suddenly she said, "I'll bring you some ice cream from the refrigerator." She brought it and sat down on the carpet while he remained on the sofa and she fed him with a teaspoon.

33

Good Henrietta was sick and I sat near her bed. Her hair was gray and coarse like the grass that is used to stuff dolls and cheap mattresses, and it was dry like the grass in the parched summer fields of my country. Henrietta never had a chance to see the Holy Land, but all its deserts were in her head, the wilderness of Judah and the dry plains of the Negev, and it is these that caused her hair to be dry. I put a second pillow under her head so that she could look out on the garden and see the trees and the trains passing on the parapet. I told her about Jerusalem and about its large public park which had once been a Moslem cemetery and about the Me'ah Shearim quarter and about my mother and my wife and about the Old City and about the kibbutzim.

"You will return there?" she asked.

"Of course. I can't very well remain here."

"And why did you come here? Don't tell me you came just to visit old Henrietta."

"I came to take revenge."

"Now?"

I did not answer at once and looked at my watch. It was after four.

"Yes, now," I said.

"Of course you will find all of them. Many remained. But what will you do? You will only get into trouble."

"Henrietta, should I bring you something to drink?"

I went downstairs but could find no one. A number of old people sat in the dining room, their eyes glued to the television set: the skaters were still skating, day and night, by daylight and by floodlight. Didn't they ever get tired? Girls in brief little skirts that swirled about their muscular thighs and men in tight black trousers. They glided singly and in pairs and in foursomes, around and around; the audience changed but they remained.

"This is cruel."

"A pity."

"Gentile pleasure," the old people sneered, yet they didn't turn their eyes away from the screen. I said to Sister Maria, "Please, let me have some coffee for Henrietta." She was delighted that I had come and went up to the dumbwaiter shaft and called to the nether world, "More coffee. For two." The chains of the dumbwaiter clanked as it rose from the depths. I asked her about Sister Elizabeth and she told me that she had already been discharged from the hospital and was now convalescing in the convent at Oberbach. Then she added that Sister Elizabeth had taken the vow of silence and that the convent observed this discipline. I was disappointed, for I had wanted to talk to her about little Ruth. Not even visitors are permitted there, Sister Maria said. Even if the mother of one of the nuns should die, the nun would not be told about it, but the Mother Superior says during the prayers, "Let us now pray for the soul of one of our dear ones." My face must have shown my disappointment, for she added, "Perhaps Father Johannes can help you get there and at least see her through a narrow window."

"Where is Father Johannes?"

"At the present he is instructing seminarians in the Magdalene Church or in the Dome."

The voice of the announcer on the TV rose to a high pitch and was seconded by shouting from the audience. The two waves of sound clashed and then subsided into silence, like Sister Elizabeth in her convent.

Only now did the old people who watched the television set put down their cups on the saucers, which emitted a hollow tinkling, like their old bodies. Sister Maria looked at her watch; then she turned off the TV set and announced in a peremptory tone, "Soon it will be Sabbath." The old people rose and their slack footsteps dragged through the corridors. I went up to Henrietta's room carrying a tray. She lay in bed, her head propped on the pillows, and she turned to me only with her voice. We drank coffee. Mr. Cohen's dogs yelped. "Now is their feeding time," Henrietta said. "Please hand me the candles. They are on the shelf, behind the J.N.F. box." I handed her the candles and noticed that the box was full. Her voice complained: "Not even a clean tablecloth for the Sabbath. The washerwomen keep changing. Were Dr. Zelig, peace be with him, alive, the first laundress who was really good would still be here." I asked when the woman had left and Henrietta told me, but it turned out that

I had already known this. Of what value is my information? Of what worth is time? Distinctions dim, and day and night become confused in the mind of a man who does not act. I told Henrietta about my weaknesses. She was surprised. "But you were always the strong one. You used to play Siegfried and Samson and you always conquered all your enemies, including terrible dragons. And you were a soldier in two wars." I told her that was not what I meant. Then she told me about her late husband Oscar, of blessed memory, whom she met in an attic in Theresienstadt. She had lost the key to her suitcase, and in the midst of all the crush and excitement he came and opened the suitcase for her. Then they were married. "Dr. Zelig arranged it all and Dr. Manheim performed the ceremony. In his sermon he said: 'May God bless you, and may the rafters of this house be your wedding canopy and may sorrow be turned to festivity. And may the sound of rejoicing be heard in the streets of Jerusalem.' Then we all wept." She stopped abruptly and asked, "Why don't you tell me about your wife?" I did not know what to tell her. When I return, my family life, too, will become orderly. Now everything is so remote and I wander around in the fog which rises from my heart.

Henrietta resumed telling me about Oscar and took a yellowing snapshot out of her pocketbook: Oscar. He looked exactly the way he should have looked, bald and fat and kindly. Oscar—for only one week he was her husband. For one week she nursed him when he was sick. People gave up their last bite to provide a wedding feast for them. Dr. Zelig even composed a gay verse to the melody of the children's song about two birds getting married and all other birds being invited to the wedding, the swallow and the cuckoo and the woodpecker and the thrush. But instead of the names of the birds who were getting married he substituted Henrietta and Oscar and their friends who stood crowded with their heads bowed in the low and narrow attic. Henrietta sang the melody to me as she used to do when I was a child, and I added the names of some of the birds of Israel, the wagtail and the bulbul and the unnamed bird of Bialik's poem.

"Oscar, Oscar," she said with a sigh, and sat up in her bed to light the candles. She covered her eyes and recited the blessing over the candles. Outside, a car ground to a halt on the gravel. "This is Mr. Grinfeld arriving for the Sabbath service," she said. All week he is busy with his cattle trade. He goes about in the villages and drinks in the taverns together with other drunks. He curses them quietly and they curse him in a whisper. Here and there he also has dealings with pretty village wenches, in barns or on the rear seat of his car, and then he presents them with lavish gifts. He is seventy, but still a bit of a rake. And it is also on account of him that a prayer quorum is maintained. He is the only one who isn't afraid of Mr. Metzman. And he has become judge and arbiter in case of any quarrel, such as who suffered more in the concentration camps, who is entitled to what and where one belongs, who is entitled to special privileges, who should lead the prayers, who should sit near a window in the dining room.

"Now, go to the chapel," Henrietta said. "They pray early here so that they can go to bed early. Then come back and we will eat dinner together."

"No, Henrietta, I can't stay for dinner."

"You are getting involved in things here."

But even if I break out of the net in which I am caught, it will still hamper me forever. I bent down to pick up the snapshot of Oscar which had fallen to the floor and in doing so I caused the air to stir. The flames of the candles flickered. I promised her to step in after the service to wish her Good Sabbath and went out into the hall. Sister Maria stood in the corner and directed me and urged me on to the chapel.

The old men were singing *"Lecha Dodi,"* and when I came in they stopped and stared at me. I motioned to them to pay no attention to me and they resumed the chant according to Levandowski's melody.

After the service I left the chapel, and two old men came up to me and announced that they had known my father. An old woman declared that she had known my aunt. Then I remained alone, for they all hurried down to the dining room. What is all this for? Why do the trees sway and the trains run? I recalled the lawn where Ruth used to sit propped up with pillows and covered with blankets while her classmates sat around her like the retinue of a queen. She had been brave to her last day. She had known that there is the fire and the knife, and also who was destined to be the lamb for the burnt offering. Tears came to my eyes. I am getting to be more and more like my father, except that he used to call people like me, who go about with many strange plans in their heads, by all sorts of nicknames which I remembered well: daydreamer, man in the clouds, disheveled head, *luft Mensch.*

Downstairs they ate in silence. What if Sister Elizabeth should refuse to break her vow and talk to me? I returned to Henrietta's room. Mrs. Munster brought her her dinner on a tray and left. One candle had gone out, the other was still flickering; then it, too, died out. Henrietta continued her tale of Oscar. One day he got up from his sickbed to attend the funeral of a good friend of his who had died. The dead were buried outside the ghetto. On the way back, he was stopped at the gate. He had no return pass, and they shoved him into a freight car that was going east. Henrietta ran to one of the S.S. camp commanders and the man told her that her husband had gone to attend his own funeral; next time he wouldn't forget to provide himself with a return pass. "Good Oscar. My only husband. We never even had a room to ourselves. I only used to come to visit him and take care of him and he held my hand. And when I got up to go, I'd bump my head against the rafter, the roof was so low." And she touched her gray and dry head.

I fed her chicken and vegetables and white *chalah*. She left most of it. I reminded her how she used to urge me to eat when I was a child: "Eat and you will grow up to be a strong man! Eat and I will tell you a story." She begged me to go down to the dining room and have my dinner. I caressed her shriveled cheek and slipped out of the house.

34

For a long time Joel lay on his back, his arm over his face, trying to regain calm, and could not. He sat up and saw her asleep, her black hair scattered on the pillow and mingling with the dark of the night, her hand resting lightly against her temple like the bud of a rose about to open.

What would his father have said of this Patricia, this daughter of strangers, this Christian woman of mixed origins, this hostage? Most probably his father's face, which resembled that of an ancient old Roman senator, would have assumed a stony expression, and he would have turned away from him as from the dead.

When still a child, Joel had loved to stand near his father in the synagogue, even though most of the prayers bored him. Only some parts of the service of the Days of Awe spoke to his imagination, like the description of the High Priest at his service, and the sending off of the scapegoat to the wilderness, or the hymn which speaks of the Rider of the

Plains. He had visualized God as a horseman of the Wild West. And now here was this horsewoman of the West, a child-woman, a mare-woman, a woman of old, as was testified by her hands and her lips. Had his father known, his heart would have broken.

He got up and without turning on the light drank some water, which tasted of chlorine. In the Middle Ages his forefathers had been accused of poisoning the wells, and now he was drinking chlorinated water in Jerusalem. He thought of the disorder in Patricia's life, her wills and testaments, as she called the bundles of letters in her closet. She had jestingly told him about them. She would will her house in Nevada to the S.P.C.A., she said; another time she said she would sell it and go to Paris and buy lots of hats. In the end she did neither the one nor the other, but worked in a hospital and ran to the call of eyes that begged, Help me! Help me!

"Water," she whispered hoarsely. "Darling, water, please. Where are you? You mustn't leave me. You mustn't . . . You should . . ."

He brought her a glass of water that sparkled like a diamond and saw her as if she were far away at the end of a long road, even though the room was very small.

"Chlorine. Jerusalem water. Holy Jordan water tasting of chlorine," she said.

"A doctor like you should know."

"I know. Come back to me."

She stretched but did not open her eyes. He watched her drink and the skin of her face was smooth and dark. Her hair got in the way and she held the glass with both hands like a child. Suddenly he realized that this was precisely how he had foreseen her, this was how he had dreamed of her all his life, and he wished almost that he were dead.

She drank a second glass and was still between sleep and wakefulness. Then she bent over his neck and murmured strange things about the whispering forest where dead birds lay alongside the trail, and the candy he had given her, and her house in Nevada. And all the time her eyes were shut.

"You are sorry you stayed here and didn't go to your native town in Germany," she whispered.

"Be silent. Don't say a thing."

"Your ego is getting bigger and fatter, like a big fat cat. You think only of yourself."

He was aroused from half sleep by the radio in the neighboring apartment, which had been turned on louder, and he heard distinctly:

"Where is it written twice . . . Who first said to whom . . ."

He paid no attention to the rest of the questions.

For verily we are to blame, he thought, in the words of Joseph's brothers, and compelled himself to think of his wife Ruth, but he felt no guilt.

Radios in other apartments were turned up to the broadcast Bible quiz and the questions invaded the room from all sides. Patricia turned away on her side, so that they lay back to back while the questions pursued one another through the clear night air of Jerusalem.

"This gives you two points."

"Next."

Joel did not go to Weinburg this summer as he had planned. He did not go to meet the dead of his native town. Whoever goes wins. Whoever stays in Jerusalem to love will never again depart from Jerusalem or from his love, and everything that he will ever do—open a shutter, sit up in bed, listen to the night, drink a glass of water—will be an act of love. There is no escape, except that the love or the lovers or the city be destroyed.

A sharp voice over the radio ordered, "Next. Now, this will be a difficult question."

Pat took his hand and placed it on her forehead.

35

The Indian and I played chess in the café under the ruin. He bounded with his knight and I crouched as during a tank attack so that he shouldn't trample me. Our argument began at once. I took him to task about the man with the tattoo, because he did not help me catch him. He accused me of dispersing his yoga group with my intrusion. He said that I lived from hand to mouth, spiritually speaking. I became angry and retorted that he lived from hand to ass. A waiter who liked both of us came and made us swear, by the fish in their aquariums and by the birds in their cages, to desist from quarreling. "Take back what you said to each other." We took it all back and the words entered inside us and bloated us. The waiter brought us a list of pastries. We read the beautiful and exotic names, the pride of the confectioner, but then the argument resumed.

"Bloated egoist!" (Chocolate-covered torte.)

"Vengeful Shylock!" (Dutch cake with cherries.)

"Your cows go among people starving to death!" (Florentine cake.)

"Homosexual!" (Angelfood with whipped cream.)

"Pakistan!" (Pineapple cake with vanilla syrup.)

"Robbers of Arab land!" (Habaniera.)

"Wretched fakir sitting on nails!" (Cherry rolls baked in butter.)

"Dealer in dead souls!" (Seven varieties of ice cream.)

The aromatic pastries finally put an end to our quarrel. I took his hand and we looked at each other. Then we looked outside. The displays in the show windows were about to be changed, and meanwhile large mirrors were put there so that people should stop and look at themselves. We talked about revenge and despair. We praised cynical man. If all men were cynics, there would be no wars.

I said that fate chose us as small stones are chosen for a mosaic. We lie to one side and we have different colors. No man—that is, no pebble—knows when its turn would come to be made part of the picture. Fate chooses us in accordance with the requirements of the picture which have all been carefully worked out in advance. Finally one is stuck into the picture and then fate steps back and says, "Nice, very nice." But you don't know yourself who the neighboring pebbles are. The Indian said, "It is good that man has a conscience at least. You must take it into your considerations. Conscience is the agent of altruism." And he added, "Our only consolation is that it is all over. When all is over, there remains consolation·only. Until one forgets the loss which the consolation was to compensate for."

36

From time to time Joel awoke. Once, he sat up and saw Patricia's face upside down—eyes and mouth in reversed position. This was more terrifying than a death mask. The lampshade was made of yellow straw fibers and looked like a little skirt.

Patricia tossed on the bed, for it was a hot night, and Joel awoke again and looked at her. Suddenly he thought of the coffee he would have in the morning, American coffee that she would prepare from cans received from overseas, red cans with a picture of a smiling Negro and the slogan "Double roasted." He touched her lightly and she responded:

"Darling, what are you doing to me?" Then, still half asleep: "Your aroma. I will put it in a can and save it, and I will go mad. . . ."

She lay on her belly and he seized her hips. Again and again his hand explored the curve of her thighs and the long channel of her spine. She would be his forever. He had a claim to her now, the eternal claim of possession; he had a claim to her feet, to her long hair, to her hands.

Other things happened that night: the guards were changed in houses on the border where rooms had become sandbagged positions. Sounds of steps and voices and passwords. Sleepy replies. Who's there? Identify yourself! People rising and others going to bed with a sigh and a squeaking of bedsprings.

In the empty lot outside their window, some night watchmen gathered and spoke in a whisper around their bonfire which lit up the trunks of the olive trees, and their quiet voices penetrated the room and calmed the sleep of the two, whose clothes lay scattered all over the floor. The clothes had been thrown down in the beginning, and every trip to the kitchen or the bathroom scattered them still more: a foot caught on a skirt and dragged it along; a shoe was kicked by a bare foot; fumbling hands hung something on the doorknob; another shoe was picked up and put on the table. A sudden breeze scattered some of the letters, one from Klein:

"DEAR MADAME,

I hope that everything is in order and that the shutter has been fixed. I hope that my friend and agent visits the apartment from time to time and takes care of things.

SINCERELY,
A. Klein"

The carpet was crumpled, like waves suddenly frozen. There was a knock on the door. Like a somnambulist, Pat got up and wrapped herself Roman-style in a sheet. Then she woke Joel. Who could it be at this hour? A telegram? Your husband? Your friend Yosel again? Mr. Cohen bringing flowers picked at midnight? "Let's play possum." Joel covered her mouth with a pillow, so that her laughter should not be heard, and went to the door. It was Yosel on one of his innumerable farewells that night, and the two friends whispered to each other.

"Goodbye. Excuse me for coming at such an hour. I have already said goodbye to Ruth. Joel, you must make up your mind, one way or the other. You are bewitched."

"Let's not talk about it."

"You must love Patricia. She said such wonderful things about you in her incomprehensible way."

"Turn on the light. Why should we stand in the dark?"

"It's better this way."

37

Suddenly I thought of Mr. Rosenbaum, the way a devout Jew recalls with consternation that he hasn't yet said his afternoon prayers though it is already getting dark. How could I have forgotten the mission concerning his house? In the memorial institute in Jerusalem he walks among the card files of the holocaust at night, and during the day he peddles sewing supplies and greeting cards. Now that New Year is approaching, he must be busy making the rounds of stationery stores and newsstands. Good wishes provide his livelihood during the day and curses at night. He lives in an attic in the house of my friend Klein, who wanders around the world.

Sitting in the café on the ground floor of my hotel, I noticed the market place coming to life with all sorts of crates and huge heaps of cucumbers. The sun was beginning to shine through the red-and-white-checked curtains, and the bells of the Church of St. Mary began ringing at random. I spread some jam on a roll and noted by its smell that it was wild-rose jam. My thoughts clambered up the tower of the church and over its carvings and saints and leaped to Jerusalem. At once, right after breakfast, I would go to the office where real-estate deeds are registered. The morning paper had a black border; this was memorial day for the victims of the great bombardment that destroyed the city. From noon on, everything would be closed. I leaped up the stairs to my room to get Mr. Rosenbaum's documents and my authorization to look after his interests.

I found my way to the law courts building, which also housed the real-estate registry office. Before I entered the building, I circled several times in the revolving door. This kind of door is just right for impractical and hesitant people like me. Finally it flung me into a large marble hall. I walked past people who begged me to excuse them simply because they happened to stand in my way but did me no harm. The people of Weinburg are very polite. If my father hadn't taken us out of the city in the early thirties, these courteous people would have sent us to the crematoria.

The doors along the corridors were marked alphabetically. The office containing Rosenbaum's records was almost at the end. I rehearsed the alphabet in my head. Because I always carry my entire biography in my head, I frequently forget the alphabet.

The walls of the room I entered were entirely concealed

by filing cabinets. Since all of us have read Kafka, we know this kind of office. Where is he? Kestler? Nestler? Bestler? The one who kicked little Ruth while the other Hitler Youth boys held me pinned to the ground. What lot does he own? On what block?

At first I saw no one because the clerk had bent down behind a partition. Then he addressed me: "Sit down, please. I will be with you in a moment. Unfortunately I cannot raise my head because I am suffering from *Hexenschuss*. A witch put a spell on me."

I went to him and sat on a low stool so that I could talk to him. "I am here in the matter of Mr. Rosenbaum's case," I said. He answered that he had been expecting me ever since he had received a letter from Rosenbaum. While waiting for me, he had been looking through the open window and a breeze had aggravated his *Hexenschuss*. "Do you have an authorization?" he wanted to know. I handed him Rosenbaum's letter. He asked me whether I had already been to the river, for Rosenbaum's house had stood near it. Nothing but a heap of stones was left of it, he told me, but underneath the ruins, like ants in a loaf of bread, life was swarming. I assured him that I had already visited the heap. He told me that he had known old Rosenbaum the butcher, peace be with him, peace to his ashes, ashes be with him. "My mother, too, was burned after she died," he added, "but she had asked in her will to be cremated. Peace to her ashes. Every year I visit the urn." I indicated that I was busy and he directed me to a ladder and to the appropriate filing cabinet: "A little to the left, now right; that's it, the one near the hat." Then I noticed the colored paper hat that looked like the miter of the High Priest, with three blossoms at the end of which hung three little bells. From his depth below, the clerk told me that the year before he had been prince of the carnival. When I got down from the ladder, he showed me a photograph in which he sat on the seat of honor flanked by two pretty blondes, maids of honor to the prince. He showed me some more pictures. "Here is the one of the carnival of 1938. Then I was only vice-prince." That was the year the synagogue was burned. In the carnival picture, they were holding aloft mugs of beer. One man was lighting a thick cigar. That was the man who set fire to the curtain on the Ark—they started to burn the synagogue the same way the Temple was burned, by setting fire to the curtain on the Ark. I made a mental note of this face.

The clerk leafed through the file which I handed him, and meantime shook his head and muttered something about Nazi hoodlums who had resumed their activities, on this day of all days. Hadn't I heard? A swastika ribbon had been found tied to one of the saints on the bridge, on this day of commemorating Nazi guilt.

38

Joel and Patricia lay in dreamless sleep. They had revealed everything to each other, emptied themselves of all that was torment and impure, lust and sorrow and distress, and all memories of childhood, all recall of an American father, a ruddy-faced captain, and all memory of a lean Jewish father with the face of a kindly Roman who was nevertheless strict in the observance of commandments (Why didn't you recite the blessing? Where is your fringed garment?), and all anticipation of terror (You little Jew swine! Take your damn cap off when a cross is carried by!). And even the face of Patricia's husband, the silent mixed-up man, disappeared, as also the face of Joel's good wife Ruth, with whom he had lived peacefully ever since that dawn in the brown, burning Negev. All these had departed from them and from the world and were no longer material for dreams. And they slept without the representatives of their past, without the actors of their distress, without the backdrop of their childhoods, and without the monstrosities of their passions.

They both hankered after a haven and were anchored in it, a haven as wide as the sea itself, yet peaceful. One of his hands rested on his belly and the other on her hip, while one of her hands lay near her forehead and the other rested on his shoulder. The dividing line between them was erased and they were mixed together, doubly jointed to each other and tied in a sevenfold knot.

Someone was running toward the house, a woman in a white smock, a light woman who seemed to be carried along in the breeze together with the loose pieces of paper and, like them, was caught against the fence. Joel got up and whispered to her from the window, "What are you doing here?" But she did not recognize his voice and said, "How are you, Mr. Rain?"

"I am not any Mr. Rain, Mina. I am Joel."

"How are you, Mr. Rain?"

"I am clouds."

She was delighted to hear him say that. But she did not recognize him, or remember the pillars of her house, or the agreement she had made with him then, or the face of Itzhak her husband, or the summit of the eucalyptus tree outside the window of her house. She took off the hospital smock and clung to the fence with her entire small, lithe body. Joel was about to go down to her when he noticed a number of people carrying flashlights hurrying toward her— a nurse, two hospital attendants, and a doctor. They talked to her kindly, but she said insistently, "I want to go swim-

ming in the sea. Why don't you let me?" They gently agreed
with her that the sea was nice, but the water was too cold,
and they wiped her with towels as if she had really been in
the water. A car came and stopped. It was Major Patterson.
Mina pleaded: "A little more, just a little more." The Major
placed his thin blue scarf on her head and she calmed
down.

"Lucky that she didn't try to cross the border," the Major
said to Joel. "Many deranged persons try to flee across the
border." Where is Itzhak? The day before, she had suffered a
sudden attack and there was no time to take her to the hospital out in the hills, and she was placed in one of the city
hospitals. The doctor said, "Gently, her fingers might break
while she is in convulsions." He gave her a sedative injection, and Major Patterson carried her away like a little child
toward the hospital.

Joel turned back to Patricia and saw that she had kicked
off the sheet in her sleep and was now lying naked and uncovered. He thought of the bodies of women, how they were
shaped for convenient childbearing—like a bell, like a sack,
like any kind of container in which a child could grow.

To think that he had almost not met Patrice at all, that
they had almost passed each other by, that he had almost
gone to Weinburg, his native town, and they could literally
have passed each other in some airport, he going there and
she coming back from somewhere. The thought caused him
keen distress. She might have gone into one underpass, carrying a small suitcase and wearing a light traveling hat,
while he went into another, and they would never have seen
each other. The moment of grace would have passed, and all
his life and all her life would have been wasted from that
time on. A minor error, a slight digression, a wrong decision,
a mood, the weather, a letter—any of these could have pre-
vented their meeting. The fear of chance which might have

caused him never to see her entered him like a knife. At this very moment he might have been in Weinburg without even knowing that he had suffered the greatest loss of his life. Overcome with this fear, he bowed down over her and she half awakened.

They talked partly in Hebrew and partly in English, with mistakes here and there, muttered words and whispers and inarticulate sounds and many vague declarations which contained the words "mine," "mine."

39

Clearing up matters regarding Rosenbaum's house and lot would apparently take a long time. A certain document pertaining to a man who had bought the house just before the bombardment was missing. But I wasn't particularly distressed about the delay. For one thing, I saw that the business affairs of others also dragged on. Besides, delay in this matter provided me with an opportunity to get a toe hold in the municipal law office, and an attack on unsuspecting Weinburg from this direction would help me to conceal my main intentions and to sow confusion and bewilderment in the hearts of those whom I was pursuing and who were pursuing me.

I boarded a streetcar and was on my way. Electric sparks shot out where the trolley touched the overhead wire. The streetcar proceeded with a hollow, gurgling sound and halted at every stop, though I was its sole passenger and no others got on. Fersil cleans. Odol cleans. The Catholic Youth Convention cleans. Though your sins be scarlet, they shall be as white as snow, Isaiah said, and who am I to contradict? I did not see people, only posters. Leonora smiled at me because her "Scandal" bra fit her comfortably. She held a can of coffee in her hand. I hadn't seen her for a long time, except in ads. The conductor looked at me accusingly, as if I had caused him extra work and it was on my account that he had to be on duty. He had already punched my ticket twice. I got off near the market square and waited for a green light in order to cross the street. Soon people in the street will lose all free will. As it is, they can walk only when the traffic lights permit and only between painted white lines. Soon a man might want to go home, but lights and lines and obstructions will guide him to another house and to another woman. Soon we will be no more free than the trains which follow tracks not of their own choosing.

I asked the hotel clerk if there was any mail for me. There wasn't any. Instead he asked me, while mumbling apologies, for my passport. An error had been made while registering me, a small matter, he said in confusion. I handed him my blue passport and went up to my room, leaping a couple of steps at a time. I was concerned and suspicious. The room was neat. Too neat and tidy. I opened my suitcase. Everything in it seemed to be in order.

I put on a tie and went downstairs. The clerk returned my passport. Outside, some stores were already closed and people dressed in black walked about among the pastel-painted houses. Some carried wreaths with ribbons proclaiming the names of the donors: Boating Alliance, Weinburg; Union of Vintners; Folk Singers Assn.; Foresters Men's Chorus; Gay Hunter Male Chorus; Fersil Cleans All; Storekeepers Assn.; Union of Catholic Girls; Odol Cleans Teeth; Trade Unions; Railway Administration.

The aroma of the flowers intoxicated me. Festively

dressed children walked earnestly alongside their parents. I was swept along by the throng and did not know where I was going. I passed by a public park and sat down to rest and think things over. In a little while Mrs. Munster appeared. When she doesn't look after Henrietta, she sits in parks. She is like a statue and nobody notices her. The rolls of fat under her eyes are like graves. She is all white. I asked her casually where all the people were going, and she answered with a proverb: "He who lives in a glass house shouldn't throw stones." Lately she talks almost exclusively in proverbs and often turns them upside down: "He who lives in a stone house shouldn't break glass," or, "A stone house is like a grave," or, "He who lives in a stone house can throw all the rocks he wants; it won't do him any good."

"He who laughs last shouldn't throw rocks at windows."

"He who cries first laughs last."

She started to weep and the tears flowed from the rolls of fat under her eyes. A mother passing by with her little girl explained to the child, "She must have lost her entire family on that awful day." Heinrele, who had been playing in the sandbox behind the bench, came running and clung to me. In that very same box I used to play as a child, but they have no doubt changed the sand several times since then. I tried to comfort Mrs. Munster with proverbs of my own:

"Company in distress makes misery less" and "When many are comforted, the one grieves" and "God took, and then took again."

But Mrs. Munster would not be consoled. Heinrele stood near her bewildered, like a young animal near the dead body of its mother. I said to him, "Go call Henrietta, or somebody from the Home, and I will give you some candy." He already appreciates the value of a bribe and so he started off at once. First he was a tractor; then he spread out his arms and was an airplane; then he disappeared from view. Sometimes I worry about his future. Will he grow up to be corrupt? Two men approached. One was Mr. Windmeyer, the assistant film director. He stopped and introduced the other one to me, a man with graying crew-cut hair, deep eyes, and wearing a conservative suit. He produced a strange impression of a mixture of military man and man of sorrow, and something about him aroused a sense of recognition. Surely I must have met him somewhere before. Something within me said, "This is your best friend; you have something in common; you know something in common; both of you were driven here by the same restlessness." We shook hands and the assistant director left. The American told me that he had heard about me and about Leonora from Windmeyer. Then he explained that they wished to photograph an excited crowd streaming in one direction for the shots in connection with the burning of the synagogue. I said I wondered how it could be done, since the expression on the faces would be different, but he assured me that taken from a distance it would be impossible to tell the difference between a memorial parade and a mob surging in anger. He also had shots of the crowd streaming to the opening of the skating tournament. He inquired about the weeping woman near me and I told him. As I was talking, she resumed reciting her proverbs and quotations:

"Tell me who your friends are and I will tell you who you are."

"Throw rocks at glass houses till they break."

We looked at her face, which was like a round white stone quietly dripping water. Mrs. Munster asked me about the man, and I explained to her that he was a film director. She at once told him about her daughter Clara, who had been an actress and had played Rebecca at the well. She looked at me and added quietly, "My good friend, she also played Little Red Riding Hood, and you were the wolf."

"Yes, I remember, and the bed I lay on nearly collapsed under me."

"After you gobbled up the old woman."

"Who ate the cake and drank the wine."

"Little Ruth played the grandmother."

"You are mistaken."

"To err is human."

Meantime Heinrele returned. He landed on the runway between me and the film director, then turned off his motor and announced, "She is sick." Indeed I noticed Mrs. Metzman, all flushed, come running and after her, like a weak old bird, Sister Maria followed. They sat down and soothed Mrs. Munster. The street had emptied and from the distance came the sound of a brass band playing slow funeral marches. At the head of the procession the old Archbishop, who used to play chess with Dr. Manheim, was carried in a canopied litter. His clerical robes seemed to weigh heavily on him. Statues and shining crosses were carried after him. The American did not cross himself—he must have been a Protestant. I remember the slap I got as a child when I failed to uncover my head while such a procession passed. ("Little Jew swine! When a cross is carried by, don't you forget to take your cap off.") Apple-cheeked boys wearing red and white surplices with lace collars followed. Then came girls in white carrying candles.

"It's all withered grass," Mrs. Munster said, and wept. The women calmed her. Sister Maria looked at me through her thick-lensed glasses which she wore as if they were a heavy cross.

"Michael on my right," Mrs. Munster said.

"And God's presence over my head," Heinrele seconded her, since he had been taught the going-to-bed prayer by Henrietta. Now came monks and seminarians singing hymns in Latin; then the Archbishop in his heavy robes was carried past a second time. I thought he looked at me, but all the others probably felt the same way. Then came the students in their fraternity uniforms, small feathered caps and brightly colored silk sashes across their chests.

It was told that the Rector of that time was the first to set a brand to the synagogue, like the Roman legionary who first tossed a burning torch into the Temple. Slowly and earnestly the procession moved toward the palace garden, whose gates are surmounted by iron angels and whose wings protect both the garden and my childhood.

Brass bands of the fire department, of the police, and of village peasants passed playing "Lord, Preserve Us." Mrs. Munster whispered:

"He who weeps first weeps always."

Mrs. Munster has an inventive mind. Henrietta told me that in Theresienstadt Mrs. Munster invented a game to pass the time while waiting to be deported to death. It was a dice game, and one gained or lost ground according to the rules she devised. "One of these evenings we will play it," I promised her. Heinrele heard the word "play" and cried, "Me, too! Me, too!"

Sister Maria said, "Let us take her back." The bands played hymns to God the great and awesome, and to Our Sweet Lord Jesus. The trumpets pealed announcing the resurrection. I whispered to Mrs. Munster, "And I will open your graves, as it is written."

She said, "You dear liar. You are just like your uncle, peace be with him, whom I knew. You know that Clara did not play in Little Red Riding Hood but in Judas Maccabeus." She shook an admonishing finger at me and smiled slyly. Sister Maria said to me, "I have important news for you. I learned that little Ruth sang much during the last days before she was sent there."

"Sang?"

"Yes, choral music, but there was no one to sing the harmony."

"And what else?"

"Liturgical songs. But she couldn't sing in two voices, for she had but one mouth."

"A mouth for laughing and a mouth for weeping, but the same mouth."

The bells began pealing loudly. Mrs. Munster sat there ready to give out with more proverbs. Heinrele played in the sandbox. The more distant bells began ringing first, followed by the ones closer to us, until the one right near us started to peal; then the ringing moved away from us and back again, like waves. I looked at the director, whose name had escaped me when he was introduced. His hair was noticeably graying. One of his eyes had a cold, martial expression; the other was thoughtful and melancholy. His eyes were like two water faucets, one for cold water and the other for warm. Mrs. Munster looked from one of us to the other. The director was giving some last instructions to a technician who stood near the sandbox. Thus we stood, like a group of singers in an Italian opera at the end of a performance, all singing together yet each shouting what is in his heart.

The tower of the church near us was truncated and it had been left thus as a reminder of the destruction. Mrs. Munster persisted with her proverbs: "All flesh is grass. Everything that happens is grass. The pitcher goes to the spring until it is broken."

Mrs. Munster suddenly fell silent and the street, too, was silent and abandoned. The nun and Mrs. Metzman took the corpulent old woman and led her away as Mrs. Metzman called to me, "You will come to see me, won't you?" "God willing," I said, and they walked off and Heinrele ran before them like a herald.

Evening was falling and the director and I went to the cemetery. In Jerusalem the cemeteries are on the hills surrounding the city: the Mount of Olives and the Mount of Rest, and Rom Hill, where Uncle Moritz is temporarily buried, and, being a *Kohen*, his monument is engraved with two hands whose fingers are parted in blessing. Only the cemetery at Sanhedriah is not on a hill. There my father is buried and there the ground is sinking and the monuments lean out of line and the concrete paving is cracked. The border is nearby, and the barbed-wire fences that mark it catch every flying scrap of paper and discarded cigarette package. When the wind blows from east or west, these scraps sway like a mobile.

We passed by a girls' school named the School for Angelic Damsels and came to the cemetery gate. Small flames in colored lanterns flickered over many of the graves. On a large grassy area stood numerous stone crosses of different sizes. I don't remember whether the inscriptions read "Lest We Forget" or "That We Remember." The souls of the dead flickered over the graves, and the sky slowly became overcast. A light drizzle began falling and enveloped us. Now I will learn all about my new friend. In talks near cemeteries I will find out all about him and he about me. The drizzle did not quench the flames. I was amazed at the way I spoke English fluently now. When I like a person, I learn his language quickly. A man came toward us wearing a hunter's cap and shouldering a staff like a rifle. "I was one of them," the man announced.

"One of whom?"

"One of the dead. Like Lazarus, I came back to life. I lay in the smoking ruin of my house. Now the ruins are still there and there is a café under them."

"Rosenbaum's house!" I cried. "You stole Rosenbaum's house."

He shouldered his staff again and repeated, "I am Lazarus come back to life."

"Don't talk to him," the director said to me. "You see he is

out of his mind. Places of destruction attract the deranged;
memorial days bring out the madmen like mushrooms."

We crossed the overpass over the tracks. What drove me
on also drove him on. We came to the southern railroad
station. This is a small station from which trains depart for
the neighboring villages. Now the road passed under the
tracks and a train rolled above us with a great clatter even as
my friend told me important things about his life. Then we
came to a street called Peace Street. Here my Uncle Jacob's
house used to stand. It, too, was still in ruins, like many others
which held personal memories for me. The city had dealt
kindly with my memory by not rebuilding these ruins. I told
the American about Dr. Manheim's house and about little
Ruth and about my wife Ruth and about all that had driven
me to come here.

We stopped abruptly, and he said, "I caused all this."

"What?"

"I destroyed the city. . . . I was in command of the unit
that shelled the city. . . . We sent them an ultimatum but the
local *Gauleiter* rejected it. We destroyed the city, and not a
man of my unit was hurt."

"More power to you."

"Why do you say that?"

"You know why I came to Weinburg."

"Call me Melvin."

"Why did you return, Melvin?"

"No one knows who I am. I came to make the film—to
prove that I had taken just revenge."

"They did more terrible things."

We walked on unaware of the light rain that continued
falling. Then we sat down near the river. Most of the river
lights were out. The lights of the tournament grounds were
out. Only a single lamp was reflected weakly in the river.
Much later I asked him whether he was alone in the world.

No, it seemed that he had a wife, yet didn't have one. They were separated. "You wouldn't believe it," he added. "But she is now in your city, in Jerusalem."

"An Israeli? A Jewish woman?"

"No. American, and a Christian like me. You may have met her there."

He took out a folder from which he withdrew a snapshot. His hands shook and a light breeze lifted the picture and floated it to the dark water. For a moment the white square was visible in the dark and then it was lost in the night.

40

Rumors followed one another. It was said that Mina had gone away, that she had fallen in love with one of the U.N. officers; others said that her lover was some sportsman at a skiing resort where she had gone.

It was rumored that Yosel had returned to Germany, that he had given up thoughts of avenging his parents, who were burned in a crematorium, and that the only time he mentioned them was to recall how they used to quarrel and fling dishes at each other.

It was said of Itzhak that he had become fanatically religious, that he held regular prayer meetings in his house, that he transformed the large pillared room into a synagogue and Talmud students were constantly in his house.

It was said of Joel that he had taken up with a woman from across the seas, a strange Lilith, with whom he turns day into night, that he can't rid himself of her, that he has sold and enslaved himself to her, that he is neglecting his work and ruining his promising career for the sake of a night of love with her.

It was said of Mina that she had committed suicide and was buried without fanfare so that nobody should know.

It was said of Zeiger the photographer that he had left the country and become a homosexual, that his current passion was a Negro boy.

It was said of Mina that she had become pregnant by a U.N. officer. And of Yosel that he had gone out of his mind and was wandering about the streets of Tel Aviv playing a fiddle.

It was said of Mina that she had never existed, that Itzhak's friends dreamed her up, and that Itzhak was really a bachelor.

It was said of Joel that he went to the kibbutz to murder his wife Ruth, that on his way to the banana grove he met Ruth's father, and that they at once resumed their old arguments about the battles in which they had both fought during the war.

It was said of Mina that she was very sick and that she stayed home all day curled up like a kitten on a bench near the window.

It was said that Joel beat up Professor Oren in the corridor of one of the university buildings, that he grabbed the famous archeologist by the beard and pounded his head against a door on which was painted the picture of a man's head to indicate that it was a men's room.

It was said of Einat that she was moving from one apartment to another but that there need be no concern about her, that she was tough and hard like all the natives.

It was said of Yosel that he had gone completely out of his mind and that he went about carrying a package dripping blood; that, like a certain Dutch painter, he had probably cut off something, perhaps the arm on which the tattooed mermaid covered his concentration-camp number.

It was further said of Yosel that he had gone back to his moored ship, where he had driven out all the rats and birds. It was said that he was seen in Eilat.

It was said of both Klein and Yosel that they were secretly employed by the intelligence service.

It was said of Dr. Golgolos, whom everybody had regarded as a careerist, that he was the only decent and sane person around.

It was rumored that Klein had acquired three mistresses and that he kept a separate toothbrush in each of their apartments.

Zeiger is trying to find himself.

Joel was trying to find himself and was trapped by this woman who would never let go of him unless one of them died.

Yosel's violin drips blood, so he wraps it in newspaper.

Mina locked herself up in the basement of her house.

Zeiger planted explosives in the new building which was put up on the site of the one he blasted during the struggle against the British, the one that contained the water department of the British mandatory authorities.

Itzhak is devoting himself to studying Cabala.

Yosel went away.

Klein will not come back.

Mina vanished.

Joel is lost in the mazes of the flesh.

Yoske locked himself in his kibbutz.

Professor Oren shaved off his beard and is on his way to new achievements and glory.

Yosel will not return.

Joel is lost for good.

Everybody went away.

41

A sharp clap of thunder released the city from its distress. My own distress remained as it was, for I did not belong to the city. Ever since Melvin told me who he was and why he had come here, I had many important encounters. Him I had not seen lately, but the fact that I was his friend gained me the confidence of many people. The thunder filled the low places in the city and the rain came down in buckets in the middle of the summer. In my dry land the earth is scorched and cracked like the lips of a dying man, and I, who should have stayed there and kissed the earth and given it life, fled from it in search of revenge. I love this man Melvin, I thought as I leaned against a doorway the way people do in a strange city. It wasn't simply a doorway; it was the entrance to the tunnel under the ruins of Rosenbaum's house. I will have to inform the clerk in the deeds office that I have discovered the buyer of the lot on which Rosenbaum's house stood, and that he is deranged.

The gay laughter of young people running to get out of the rain reached me but I did not see them, for my eyes were fixed on the puddle that had formed on the pavement before me. Where is Leonora now? I must look after her. The lightning and the thunder about me were just as in a Shakespearean play but nothing really happened. I had killed nobody and the ghosts were still within me. In the entire city there was no room for ghosts. In his own time my friend Melvin caused thunder and lightning with his cannon that destroyed the city. I love the man.

I entered the tunnel and took off my thin raincoat and shook it. In the display window where bathers lolled on a Mediterranean beach, the light blinked on and off. There was even real sand.

I phoned Mrs. Metzman. Hello. How are you? Fine. How is Henrietta? Still confined to bed; when will you come? I will come. Here is Mrs. Munster; talk to her.

"Hello, you dear liar."

"How are you, Mrs. Munster?"

"I wanted to tell you that Clara played in the Hanukkah program. I know. The jug returns to the spring until it breaks. When the Russians liberated us, Clara was all crimson from the cold. One of their officers came and gave her a sip of vodka; she drank it and coughed. I told him that my daughter was not used to drinking vodka but he gave her an entire bottle. This helped her live a few days more."

Through the glass door of the telephone booth I saw Leonora and an Egyptian talking pleasantly to each other. The phone booth was set into the wall like the fish tanks and the bird cages. I was both a bird and a fish. I said to Mrs. Munster, "Good that Clara lived only a few days longer and died free."

"She died on my knees," Mrs. Munster said. "We sat in a little abandoned railway station where no trains came. All the other people had fled west from the typhoid epidemic. I don't remember what the place was called. The sign had fallen from over the door, and snow slid off the roof. She died on my knees. My knees were like an altar. Come, come and visit us and we will play the Theresienstadt dice game in Henrietta's room."

I patted the receiver soothingly and Mrs. Munster was calmed and the conversation ended. I went out of the booth and apologized to the Egyptian and took Leonora with me. The thunder retreated but still rumbled in the distance. The rain continued to fall and there was no one in the street.

Skipping and jumping, we came to the church where Father Johannes was supposed to be. The entire building was constructed of reddish sandstone. It would be good if everything in the world were colored red, all buildings and plants and stones, so that the blood on them shouldn't show. We skipped up the broad steps and stood breathing heavily in a wide doorway of carved stone. Leonora removed her hat and shook her heavy tresses; she stood near a pillar and resembled an angel. We pushed against the heavy doors with our bodies and entered. The church was nearly empty; only here and there a few knelt in prayer and their heads rose and fell among the waves of empty pews. Organ sounds came, mellowed by the distance. Advancing from pillar to pillar, we approached the lights and the glistening gold. Many young student priests marched sedately back and forth reciting prayers. An old woman whispered to us, "These are seminarians and they are rehearsing the rituals."

The young men bowed their heads; then they knelt and prostrated themselves. An older priest observed them like a ballet director and gave whispered instructions: "You forgot to raise your hand! Slower! Again! Once more!" Sometimes he indicated his wish with a mere flick of the finger or a movement of the chin.

I was reminded how at the conclusion of the *Amidah* one takes three steps backward and then three forward, after lightly bowing at the beginning of this prayer, and how one hops during the *Kedushah*, and how one prostrates oneself during the High Holy Days service, when Cantor Hildesheim, who was a corpulent man, used to touch the floor with his forehead even as he was intoning his chant. Because he had to keep his feet touching each other while doing so, his voice would become choked. Two members of the Sacred Congregation of Weinburg would stand on either side of him to help him rise, and after he gasped like a fish out of water and filled his lungs, he would cry out in a great and liberated voice, "For He is our God, and there is no other, truly."

One of the student priests became confused and stumbled over his cassock. Two of his comrades snickered. The instructing priest clapped his hands and they fell silent. Then he noticed us and raised one eyebrow questioningly. I lowered one eyebrow in reply. He took my hint, for he said a few words to the student priests and they disappeared whispering among the dark waves. A woman rose and walked out, and the bench creaked after her.

I told the priest that I was looking for Father Johannes. His face was immobile and he asked who had sent me. I told him. "You can talk to him in the confession booth," he said, and directed me to it.

I felt greatly depressed, but for the sake of little Ruth I would not be silent. I sat down on the pillow which was there to kneel on and I heard a rustling behind the partition, a rustling of paper and also of cloth. I coughed politely and the unseen priest muttered a prayer.

"I came from the land where Jesus was born."

"Yes, my son."

"I was sent here. I am Jewish."

"Many saints were Jews."

"Little Ruth, too; it's on her account that I came."

"Yes, my son."

I told him what I wanted.

"It's a serious request you are making," he said, "a violation of sacred rules and vows."

"Please, do it for the sake of little Ruth."

Silence. And then the voice said, "Tomorrow at ten, be at the southern gate. Someone will meet you there and lead you. Now go, go."

The voice began murmuring prayers for the forgiveness of

sin, as is customary after confession. Leonora stood waiting near a pillar. The rain had stopped, apparently, and a number of people came into the echoing hall. Leonora left me, saying she had to go to the tournament, which was being resumed near the river.

"Oh, that terrible tournament."

"Why do you say that?" With this she went out, creating a breeze which put out one of the candles. The organ opened up with a big and inviting melody. I followed in Leonora's footsteps. Outside, clouds pursued clouds but there was no rain. The day was slowly sinking into its true darkness. An illuminated streetcar stood waiting and I vaulted into it. Leonora was already seated in it. The stores on either side of the street glowed at each other with lighted windows. Leonora faced her picture in an ad in which she was gaily sipping wine. Near the bridge she got off without saying goodbye to me. I will go to the Home. I will go there and play Theresienstadt with Mrs. Munster and Henrietta.

42

A dispute broke out among the players seated near Henrietta's bed.

"I am entitled to cast the dice an extra time."

"That's not so."

"That is, too. I am on 17. I should know. I invented the game." Saying so, Mrs. Munster pulled out the sheet of instructions and read, "When one gets to 17, one becomes a relative of a Capo and is entitled to move to a warmer barrack and to cast the dice a second time."

"Easy, you only have the right to move two numbers to a warmer barrack."

"You are telling me?"

Mr. Cohen was silent. They had invited him to join the game because there was no one else around; otherwise they don't talk to him. Henrietta intervened in the dispute. She is not allowed to leave her bed, but she sat up and restored peace. We were sitting around a small shaky table. Mr. Cohen got up and looked into the garden. His face became relaxed and he smiled. He no doubt visualized his puppies eating and wagging their tails. "Mr. Cohen! It's your turn!" The old man sat down and cast the dice. The heads of the women bent avidly over the board like predatory birds. Mrs. Munster was happy, and from time to time she patted my cheek. I sat on the edge of Henrietta's bed and protected her face from the rolling dice. Her eyes were getting dull, and only the sound of a passing train brought a spark of life to them. It was now Mrs. Munster's turn. She cupped her hands and vigorously shook the dice before casting them. Seventeen, and she seized the small cardboard figure painted to look like a concentration-camp inmate, in striped pajamas and with a minute yellow patch on his chest. She didn't at once place him on 17, but slowly moved him from position to position, enjoying herself immensely. She knew all the privileges and penalties of every position; nevertheless she enjoyed placing the figure in each circle.

"29—the latrine is occupied; you lose one round."

"30—you distinguished yourself in packing ammunition; advance three positions."

"31—the person sharing your bunk died; you now have more room; advance to 34."

"32—you are infested with vermin; return to quarantine on 20."

"33—no change."

"34—no change."

"35—unsuccessful attempt to escape; the dogs rend you."

"But you have a chance to return to life."

"Yes, Mr. Cohen, but only if you have a winning ticket."

"The only one I have says that repentance and prayer cancel the evil decree."

"That's good."

"I also have one about miracles."

"Not worth much."

"37—you broke a leg; stay where you are."

Mr. Cohen suddenly cried out, "You were burned! You were burned in a crematorium!"

43

Lying in bed near the latticed window in Klein's apartment, Joel thinks, We belong to a generation that acted before it matured and now our youth is belatedly catching up with us. We are like the tribes of Gad and Reuben and Menashe, which left their private lives in the fertile lands east of the Jordan and joined their fellow tribesmen to conquer the country to the west. Now that the conquest is over, they can't find their way back.

Patrice sleeps and one of her hands grasps a bedpost, as if reaching for solid earth from amid a great white sea.

Patricia's body also thinks. The various objects in the room think—the dresser with its door open a crack, the big black trunk which Patricia covered with a colorful cloth and put a small plant on it. Everything thinks, the gay dress and the somber one, the skirt made of sailcloth and Joel's unlaced black shoes near the bed. (These he bought in Barcelona, near a statue of Columbus in the port area.) The stone on the window sill thinks, as does the leaf petrified inside it.

Joel is becoming remote from his comrades. This is obvious from the liberated expression on his face when he is with his beloved. They have sensed it, and some have accused him of betrayal. Itzhak's face is becoming more severe; his skullcap seems to be growing bigger on his head. Zeiger's lips are chapped.

"You should put some cream on them; the Jerusalem wind is torrid."

"What do you care?"

"Only about your lips."

Patricia said to Joel, too, "Your lips are chapped, darling." And she would take one of the many jars that lined the shelves of the medicine chest in the bathroom and spread some of the cream on his lips, for the drought lasted all that summer.

Patricia's thinking body lay curled, her knees pulled up. Thoughts and memories sank into her body and rose from it like Jacob's angels. Her black hair was also deep in thought. Her girlish breasts (her great disappointment) were uncovered and she brought back memories of a college girl: white woolen socks, black-and-white tennis shoes, books carried against the belly like a pregnancy.

One of her elbows was hidden in the shadow of her bosom, for she lay rounded like an infant. Her hips rose high and bony, and her entire body became threatening and lobster-like, with arms like pliers and thighs like pincers that could hurt and heal at the same time. Whoever sinks into her will do so without warning, without defense, without restraining handhold. He will fall and sink from tenderness to harshness and then to a still greater, more primeval tenderness, the softness of the egg cell and of the dream and of the endless end; without halt, without rest, without defense.

During the night she sat up to deliver a speech, as Joel called these declarations. She sat up, but all she said was "Beautiful, beautiful," and he did not know whether she meant him, or the experience of her love, or this night in its entirety. For indeed this was the night of nights, a night which is a collective noun and has no plural.

And then she said strange things in praise of their love in Jerusalem in the middle of the twentieth century, a harsh and despairing love and also a tender one that brings oblivion, and other words, half asleep, about a curtain which she meant to change the next day, and a broken toilet seat which Joel, as agent for the apartment, should have fixed.

And where right now is Ruth? Whom he had met during the war in a sandy valley. Her braids were brown and her eyes shining and innocent of the knowledge of hell. Later she had visited him in the Dajani military hospital in Jaffa when he was recovering from a leg wound.

Now Patricia was caressing the scar on his leg, and he knew that in his heart he would have to rewrite his biography in the light of his love for Patricia, to forget some things and to recall others, just as after a revolution the history of a nation is rewritten. Falsification? Perhaps, but he knew no other truth than that of his love. Therefore, when he awoke, he would suddenly forget his comrades and his disputes with them and would recall other things from his childhood: little Ruth, for instance. Would she consent to his love? And other children with whom he had gone to school and most of whom were burned: Lore Kleiman, the daughter of the horse dealer; and Heinz, who was a handsome child and who, Joel recalled with happy surprise, resembled Patricia— the same long lashes, the dark skin and long nose, and the almond eyes.

Dawn was approaching. A dog barked, and cries were heard from afar. A flock of wild birds passed outside with a whir of wings. Wild pigeons, perhaps. Rapid steps of night workers and the clink of milk bottles.

From the hills a breeze came and rustled the curtain and a strand of hair on the woman's forehead. Other light things in the room fluttered and settled down—a letter on the suitcase, the sleeve of a shirt. For an instant they told which direction the breeze came from, as at an airport where the direction and strength of the wind are constantly measured. Then all was silent again.

44

The long night of love is coming to an end. Somewhere in the distance a dog is barking. A car screeches as it makes a sharp turn. There is a light chill in the air and the blank wall outside is turning gray. The scraps of paper caught against the fence fall to the ground. The first faucets are being turned on in houses. The waves of the night carried Joel and Patricia in their sleep to the shore of day and now they lie on the crumpled sheet tossed out by the black sea, and their bodies reveal the movements of the long night, like the bodies of the people in Pompeii who were caught and became petrified in their unsuccessful attempt at flight.

Such were the bodies of the two lovers: a leg bent as in a leap, remembering the night; an arm curved in a gesture of embrace; a face offering itself to the kiss.

Patricia woke first. Eyes still closed, she languidly rolled over on her back. Her left leg rose at an angle, the flesh of her hip was heavy and relaxed while the muscles of her thigh came alive. Without opening her eyes, she let her body remember the night.

Joel awoke and in his mind was one word, "Venice." He must have dreamed of that city so exactly the opposite of Jerusalem, so perfectly the reverse of the holy city of rocks desiccated by hot winds. Venice! Patricia is Venice. A Queen of Sheba who miraculously appeared from Venice, over the sea, in a ship of black and gold.

"Venice," he whispered. "I will call you Venice," and the two had not yet opened their eyes to see. Slowly and heavily he came to her and she received him, still half asleep. And as their lust was aroused they, too, awakened. Now their movements were calm and restrained. She lay on her back, wide and receptive, while he arched over her, barely touching, heavy and light at the same time. His toes grasped the edge of the bed and his body was over her like a taut bow. The muscles of his legs alternately tightened and relaxed and he entered her more and more and again and again until they passed all boundaries and reached the great and endless freedom and fulfillment.

Light began to seep into the room. The double rows of books on the shelves became visible, books on sociology and philosophy by people who think and people who love, and a row of valuable first editions in leather bindings, and the small ladder by which one reached the upper shelves.

The morning was progressing. There were sounds of coughing and sounds of complaints, parents complaining about their children and children about their parents. Constant complaints and recriminations, as in a generation of desert wanderers, complaints which only love could silence. Sounds of people walking, of beds being moved, of toilets being flushed. The curses of morning came to life, like the curses of

Jeremiah and Job, and only love could transform them into blessings. And Joel was arched over her again, and she sobbed uncontrollably, "Please . . . please . . ."

And then he came to her the last time. The door of the dresser was open and the mirror saw all. Outside, under the olive trees, the night watchmen drank coffee. The first laborers began to arrive. The milkman clanked his empty bottles on the stairway. Employees of the electric company sawed off eucalyptus branches that touched the high-tension wires. Entire families came to life like occupants of birds' nests.

Patricia went into the still-darkened bathroom and stayed there some time. When she returned, her hair was combed down on both sides of her face. Now their eyes were fully open and he saw her tanned body and the pale areas that were shielded from the sun by her bathing suit. She allowed him to look deep into her eyes, down to their lowest level.

"Patrice."

"You are mine."

"Yes, Patrice."

And suddenly, like a frightened little girl, she said, "Don't leave me. You must never leave me."

He took her face in his palms and looked at it to see once more the great freedom and the broad spaces which it held out.

"Where did you get these shoes?" she asked suddenly.

"In Barcelona; I bought them in the port area."

"Joel, why are you afraid to be happy?"

"It will come, in time."

Her lithe body leaped away, followed by the kitchen door slamming and water running from the faucets and her voice humming a tune. He remained lying on his back. In a little while he smelled the aroma of coffee. Children were skipping down the stairs on their way to school, and he felt suddenly happy that he didn't have to go to school. "Coffee is ready," Patricia called and he went into the kitchen. She stood facing the stove; a brief smock made of toweling material barely covered her nakedness. He sat intoxicated with happiness under the picture of blue horses with long arched necks. A cup stood before him, another before her, and the jar of jam between them. She sat opposite him, a smile in her dark eyes and her lips opened as if about to speak. But she said nothing and his heart suddenly cried out in terrible joy, "Our Father, Our King; Our Father, Our King." This prayer from the service of the Days of Awe his heart cried because he was infinitely happy and because his heart could not think of any other words.

45

Good Melvin. His mixed-up love for his wife drives him to wander about the world. Like Cain. His love and his destruction of the city. Love drives him to action, and action to love, the way it befits a man. He will never be able to love another woman. "Had you known her, you'd understand," he says. Why is he not with her, then? And why doesn't she stay put in one place? "We can't stay together and we can't make a final break," he says.

My friend Melvin is not a typical American. My Indian friend is not a typical Indian. And I am not a typical Jew. Therefore our paths crossed.

We drank in silence. Through the glass wall I saw the lighted tunnel and I waved my hand in greeting to the shoeshine man. He answered my greeting. The day I arrived, he seated me on a throne and now he is shining the shoes of a fat man who stands between us. "What did you say?" Melvin asked. "I only mumbled." "What?" "Our Father, Our King, for Yours is the kingdom forever and ever." He remarked that it was strange that I should be mumbling a prayer at the very time when he came to meet a Jewish chaplain who had served in his regiment. He had invited him to consult about Jewish prayers and rituals in connection with the film.

People walked through the tunnel. Men lugging bulky suitcases and women carrying baskets and handbags. I examined all of them from my elevated position, the guilty and the not guilty. Banging with a teaspoon against my glass, I ticked them off. Guilty. Not guilty. Guilty. Guilty. This one knew all. This one heard something. This one heard much. This one knew and was silent. The fat man who was having his shoes shined shifted his weight to his other foot.

Melvin suggested that I come to America with him and go into film making.

"What do you think of Israel?" I asked him.

"I only go there for a few hours at a time, mostly at night, and then I come back. My friends in the Air Force put a plane at my disposal."

"It must be like a dream; to come to a strange country, to talk to your estranged wife, and then to return. Won't you ever decide what to do?"

"I don't know. You'd have to know her."

"Perhaps she will still be in Jerusalem when I get back?"

"No. She is looking for true love."

We were silent. My friend's trips have still further confused my timetable. She is in Jerusalem; he is here; and, as for me, I move sluggishly. Sometimes I think that all that is happening to me is taking place in the course of a single night of disordered and confused dreams. Had I remained in Jerusalem, the summer would have passed peacefully and I would have known what I was about. Our Father, Our King! Yours is the kingdom!

I must go to see the old synagogue. When still in Jerusalem, I was told that it had been burned during the Crystal Night, the night the glass splinters fell on Ruth. The Rector of the university tossed the first torch into it, and was followed by the man whom I saw lighting a fat cigar in the picture of the carnival.

Mr. Bergner also told me I'd find the Weinburg synagogue destroyed. On Crystal Night his wife was seized with labor pains. Now he lives in Jerusalem and is a director in some government office. He is also an official in the little synagogue where my father used to go to pray.

Mr. Rosenbaum, too, told me about the burned synagogue, and also Mr. Mendelson, the margarine salesman whose red-haired daughter plays the tuba.

Melvin got up and I accompanied him to his car. The train bringing the chaplain was late, and he drove me to the entrance to the alley of gates near where the synagogue had stood. We assured each other that we were friends, and that it was a miracle that we had met in the course of our wandering in the world.

I passed by a locksmith's shop which remained intact, and on its wall verses were scribbled in ornate Gothic script which appeared to have been freshly redone. Then I passed a small gate which blocked one of the side entrances to the synagogue. On it hung a knocker in the shape of an iron fist. Had I had my way, I would have hung on the gate Ruth's artificial leg or Dr. Manheim's glasses for a knocker. A plaque on the doorpost proclaimed: "Here the Knight Von Tuchtolz Fought His Last Battle." Standing before it, I heard a woman yelling, "Sibyl! Sibyl! Come home!" But I saw neither Sibyl nor the woman calling her.

I pounded the iron fist on the gate but only a dull echo answered me. I then went to another entrance that was open. Sounds of piano playing came from within. An old man who served as doorman addressed me: "You must have made a mistake, sir; this is a dancing school." I told him: "I am a ballet teacher from abroad and I wanted to have a look." "Look, look," he said and went away. As I walked up the creaking wooden stairs, I realized that in the past the Jewish school had been housed in this building, and tears scalded my eyes. The gloomy halls were dimly lit by weak yellow bulbs and the odor of the school still hung in the air. I passed my hand over the banister, which was smooth from much rubbing. As a child, I used to slide down it, until one day the principal caught me at it and caned me. I opened the door of the classroom where I had been a pupil and saw a number of girls of different ages in black ballet costumes. They stopped and a thin, graceful woman said, "What can I do for you, sir?" I informed her that I was Señor de Rosario Galardo de Choka Chika (whose suitcase I had noticed in the entrance to my hotel). She was delighted. "It is a great honor to have you visit our school," she said, and had the children go through some motions with their hands and feet. I praised them and she said, "What a pity that Sibyl isn't here; she is my most outstanding pupil." One of the children said excitedly, "She has already appeared in recitals and can dance on one foot for a long time." The teacher explained that it was indeed so; Sibyl could switch from one foot to the other so rapidly that it seemed she was dancing on one foot. I told her that I was particularly interested in this kind of dancing. She smiled and apologized: "I forgot to introduce myself. Maria Von Tuchtolz-Baldheim." I asked her and she confirmed my guess that she was a descendant of that brave knight. I pressed her hand with the delight of one aristocrat discovering another in a petit-bourgeois world. I told her that I loved old wooden houses with creaking stairs like the one we were in, that they were more human than the modern glass houses, that creaking stairs echo the voices of human beings, and wooden walls are permeated with joy and sorrow, that a house like this one was simply made to be a dancing school. She smiled, then shouted at the children to be quiet, then smiled again.

"Do you know what was here before, Count?" she asked.

"Wasn't it always a dancing school?"

"A school, yes; but not for dancing."

"What, then?"

"It was a school for Jewish children."

"You don't say."

"On these creaking stairs the poor little circumcised children went up and down. And just outside this window stood their synagogue."

She led me to the window and pulled the curtain aside. I saw a huge pit in which three bulldozers worked while over them towered a huge crane whose glass cab was level with the window. The crane operator waved at us and Countess Von Tuchtolz threw him a kiss. "A wonderful man," she said. "A new generation of city builders is growing up here."

"What are they building here?"

"A supermarket."

The children became unruly and the instructor closed the curtain, and once again the room became dim with weak yellow light. Then she formed the children in two lines and they began circling. My eyes burned. I explained to the ballet teacher that each time I saw girls dancing I was reminded of my little daughter Anna, who died in an accident at the age of eleven. I described little Ruth to her—her delicate chin, her braids, her pug nose, her freckles, and the way her hair was parted exactly in the middle in the manner of ballet dancers. The teacher clapped her hands in amazement and cried, "An exact description of our Sibyl! I told you about her. A real little star. A great future is before her." "Why didn't she come today?" I asked. She answered that Sibyl no doubt was in one of her moods. Then she invited me to have lunch at her house. Her husband is away and marriage these days isn't what it used to be. "Count, just consider. The synagogue of the Jews used to stand here and now they are building a supermarket. Nothing is permanent. Everything changes. Here am I, a woman married to the entire world, and I lift my body like a beaker of wine to your health, Count, and to the memory of your poor little girl Sibyl."

I corrected her: "Not Sibyl but Anna." And in my head I made another correction: Not Anna but Ruth. Had Ruth learned to dance, perhaps she might have evaded her cruel death.

The girls became unruly and their teacher turned to them to restore order. I utilized this opportunity to get away. I went down the creaking stairs. Here was the school auditorium where the plays about Eliezer and Rebecca and Judas Maccabeus were staged. Here flared the great conflict between me and red-haired Siegfried, because both of us had been promised the role of Judas and the teachers were afraid to rule in my favor because he was the son of the strict principal. On the morning when the final decision was to be made, Ruth said to me, "Let them have it. Fling the role in their faces." "What?" I protested. "After I have memorized it all?" "You don't understand," she insisted. "You don't understand. Show them that you have character." "Character? What do you mean character?"

This conversation took place in the morning as we walked to school through the Palace Park. It was a cold morning, and snow began falling, a bitter morning of misfortune.

46

The street lamps remained lit though it was already bright morning. Somebody in some remote office had forgotten to press a button. Joel walked down the steps on the way home, which was no longer home. The night watchmen had already gone away, leaving behind them smoldering embers and ashes where they had sat around the bonfire at night. Shutters were raised like guillotines being made ready for fresh beheadings. The new buildings are getting ever more numerous and the Arab houses are lost among them. He walked as far as Salameh Square, which is ostensibly open to both sides but is actually open only to the west, for on the other three sides is the border. Therefore one shouldn't pay much attention to the cars dashing to the east. Let them run down King George Street with a screeching and howling and rattling. In the end they will have to stop or turn back to the west, skulking with tail between their legs. Joel went westward.

He had left the house of his beloved. One of his shirt buttons had been torn off during their wild struggle early in the night. Delivery trucks carrying ice and milk and kerosene were beginning to fill the streets. Heavy buses rumbled down toward the valley. People relieved each other at their posts, for everybody was on some duty roster. They did so without end and without purpose, near the wall of the Old City, near no man's land, on the highway to Jerusalem, which passes under the watchful eye of the tower on the grave of the prophet Samuel. The living changed posts, and also the

dead on the Mount of Rest. Were it not for the heavy tombstones, the dead would roll down and fill the valley below.

Joel approached his house. The sun was pale and white like
an albino. The sun was bored with itself and with its light.
This sun was not good for Patricia or for Joel.

Joel got only as far as the mailbox. He did not want to
look into his empty apartment. In the mailbox he found
a note from Mrs. Gutman, his mother's friend and emissary,
in which she reminded him in a single line that this day was
the anniversary of the death of his father. He glanced at his
watch and went upstairs to get his phylacteries. He stopped
before the door and listened a moment; then he entered with
a sudden rush, like a soldier about to make a search. He
noticed at once that the beds had been untouched during
the night. Then he looked for the phylacteries. From year to
year he forgot where he had put them away and, indeed, it is
hard to assign a place to things which one needs but once a
year.

Feverishly he searched for them until he located the
velvet sack containing them, on which his name was embroidered. He passed his hand over the golden letters of his
name, which stood out in relief; and then he went out toward
the small synagogue standing amid eucalyptus trees that had
been planted young when it was built and now towered over
it.

He mentally rehearsed the order of putting on the
phylacteries: first seven loops around the left arm and then
the phylactery of the head. The benches in the synagogue
were low while the pillars were disproportionately high;
when the worshipers sat, only their skullcaps could be
seen.

The first *minyan* was finishing its prayers and the second
minyan was just starting, so that the prayers of the two
groups came in confusion. Furthermore, the worshipers of

the early *minyan* of super devotees stretched the regular service with additional psalms and hymns and mourners' *kaddish*, and then more and more, the way a dedicated housewife adds many spices to make the dish tastier and richer.

The old *gabbai* looked at the synagogue clock, then at his watch, which he pulled out from his vest pocket, and addressed Joel in his gravelly voice: "What? Another year has passed already?" The number of regular worshipers is small, and most of those who come are either mourners who come to recite the *kaddish* or boys practicing how to put on phylacteries. There was no prayer quorum yet, and Joel went to his friend Itzhak's house. He found him at his desk. Lately he had become engrossed in mathematical philosophy. On his desk, suspended from a small bar, hung a triangular piece of tin punctured with holes of various sizes. Opposite it was a square piece of metal from which strings dangled. Itzhak began to explain the meaning of these objects, but Joel didn't understand and asked him to accompany him to the synagogue to help complete the *minyan*. Itzhak smiled and touched his mathematical construction, which gave out a tinkling sound. Then he took a bag containing his prayer shawl and phylacteries and went with Joel. It was good that there were people like him, and like the others of their group. In a pinch they always came to each other's rescue, whether it was as boys during an exam in school, or in their involvements with women, or in war.

With echoing footsteps the two friends walked through the spacious rooms of the house. "A long night . . ." Itzhak muttered. "Four times I was called to Mina. I don't believe that . . ." and he didn't finish his sentence.

When they reached the synagogue, the prayers were at their height and they sank among the rows of worshipers as in waves. Indeed, they were already reciting the *Song of the*

Sea—"Horse and rider He cast into the sea." The straps of Joel's phylactery of the head were tight. Each year his head was growing bigger, it occurred to him. A gilded, seven-branched candlestick stood before the cantor and on it was engraved a bunch of grapes.

Joel heard his mother cough somewhere behind him, for he sat not too far from the curtain which separated the women's section. He coughed to let her know that he had arrived. When it was time to recite the first *kaddish*, the *gabbai* told him: "Shout, otherwise Mr. Wurm's young son will drown you out." Mr. Wurm had died some weeks earlier in the bed of his mistress; he died and sank in her like a ship. The father was dead and the son was praying for the elevation of his soul.

Joel opened the prayer book. An oval stamp proclaimed the name of the donor of this torn volume. Mr. Mosner, who is also from Weinburg, came up to him and loosened the straps of the phylactery on his head. Mr. Mosner sells elementary-school textbooks. Now time weighs on his hands for he has sold all his used books. His entire business exists for the sake of the few weeks before school opens. Then his door is never locked. Were he to lower the iron shutter on his store door, he would strike several children trying to get in. During these weeks the store is full of children's arms and heads and other parts. When one child finishes buying his books, he is catapulted outside like an arrow. All children are made of springs. Above this pandemonium, which resembles nothing so much as a stormy sea, briefcases and books float like objects on turbulent water, or like bits of straw over a mass of ants. Mr. Mosner directs all this confusion. His clothes are torn from being pulled at from all sides. "Mr. Mosner! A fifth-grade arithmetic book! A history! A nature science book!" This one month provides his sustenance for the rest of the year.

Joel's and Mr. Mosner's fathers had been friends. Old Mosner was killed during the bombardment of Jerusalem in the War of Independence, and Joel's father was the only one to brave the shelling and go to the funeral. The old man was buried in the garden in the back of his house where children's toys lay scattered.

When he came to the *Shema,* Joel covered his eyes, according to custom. For the *Amidah* he rose, together with the rest, to the sound of squeaking springs. From year to year he recalled the ritual procedure, and even beat his breast with a lightly clenched fist when he came to the confession.

The synagogue windows were small and placed high, almost near the ceiling. To open them, it was necessary to set in action a complicated apparatus of bars and wheels and hinges that resembled an artificial limb, like Ruth's artificial leg.

Patricia, the American doctor, daily visited Dr. Manheim, Ruth's father, to inquire after his health. His own doctors didn't inquire—and they knew that she took a special interest in this man who was about to die. Patricia would come at an hour when there were neither visitors nor doctors in the large ward, and only the coughing of the sick and the old filled the room up to its arched windows.

Joel turned the pages of the prayer book and noticed anew that it contained the entire year, Purim and Passover, prayers for rain and for dew, for summer and for winter, for Days of Awe and for joyful occasions. Side by side were mourners' prayers and hymns to celebrate a housewarming, grace after a meal and prayers for fast days; without sequence or order, day and night, morning and evening were ranged in confusion even as there was no order in his heart. And he strongly wished that he, too, could contain everything, lose nothing, bind everything together, childhood and youth, man and beast, peacetime and wartime, memories of the past and visions of the future.

He heard his mother cough. This meant she was inviting him to have breakfast at her house and then to go with her to the cemetery at Sanhedriah. The beggars began coming into the synagogue and the worshipers placed coins along the line of their march. Well trained, each beggar took but one coin and no more. With them came the young yeshiva student who collects donations for charitable purposes as an exercise in modesty and humility. His face was pale between his black earlocks. The synagogue clock rang politely in the midst of the great silence of the *tachnun* prayer. Seven times it rang. What happened at seven the day before? He had met Patrice as she sat on the steps awaiting his coming; that was before everything.

Now it was time for the mourners' *kaddish*. Mr. Mosner showed him the place in the prayer book and he recited from it. Then he took off his phylacteries, carefully folded the straps about them and put them in the velvet bag.

He walked with his mother to have breakfast at her house. In the garden adjoining the President's house a group of soldiers were rehearsing some complicated drill, for in another hour or two the ambassador of some country would call to present his credentials. The military band was also there and in its midst was the red-haired daughter of Mr. Mendelson from Weinburg. Her tuba was wrapped around her like a snake and its huge mouth gaped over her head. She looked like an angel in the heavenly military band. As Joel walked by, she blew a few short blasts in his honor, and he waved his phylactery bag at her.

His mother looked at him and remarked that he was increasingly resembling his father.

After breakfast they quietly rose and went to the cemetery. Because of the wars, cemeteries in Jerusalem are scat-

tered throughout the city. With the exception of the old one
on the Mount of Olives, new burial places are constantly
being established. Uncle Moritz is buried in Sheikh Badr,
where the dead were interred during the War of Independence. This temporary cemetery is now the most secure spot
in Jerusalem. Other nations in other countries form a defen-
sive circle about their women and children. In Jerusalem a
cemetery near an abandoned quarry was the center of defense.

Then it was decided to locate the city cemetery in Sanhedriah, near the tombs of the Judges. Before that, this area
had served as a botanical garden and is still marked by
handsome alleys of cypresses and long glass structures
which served as hothouses and nurseries. In one corner there
still lies a big heap of rusty signs bearing long Latin names
of various plants. Near these is a pile of signs bearing names
of the dead on whose graves permanent tombstones have
already been set up. And there is also a heap of old spades
and stakes and picks and cans of paint and baskets made of
old tires.

The main gate was locked, for it is opened only when there
is a funeral. Joel and his mother entered through a side gate.
Joel donned a skullcap. Some people who have no skullcaps
tie knots in the corners of a handkerchief and use this to
cover their heads, a kind of dunce cap for funerals and cir-
cumcisions and weddings.

Joel's mother was calm and relaxed here. Her entire life is
constantly astir within her, so that her wrinkled face now
looks like a large railroad junction photographed from the
air.

As they walked down the paved path, Vicky suddenly appeared and walked before them, occasionally turning to look
at them the way a dog does. She was going to the ruined
house near no man's land. The cemetery is near the border,

and where there is a border there is a no man's land. Vicky is an expert at these. The entire world of the adults is a no man's land for her; therefore she felt no reverence for Professor Oren or fear of her parents. Joel she loved and therefore was mightily jealous of the American doctor. The city was a no man's land wide open to winds and to enemies and to lovers.

Vicky disappeared among the tombstones, some of which were leaning badly on cracked concrete bases. Here, too, the ground is sinking. The wife of the cemetery watchman kept yelling at Vicky, who had apparently knocked a sheet down from the laundry line as she ran.

The cemetery invades the no man's land like a peninsula. Within a few months the ground here will be covered with flowers and tall grass, but it is just as likely to be rent by exploding shells and to be torn by soldiers digging foxholes and peopled by others seeking safety behind the tombstones.

When did this great turn in Joel's life begin? The question rose in his mind and just as quickly subsided. He looked in the direction of Mount Scopus and suddenly longed to be there amid the abandoned buildings, in the forbidden and closed world, to look from it at the wilderness of Judea rolling like a sea from the amphitheater to the Dead Sea. Should he perhaps ask to be sent to Mount Scopus with one of the companies that go up to supervise the packing of antiques that still remain there? To visit those buildings where he had once studied and which now are empty and crumbling? To walk through the empty halls, to come into an empty room, an echo within an echo, to be there and there to decide?

When did the great turn in his life begin? That turn which leads to the abyss or to the great freedom? He asked his dead father, and the living mother at his side, but received no answer. What brought on the beginning of the great turn in his life? Was it his first sight of a dead man? The end of his childhood? His first battle? Being wounded? The first girl he loved in a shed among the orange groves of Rehovoth, who later left him? All these had shaken him and raised him high in their day but had finally set him down again and returned him to his usual self. No, it was not these that brought on the great turn.

He looked about him to the square tower of the English College, which resembled the tower of an Anglican church, and to the Italian-style turrets of the hospital, which seemed to have been picked up in Italy and deposited in the Holy City. For Jerusalem is like a woman who adorns herself with the gifts of her lovers from all over the world.

His mother returned home. Joel went into a Hungarian store and bought a bottle of wine and went to Patricia's house. Perhaps she was not at home. Perhaps she had waited till she had despaired and then fled to some owl-like friend. Perhaps her apartment is full of visitors, transient, gum-chewing, guitar-playing, loud-shirted Americans, or individualists or eccentrics. Or perhaps Mr. Cohen and his flowers, or the painter Meinzer?

She had given Joel a key to her apartment on a blue string. Nevertheless he rang the bell. He heard no steps, but the door opened as in a dream and he sank into her voice and arms.

"Darling. Darling. I was afraid you wouldn't come."

"Why?"

"I was afraid. You saw your wife. Don't lie to me, please; you don't have to. But I can't allow myself to lose you. Say nothing, darling, please don't."

She drew him after her to the kitchen and he beheld her, barefoot and in her little apron. She wiped her hands on the apron and this gesture, too, was a motion of love and finality, like everything else she did, fit to be the very last and to be engraved on his memory forever.

Pots hissed and bubbled. A piece of meat sizzled in a pan and shot sparks of fat all around. The smell of frying filled the kitchen.

Overcome, he embraced her hips and belly and she laughed, "Careful, the meat will burn." He started talking about Venice, where they would go together, and she told him they had already been there. They had been everywhere together. Then she talked of a small neat hotel in Paris, and a neighbor came in and brought flowers from Mr. Cohen.

"Foolish, silly Mr. Cohen. I have told him to stop and he keeps on sending, and even adds that he knows it is hopeless."

He led her after him and lifted her and put her on the sofa, where her clothes lay piled. There were times when a frenzy about clothes overcame her and she took out everything she had from the closets. But she would not let him come to her, and urged, "Wait; first we will eat; be patient." They returned to the kitchen and she hummed an American popular song that had much to say about baby and love, and she sent him back to the other room. He sat in the upholstered chair with the weary springs, his head thrown back, and he saw the lampshade which was like an African grass skirt and the papers and reports on her desk, and he was afraid she would leave him. And just then she came in and set the table before him and tied a big napkin around his neck and laid out the silver, and then she returned bearing the meat garnished with parsley and little brown fried onions, and a third time she came in on her bare feet bringing the rice in a small dish, rice browned like honey, each grain distinct. She poured from his wine and from hers, and he felt like King Henry VIII. He drank and ate much with gusto. But, unlike King Henry at table, she sat opposite him, his queen and mistress, very near yet remote as only queens can be, and he was her king and her nation. And even before the meal was finished, they collapsed together into the upholstered chair and filled it with the confusion of their passion. Then they calmed down and ate ice cream, after which she brought out a box of snapshots. "Here I am in front of our house in Nevada. And here in a tennis costume. I am a good tennis player." They tired of this, too, and she sat opposite him, a sly yet loving look on her face, and once again, as they sometimes liked to do, they talked without verbs.

"You—me?"

"Yes."

"My hair, too? And my fat thighs?"

"Yes."

"Always?"

"Didn't you say you'd give me only one night?"

"This, too, is part of that night. One long night."

"Without end?"

She nodded and he suddenly remembered Dr. Manheim's speech and his ailment, and little Ruth and his wife Ruth, and finally his father, the anniversary of whose death was coming to an end, and a great pain seized on his heart and he did not know what caused the pain, memory of his father or love for Patrice.

47

"Sibyl! Sibyl!" A woman's voice resounded in the alley. I stood partly hidden so that Sibyl could come without seeing me. I listened for her footsteps. Strange that a little girl should be named after an oracle of doom. But there were no footsteps and the mother's voice fell silent. Rain started to fall. Out of habit, I turned up my coat collar. One day, when atom bombs start falling, people will turn up their coat collars for protection and it will be no less useful than hiding in shelters. A young man carrying a briefcase approached the entrance of the house where I was standing. "You are waiting for Professor Laufer's seminar? He won't be here." I told him that I was very sorry, for I had come from abroad to attend Professor Laufer's seminars. Would he be away long? The student directed my attention to the bulletin board inside the door and wanted to know what country I came from. I smiled and told him that it was a faraway country. The student began telling me about Professor Laufer and what a unique psychoanalyst he was. I asked him about the effectiveness of the Laufer Test. I took it for granted that every soul healer must have some test named after him, and my guess was right.

The student went away and I turned to the bulletin board. "Psychoanalytic Institute of the University of Weinburg," it read. Among the various announcements and notices was one declaring that Professor Laufer's lectures would be discontinued till further notice. A coin fell out of my pocket, and as I bent down to retrieve it my back brushed against the board and it fell from the wall. I picked it up and felt for the hooks to hang it on. My fingers discovered my name scratched into the wall with the point of a nail, and I realized that in the past this had been the entrance to my father's store. As a child, I had scratched my name on the wall and it was still there. I carefully fingered the letters; then I hung up the bulletin board.

A big truck stood in the inner court and a couple of hefty men rolled barrels of wine from it into a cellar. So under this building, too, there was a big wine celler. Suddenly two small warm hands covered my eyes and my face from behind. I gently pushed them away and looked back. A girl of about eleven stood there laughing. "Don't you recognize me?" "No, I don't recognize you." She was disappointed. "Aren't you the American actor? We played together when the scene near the railroad station was filmed."

"Ruth! Ruth!" I cried out.

"Then you called me Ruth, too. But my name is Sibyl. Mr. Melvin, the nice American director, also calls me Sibyl."

"Why didn't you go to your dancing class?"

"How do you know?"

"I know everything, Sibyl. Your mother was calling you."

"She is always calling me. I live here, in the old house."

"Above the institute?"

"Yes. Sometimes they bring madmen here, real crazy people."

Then she told me that Melvin wanted to shoot a number of the scenes a second time but that she was fed up with it. The day before, she ran away and hid in a junkyard, but two S.S. men came and dragged her out by force. "I cried quietly; I really cried. Melvin told me not to yell and that I was doing very well. A week ago he told me to yell 'Daddy,' 'Mamma,' and then I heard him tell his assistant that he decided to change my role after talking to a man who came from Jerusalem, and that from now on I would have to cry quietly and pray to the Jewish God. He also said that now my role would be a rabbi's daughter."

Her story was getting all mixed up as she told about her dancing lessons and her school and her braids, which she wanted cut off, and an American dress that one of Melvin's assistants brought her. She also said that she really cried when an old woman told her that they were all about to be gassed.

The rain stopped altogether. Sibyl brushed aside a lock from her forehead and walked with me to one of the ruins.

Once, this had been a fashionable café named the Alhambra, a café for men only, all done in marble, with tall pillars supporting a high ceiling. The tables and chairs were of marble and metal. There my uncle, my father's oldest brother, used to spend much of his spare time playing chess with the director of the Weinburg high school, while in an adjoining billiard room men in shirt sleeves stood over the billiard tables with the expression of generals over their maps.

Only a few pillars of this café poked their heads sadly from among the rubble. Sibyl let go of my hand and ran to play in the ruins. Now and then she appeared between the pillars and mischievously called to me. From there we went to a court that was known as the Brothers Court, and after climbing over some more ruins we came to the locksmith shop bearing an inscription which I now read for the first time:

> I am a locksmith
> Good as can be;
> I make lock and key
> With dexterity;
>
> If only I could
> Make a lock for man's mouth,
> My business it would
> Reach the ends of the earth.

Then we were back to the steam shovel which stood on the spot where the synagogue had been. Sibyl explained to me that it was excavating for the foundation of a big American-style supermarket. I walked up to it but Sibyl was reluctant; she was afraid her dancing teacher might see her from the window. I reassured her: "I know your teacher, Mrs. Von Tuchtolz. She is a friend of mine, and I will get you out of trouble." Sibyl caricatured her teacher's name, "Von

Tuchtolz," "Von Rucholtz," "Von Ruchshtolz." With shining eyes, like an adult, she complimented me: *"Sie sind ein so netter Mensch."* We came to the outer wall of the synagogue which remained alone like a Wailing Wall. A sign warned us: "CAUTION! DANGER OF COLLAPSE!" We were cautious and the wall did not collapse. Sibyl walked alongside me—Sibyl, the oracle of the end of time and of the Last Judgment. (At that time a big shofar will be blown and the dead will emerge from their graves, when the time comes, when the time comes.)

"What will happen when the time comes? What are you talking about?"

"Did I say anything? I was talking to myself."

"Macht nichts. Sie sind ein so netter Mensch."

There were tears in my throat and I dropped Sibyl's hand as one drops a fruit.

Cautiously we went down into the excavation. The laborers who worked with air-pressure hammers called to us gaily, for they knew Sibyl. She tried to grasp my hand but it was clenched into a fist. She noticed that I was sad and she, too, became sad. Suddenly she stumbled against a wooden box which the laborers had tossed aside. I kept her from falling and I kicked the box. It broke open and the wind blew papers from it. Sibyl bent down and picked up a few of the sheets and handed them to me. The writing was blurred from the rain. She stopped and read aloud: " 'Lord God of heaven, preserve us in time of trouble for the waters encompass even the soul.' " At this point she had to skip some words which were too blurred, then continued: " 'And as the sound of the shofar is heard, let every heart arouse itself to full repentance. . . .' Now it is blurred again. . . . 'May it be' Thy will. . . .' And here is something in crazy letters."

Rabbi Dr. Manheim's sermons! I leaped to grab the pages which were quickly becoming soaked in a puddle; the others the wind had scattered. When Sibyl saw my excitement, she grabbed as many pages as she could. She thought it fun to dash about and catch scraps of paper being carried by the wind. A whistle announced a break in the work and the laborers sat down to eat their lunches wrapped in newspaper. After we had collected as many of the sheets as we could, we sat down in silence. Dr. Manheim's sermons! My God! I smoothed the remaining scraps while Sibyl watched me in sad wonder. To distract her, we went into the cab of the steam shovel and the operator consented to lift us above the ruin. I thought, Now we are on the level of the women's section; now on the level of the choir gallery where I sang as a child. We were moved here and there in the space which had once been the interior of the synagogue. I felt like a soaring angel. Clouds moved over me, and smoke curled alongside me.

We were lowered to the ground. The laborers returned to their work. Perhaps I would find the speech which Dr. Manheim had prepared for my Bar Mitzvah and which he hadn't had time to send to Jerusalem. Or is it too silly to run after sheets of paper carried by the wind? Is there anything more ludicrous than a man chasing his hat which the wind has blown off his head? Or papers that have fallen from his hands in the street?

I sat down and became immersed in reading the sermons I had recovered. Here was one for Hanukkah: "On this festival of the Maccabees, every Jewish heart beats with pride. The miracle of the light became the symbol, throughout the generations, of the spirit of the Jewish people ever since Sinai." For us, the children, there was no symbol involved. We were interested especially in the battles and the war elephants, and because on Hanukkah, in addition to playing at wild Indians, we could also play at being Judas Maccabeus and Nicanor and Antiochus. On the eve of Hanukkah the misfortune occurred. That morning the conflict broke out about who was to have the role of Judas—I or redheaded Siegfried, the son of the principal. The moment of decision had arrived. Near the wooden balcony of the school, which is now a dancing school, Ruth tried to persuade me for the last time to renounce my claim to the role, to fling it in their faces, and I refused. We quarreled and to get even with me she rode off on Franz's bicycle. It was snowing then and Ruth rode off in the snow. Some years later, I have heard, Franz was burned. That was a hard winter with much snow and the city became like one big apartment. The streets were like corridors and the squares became rooms. All wheeled traffic stopped and the layers of snow absorbed all sounds.

Thus I sat in the ruins of the synagogue giving myself alternately to remembering and forgetting. Memory of the falling snow which covered everything blotted out all awareness of my present life and of Jerusalem. Memories came powerfully, and just as overwhelming were the attacks of total oblivion. Now that my army has dispersed, I no longer need it and am alone with remembering and forgetting, which consume me and hasten my death like two terrible ailments.

The rattling of the air-pressure drills that were digging up the remains of the synagogue foundation resumed and woke me from my reverie. From the expression on Sibyl's face I realized that the abyss of remembering and forgetting which had opened up before me lasted no more than a few seconds. She remarked suddenly that the sound of the drill reminded her of a machine gun.

"What do you know about machine guns?" I asked.

"Everything," she said. "We were taken to an abandoned quarry and were made to remove most of our clothes. We were left in only our underwear. At first I felt terribly

ashamed, but Melvin looked at me angrily and I can't stand
to see him angry. Then came the rattling sounds and we all
tumbled into a pit. It was funny at first, you know; suddenly
everybody is dropping. And Mr. Windmeyer yelled at some
who didn't tumble properly, 'What's the matter with you?
Are you drunk?' And he yelled at me, too: 'Stop laughing or
I will send you away.' I stopped laughing and they even
photographed me from close up. Melvin explained everything to me, and I cried and later quarreled with my parents.
He also explained to me that the filming of the railroad scene
belonged in the beginning and that the scene in the pit came
at the end of the picture, but that he could cut out some
parts and shift others around."

She pointed to the entrance of a house where she had
hidden. Maybe Ruth hid in the same entrance. We got up
and moved over to the western end of the excavation. Here
had been the gallery where the choir faced the Ark. Sibyl
began to sing a nursery rhyme: "Fox, you thief,/You stole
the goose/Return it without delay/Or the hunter will come/
With loaded gun/And shoot you this very day."

I sank back into the well of memory and recalled the slap
in the face I received from the choirmaster because of a false
note which, he said, destroyed the entire hymn "Our Father,
Our King." Mr. Mendelson, the margarine salesman in Jerusalem, was then a young man and stood directly behind me.
Mr. Goldschmidt, the tailor with the triangular skull that
made him look like a death's head, used to stand to my right,
and his shrunken body gave forth a surprisingly tremendous
and echoing bass voice. The choir gallery ran along the
western wall, about half as high as the women's gallery. A
huge clock hung over our heads like the eye of some peren-
nial angry god. We sang the melodies of Levandowski and
Sulzer and other liturgical composers of the nineteenth century. The choirmaster towered over us, and we faced him

like so many music scores open at the same time. As we sang, our mouths were red and dark, and from below the voices of the congregation bent over their prayer books came up like ghost voices to us. I would look at the huge curtain over the Ark embroidered with gazelles fleeing before the lions that stood on the marble pillars on either side of the Ark. All of these the Rector of the university burned on Crystal Night, so that only the four soot-covered walls remained of Dr. Manheim's synagogue and grass began to sprout on the mounds of ruins. What remained was destroyed in an hour with the rest of the city by my friend Melvin and his cannon. Melvin, my friend, my twin brother, did what I should have done long before him, and left little room for me to take my vengeance.

"Why do you call me Ruth?" Sibyl suddenly wanted to know.

"I used to know a little girl named Ruth."

"Good. Call me Ruth and not Sibyl. We will tell no one about it. It will be our secret."

"Now you have to go home, Ruth."

"In a little while."

"Your mother will worry, Ruth."

The rattling of the air-pressure drill resumed.

And then there was the strange and mysterious blessing of the congregation by the *Kohanim*. In Germany it was the custom to recite this blessing only on holidays. In Weinburg the *Kohanim* advanced in festive processions on both sides of the Ark. Then they turned to the congregation and pulled their prayer shawls well over their heads. This produced a solemn and frightening effect. The blessing, pronounced in deep tones, emerged out of the caves of their prayer shawls. As they blessed us, they held their hands extended, fingers outspread as in a spasm of love and terror. The cantor first recited: "God bless you," and they responded with a prolonged "Oh-h-h." This, too, was a ghostly sound, monotonous, penetrating the heart with all its sweetness.

All this was burned and collapsed on that great night of the god of vengeance under the fire of Melvin, the American artillery officer. Many Philistines were buried in the ruins. It would have been right had little Ruth stood between the pillars and proclaimed: "Perish my soul with the Philistines." But she was not there, and her hair had been smoothly combed, unlike the unruly locks of Samson.

Ruth had seen many horrors before she died. Those who died like her removed many of the horrors from the world; they had seen these horrors and taken them along into their great oblivion, the scenes of carnage and the images of their murderers. In vain will my friend Melvin ask the best actors to simulate the faces of beastliness. He will not succeed. He may perhaps arouse genuine terror in the heart of Sibyl and bring tears to her eyes, for she is a sensitive and generous child, but no more.

When I was three years old, they brought me to the synagogue for one of the finest rituals practiced by German Jews. My father took me up to the *bimah* in the center of the synagogue, where the reading of the Torah was done. As the scroll was rolled up, my father lifted me and I was given a broad ribbon to tie about it. This ribbon had my name embroidered on it, the year of my birth, my parents' names, and a number of texts. This was a kind of first identity document for me. Between the letters were flags and flowers and other colorful designs, embroidered by my mother during many an evening as she sat by the window, the straw basket with the threads at her feet.

I tied the ribbon around the scroll. Somebody older tightened the knot so it would not slip. Then a kind of white robe was pulled over the scroll, and over this a heavy velvet covering embroidered with silver and gold threads and set with small pearls. Then a crown with many little bells was installed on the top. The chief cantor, Herr Reuven Moshe Hildesheim, a man possessed of a powerful tenor, lifted the Torah and intoned: "Magnify the Lord with me and let us glorify His name together." If it was the beginning of the year, the scroll was light on the Genesis side and heavy on the Deuteronomy side. From week to week the weight shifted from one side to the other. So, too, has it been with my life, which constantly moves between past and future again and again. The scroll remains the same and the text does not vary.

Finished with the ceremony, my father returned me to the women's gallery, where my mother waited with open arms to take me home.

"And what did you do when the ship began to sink?" Sibyl asked.

I was aroused from my thoughts and realized that I had been telling her an imaginary tale, and now I couldn't recall it.

I took Sibyl's hand. "Let's go," I said. "The story is finished." One of the laborers came up and told us to move, as the steam shovel was about to start working in this corner. I sent Sibyl home to put an end to the cries "Sibyl! Sibyl!" I walked down the street which was the one I liked most, it was so postwar European and genteel. The stores displayed wares in delicate colors and everything was arranged in such pleasing order. Lightly dressed young people, light-footed and friendly-eyed, passed by. The girls carried large art books and records of very ancient and very modern music. One store displayed fashionable wares and unusual art objects, African statuettes and porcelain pearls and asymmetrical porcelain earrings and daring woolen skirts and a mixture of peasant art from Sweden and Scotland and Bikini, and American Indian work. Nearby was a bookstore, and in its display window were poetry and philosophy and art books and announcements of a reading of modern South Korean poetry and a meeting of devotees of Zen Buddhism and yoga.

In one of these places I stopped near a pillar, and a hand on my shoulder aroused me. My Indian friend announced cheerfully: "I've been looking for you in the café and all over. I thought you might be interested to know that this has writing in your language." He handed me a crumpled sheet of paper that had been smoothed out. I took it and went to the store window, and by the light of the daring skirts and the unique strings of pearls I read one of Manheim's sermons: "At this time let us recall our dead. May they repose in peace until the day when they rise from their graves, as it is written, 'Behold I will open your graves,' Amen." I asked the Indian where he had found the paper. "In the heap of rubble over the café," he told me. "It was caught there. Sometimes I look for letters that have been blown away by the wind, or that have been tossed into the wind. I have found many statements of despair in this way. Tell me, is there despair in this one?" I recalled little Ruth and Henrietta and the past, but even as I remembered I forgot, and the white snow of my entire life descended upon me as I stood on this summer night in the tastefully modern street in Weinburg.

48

I waited for Yosel in the Weinburg railroad station and suddenly felt that soon I, too, would have to travel again. What had I accomplished? And what would become of my plans?

Wasn't I unraveling the complex web of vengeance plans that I had woven? It occurred to me that the past of those here was now my present, and my enemies of yesterday are my friends of tomorrow. It is quite possible that my coming here didn't in the least advance the cause of vengeance, even though I had managed to lay the groundwork.

Most of the train platforms were empty and there was very little traffic. Porters slowly pushed baggage carts. A train arrived and discharged empty bottles and took on newspapers and rolls and full bottles, but not a passenger got off. Through the train windows I saw people whom I would never see again. I should have stayed in Jerusalem and spared myself this pain. Anyone who goes on a trip opens himself to the pains of distance, to the sorrows of never-to-see-again, which are like the sorrows of love. A loudspeaker announced the arrival of the train from Frankfurt. I paced back and forth.

I hadn't seen Yosel for a long time. Now the train bringing him arrived, but it stopped before pulling up at a platform. I was dressed neatly and correctly, as befits a member of my generation which is already ruling everywhere in the world. We should have attained power when we were younger and had more faith. But it is only now, when we are beginning to realize that things are not the way we believed they were, that we are getting power. A sad and beaten generation mine: at least two wars per person. My age group in Germany were old enough to murder Jews; my age group elsewhere are now generals and ministers and corporation presidents.

It is good that there are such people; this makes it possible for a person like me to wander around the world like a pupil dismissed from a history class, without responsibility for time and action, free to move time forward or backward, to dream a bit by the side of the road, and always to be on the go. All the same, I am proud of my age group who now rule everywhere.

The train finally glided into the station. Some people got off. I stopped pacing, for I thought that it is best that one of us should move while the other stands still so we can find each other. Then I saw Yosel coming toward me. I thought he had gained weight. He stopped and faced me under a sign which read, "PARIS-MUNICH-ROME EXPRESS." There he was, my good friend Yosel. In one hand he carried a valise and in the other his violin case. The temperature of my friendship for him rose and I suddenly remembered everything I had left behind in Jerusalem, all the things that I always feared would get broken. We descended into the underpass and started a friendly argument about who was to carry the heavy suitcase. Then we went into the terminal post-office station. Letters had already arrived for him. The small modern concourse was nearly empty and induced the pleasant sense of reverence one feels in a church. A number of times I addressed him with unfinished questions, such as, "Look, Yosel, what about . . ." Or, "Listen, about your plans to . . ." But I didn't finish any of them.

We rode together in a yellow streetcar in the city of my childhood, and I took Yosel to the café under the ruins of Rosenbaum's house. The Indian waited for us, and he and Yosel at once engaged in conversation. The espresso machine hissed and the birds in their cages on the wall chirped, the way birds always do in school children's compositions. Yosel told me about Mina—that she sits all day in the garden, crushes eucalyptus leaves between her fingers, and recites poetry.

Later the waitress suddenly addressed me: "They have already left." "I also left," I said, and I paid her and went out. Near the door stood an old farmer selling cherries. He weighed some for me and put them in a paper bag and I sat down on the ruin and ate. Some of the cherries I hung over my ears, the way I used to do as a child. I was about to throw away the bag when I noticed that its paper bore one of Dr. Manheim's sermons. It was stained with cherry juice as with blood. From the few words that were still legible, I realized that it was the Bar Mitzvah speech he had prepared for me: "My dear boy . . . you read before us . . . when Jacob wrestled with the angel . . . This is a symbol . . . the clean and the unclean . . . Close bonds unite me with your father's household . . . Verily, this is a place of awe. . . ." At this point the paper was soaked and disintegrated.

Then I washed my face in the fountain of the four cisterns, and there I also met the clerk from the deeds office, who informed me that the matter of the ownership of the ruin of Rosenbaum's house had been settled. As he talked, he took out a small package wrapped in paper and I realized that this was also one of Dr. Manheim's sermons and I begged him to give it to me. "Mr. Rosenbaum will collect a tidy sum. Why do you want this wrapping paper?" he asked. "To read what's on it," I assured him. "What does it say?" " 'Do not pass judgment upon us, for Thou art a merciful God.' " "Yes, mein Herr, we all need heavenly mercy. When are you going back to Jerusalem?" And, saying this, he tipped his hat and walked off.

I went down to the river to inquire when a boat was leaving for the convent at Oberbach. I examined a timetable near the dock and made my plans. I decided to go there by boat and arranged for the priest to meet me.

A sheet of paper floated on the water and I knew what it was. With the help of a boy who was playing nearby, I fished it out. The writing on it was all blotted out. Ever since I broke the box containing Dr. Manheim's sermons in the ruins of the synagogue, I find them everywhere. An old man stood near the skating arena and a lone Frenchman circled in it.

I went into a store and bought a bottle of wine for Henrietta. The clerk wrapped it in Manheim's beautiful sermon on the exodus. The exodus from Egypt, it said, implied physical liberation from slavery and spiritual liberation on Mount Sinai.

I was weary, and didn't stop the clerk from wrapping the bottle in a sermon.

49

The urge to action which overcomes me is like a match. I rub it against my memories and they catch fire. But there is danger that the fire will consume the urge itself. Therefore I am anxious to complete my activities in Weinburg. One important operation is left—a visit to Sister Elizabeth in the ancient convent in Oberbach. This is a major operation, and perhaps the last.

I stood near the anchorage and waited for my army. For this operation I had invited all of them. Let them help me hear about the fate of little Ruth directly from Sister Elizabeth or from the intermediary between us. The captain already stood on the deck of the boat which rocked under his weight. He checked the little motor and rattled an iron chain. I asked him what the horsepower of the motor was and he told me, and also that for many years he had been a sailor in the merchant marine and now, in his old age, he had been reduced to carrying excursionists on the river. He put on a cap that was vaguely reminiscent of a ship's officer's white cap with an anchor. His face was flushed and he breathed heavily. Then he erased a number from the time-table bulletin and wrote another in its stead. He was postponing the departure because my landing forces had not yet arrived. I thanked him for it.

Leonora came walking down the dock. A fashionable handbag was slung over her shoulder and swayed in rhythm with her step. She came toward me and fell into my arms like a very tired little girl. Then she took from her bag a heart-shaped cookie trimmed with almonds and walnuts. Written on it in powdered sugar were the words "I Love You." She handed it to me. I broke it and handed half to her. We sat down and dangled our feet against the dock. Why does she continue to circle in the arena, just like the earth? She was more beautiful than usual, and prepared for the journey. Soon she would leave for destinations far more remote than Oberbach, where one does not meet even far-ranging travelers like me. A wind rustled the tops of the linden trees that grew along the river. The captain started the motor, and now no one could hear whether Leonora was crying or laughing.

I jumped into the boat and held out my hand to Leonora, who leaped after me. Benches stood on the deck along the railing near the flag, which drooped mournfully. The captain asked us to sit on opposite sides so as not to tip the boat. An American Negro soldier appeared on the dock. I signaled to him to come along. He bared his teeth in a smile and brought along his buddy, who appeared, too. They came down without making a sound, for their shoes had composition heels. I should have worn noiseless shoes like these— blood avenger's shoes. For one must observe silence when descending into the ghostly past.

Long flat river boats loaded with coal and sand floated by. Barges passed, pulled by small insolent tugboats whose horns bellowed deeply. The two Negroes sat talking to each other. They were in my army without knowing it. When we cast off, I would explain to them my plan of campaign. Meantime I mentally gave them orders.

Leonora knew where we were going. We conversed quietly, since not all my army had come yet. "You will never rid yourself of this system which you are trying to impose on life—the system of reward and punishment," she said.

"Look at the Castle of Saint Mary, which towers over us. Soon the grapes will ripen on the slopes. If you are here late in the fall, you will see the grape festival when the entire city is drunk with the wine from above."

"Vengeance can be turned into anything—wine, flowers, honey."

"Not mine."

She took out a comb and combed her hair.

Then Yosel came, and the captain seated him opposite me for the sake of balance. I complained to him because he had vanished from the café, and he became angry and said, "You are not at all interested in my friendship. You maintain contact with me only because someone like you likes to associate with someone who leads a bohemian life like me. It provides you with a sense of security and satisfaction in your orderly life."

"You call my life orderly?"

The old sailor rang a bell. Six young chattering nuns came running daintily. They laughed as they walked down the steps to the boat the way only young nuns laugh. The motor was now started in earnest, and after some sputtering it settled down to a regular hum. The nuns came down the steps and were seated three on each side for balance. The Indian also came, but he nearly missed the boat. He held a brief-case full of papers. I was proud of my army. My blood was ripening within me like the blood of grapes ripening on the opposite slope.

A boat passed alongside and its wake rocked us. The Indian whispered to me, "I have a feeling that today I will conclude my great work on despair." The captain looked at his watch and asked, "Where is he?" And just then Father

Johannes, who had arranged the meeting with Sister Elizabeth, came. He raised his hand in blessing, like Saint K.; but
I could not see his thoughts. The Indian was feverishly writing something in his notebook. Leonora sang quietly and
dipped her fingers in the water.

The captain's young assistant untied the rope from the
stanchion and quickly leaped into the boat, which began to
move. I addressed my army, the way commanders always
do, but they didn't hear, for the words remained inside me.
We moved forward and Leonora's hand trailing in the water
served as an additional rudder. She was beautiful and calm
and dreamy, and her lips moved as if she wanted so say
something.

What is in the river? Remembrance or forgetting? I didn't
know. Yosel said, "Everything is in order," like an adjutant
reporting to his commander. We approached the bridge of
the saints, and the golden implements in their hands glistened in the afternoon sun—a sword and a bow, scales, a
cross, a spear, and a shepherd's crook.

We passed under the bridge. The Negro soldiers took
snapshots, with my permission. Leonora's hand cut a small
furrow in the water. I whispered in her ear, "Leonora, come
back with me to Jerusalem. Give it another chance." She
answered, "I have already tried everything. I will not return."

The captain held the steering wheel, his cap carelessly
pushed back. He looked at Leonora and remarked that it
was lucky that the beautiful Lorelei sat on the deck of his
boat instead of on a cliff or the bank, or the boat would
crash. Then he scratched the back of his neck and winked at
me.

We glided close to the shore and passed the tennis courts.
Gradually we left the city behind us. The vine-clad hills
moved away from the banks of the river and the railroad

tracks alternately approached and receded. Once, a train passed over us on a bridge. I asked to steer the boat a while and was given the wheel, but then the river began to zigzag and I returned it to the captain.

I sat down and a heavy snow began falling on me. In the midst of a summer day, on the river of my childhood, the snow descended on me. Memory has its clouds and wind and snow, like a theater stage. For some reason my memories were associated with snow and my heart became covered, then sank into the white flakes.

At first, when Ruth lay in the hospital, it snowed a good deal. The stores of Weinburg were decorated for Christmas with angels and stars and white powder. Then the world became divided between what was in the window displays and what was outside in the snow. Henrietta gave me a fine present, a game that answers questions, a kind of ancestor of latter-day electronic brains. When the correct answer to a question was punched, a light flashed on. Never again did I receive such a present, and only rarely do lights flash onto my correct answers. In fact, questions and answers remained a game for me ever since, and that is my trouble.

We passed by the red-roofed factories and the forest approached the river. People swimming in the river bobbed in the waves we left in our wake.

The synagogue choir was then preparing for Hanukkah. We rehearsed the Hanukkah songs in four parts: Mr. Mendelson, the margarine salesman in Jerusalem, sang tenor; Mr. Goldschmidt, whose skull resembled a death's head, sang bass; and there was Mr. Rosenbaum with his hoarse voice, and the others.

The river is the only one that did not take part in the deportation of the Jews of Weinburg, because it flows west. From the west, too, came Melvin, the commander of an artillery regiment. In two hours all his heavy vehicles crossed the river on a pontoon bridge which the engineer corps had put up. Melvin must have stood there wearing a steel helmet with an eagle on it to indicate his rank, speaking quietly, hands on hips. My friend Melvin had not joined us on this excursion. He is a strange man. Dreaminess and confusion are within him alongside cold and efficient calculation. All this makes him a good film director, but he is too straight-forward and independent to make the grade in Hollywood. He avenged my wrong and derived no satisfaction from it; he loved a woman and had no satisfaction from his love.

All the Hanukkah festivities were then canceled, the singing of the Hanukkah hymns in four parts was called off, for little Ruth was already in the hospital where they amputated her leg on that snowy Hanukkah evening. What a baby I was—I was actually strangely proud that her name was mentioned in a special prayer for her recovery.

At home we sang the Hanukkah hymn "Maoz Tzur" in weak and choked voices, and there were no games, either of questions and answers, or spinning tops, or bell and hammer.

Bathers stood on the bank. They undressed in the bushes. Garments were tossed above the green bushes like some strange huge butterflies.

Yosel asked, "How much longer before we get there?" I passed the question on to Father Johannes, but he was deep in thought and did not answer. I pressed Yosel's hand out of deep gratitude that he had come with me.

I was beginning to harbor doubts. Was I really getting nearer to a great exploit? Perhaps I am already in retreat? Perhaps my army is already defeated before it saw action? Before it even realized it was my army?

50

The captain rang a bell and the boat veered toward the bank. On the dock a man stood ready to catch the end of the rope which the captain's assistant threw to him. We climbed to the dock. The town of Oberbach dozed in the heat of the afternoon.

Suddenly there was a downpour of rain, and before I knew what had happened my army dispersed to find shelter. The nuns were the first to run and their childish glassy laughter receded in the alleys. They could have helped me even though they did not belong to the order vowed to silence. For instance, they could have smuggled weapons or secret documents in their habits.

A peasant girl ran by, her braids flying. She looked for some doorway or niche but all the sheltered places were occupied by the soldiers of my army, and she ran on in the rain laughing loudly. I dashed from one shelter to another. Under a wide-spreading linden tree, I found my friend Melvin. I was delighted and told him about Yosel, the violinist, who had come to Weinburg. We both ran from doorway to doorway but couldn't find any of my army. I looked at the clouds and saw that it would be a passing shower.

We came to a small tavern where Yosel and the two Negro soldiers were already drinking. Melvin remarked that he had long been searching for heavy-lidded Jewish eyes like Yosel's. What for? For his film? No, he said, in order to weigh down the conscience of the world, which is lightweight and tossed about by every breeze.

Melvin gave me a thick American cigar and I thought, I will blow a shofar to summon my army, as they used to do in the Bible. But I said, "Let's order beer." The tumult of the drinkers and the smoke rose about us. Before my eyes was a deeply creased red neck. I prophesied, "Red neck, you who witnessed the burning of the Jews will end by being severed from the head." I looked at Melvin's face and calmed down. His face was handsome and virile but his eyes betrayed the confusion and the softness within him. A strange American. Then a woman with bulging buttocks brought us mugs of beer.

Two men came in and hung their raincoats and umbrellas on buffalo horns.

I remained alone with Melvin amid the clouds of smoke.

"I haven't told you, have I? My wife and I are getting divorced," he said.

"This is definite?"

"Yes, this is final. She has some traits of finality in her character."

"And what will you do?"

"I have to finish this film. Then I will go to Japan to make films there."

"And she will remain in Jerusalem?"

"It's not clear. I have the impression that she finally found the great love she had been talking about."

Then he said "Cut," the way he orders his cameraman, and the conversation was at an end.

Nervously I began to spin the coaster until it fell. Melvin took another coaster and drew strange designs on it. "Do you know," he said, "that during the war I was in this very tavern? We spread our maps on one of the tables, and on that other high one we set up our telephone switchboard. It was right here that I received the order to direct my seventy-fives and one-twenties and howitzers against Weinburg. I remember that when the order came I was asleep, and my young adjutant woke me. I thought he was bringing news that the armistice had been signed, for in preceding days we had been advancing unresisted. All my men, officers and privates alike, acted like children detained after school when they heard the order. And exactly at six we began the shelling. It was a mighty concert and my shells danced in the streets. I moved the forward command post to Mary's Castle. I couldn't see a thing because of the smoke. We entered the city on the following day, when most of the fires had burned out."

The rain stopped and I raised my hand to signal to my troops to get up. But only Melvin had remained with me. We went outside. The two Negroes were taking snapshots of the ancient buildings and paid no attention to my orders. The clerk from the deeds office lay drunk under a bench in the tavern. The tavern owner came and cried, "He's in here!" "We'll come for him afterward," I shouted back. "When? When is afterward? After what?" he wanted to know.

My army had truly shrunk. Perhaps it was better this way —like Gideon putting his army to the test of drinking and thus reducing its numbers. An army that disperses because of rain and gets drunk on a bit of beer is in any case not an army. We walked through a small park that had once belonged to a local nobleman and was now a public garden. Swans moved on the water. Then we came to an avenue of poplars along the river and followed it till we came to the wall of the convent. Father Johannes stood near the gate and greeted us with an earnest smile. I felt tired and thought that my army must be tired, too. During the war, I once served in a unit that marched all night through deep sands in order to strike at the enemy at dawn. But when we got there, we were all exhausted. We were like a tired fist at the end of an arm that was too long. We could not strike the enemy and retired with heavy losses.

51

"Then I started to run home. I couldn't stand the sight of all the blood that was on the pavement. Do you hear me, Sister Elizabeth?"

The old woman nodded. "I realized that the festivities would be canceled. There would be no Maccabees, no Judas and no Mattathias. Everything would be canceled." I noticed a questioning look in Sister Elizabeth's old eyes but she was vowed to silence. "No Maccabees and no Saint Nicholas and no three kings coming to Bethlehem." Her old eyes lit up and cleared. Now she understood. She was very old and her eyesight was failing. She would never get up from this bed.

"Snow," I told her. "It is always snowing in my mind." The old woman nodded her consent and pointed to her heart, as if to say that there, too, snow was always falling. She was happy lying there in her bed. Someone had propped her head with some pillows so that she could see me better. I had been sitting there for more than an hour telling her about little Ruth, for she was forbidden to utter a sound.

"You are an old woman, full of memories." (She nodded.) "But memories grow dim and vanish." (She nodded again.)

"In the snow."

She nodded vigorously, so that I repeated the word "snow" several times. I beheld her, old and fragile, and she, too, was a white and precise angel, like Sibyl and Leonora. Where was Leonora circling now?

The nun who mediated between us entered and brought darkness with her, for evening had fallen outside. She asked me to wait outside until Elizabeth had said her prayers. I went out into a court surrounded by a porch. I sat down on a low wall and Melvin stood near me by a rose bush.

"Have you finished?" he asked.

"In a little while."

"Haven't yet finished the parade of the past?"

"They are praying now."

"Tell me more about little Ruth. I am thinking of doing a film about her. Are you angry that I am being so practical about it?"

"No."

We were silent a moment and then I proceeded to tell about the time little Ruth was in the hospital when her leg was amputated. "Some days later I was told that she wanted to see me and I was terrified. My mother gave me a bouquet of white carnations. 'Bring her these,' she said. I took the bouquet, which was wrapped in a silky kind of paper, and went to the hospital. I hesitated at the gate for a while, then took courage and walked in. The gate shut behind me. I walked down a path of white gravel between chestnut trees. I was led on it as one walks at night. I knocked on the reception window, for this was not during visiting hours, but the gatekeeper knew I was expected and opened the door for me. I found myself in the midst of hospital odors. As a matter of fact, it was an enchanted castle where Ruth had been bewitched. Wheelchairs rolled by me silently. Then Sister Elizabeth came and put her hand on my head and I knew she would guide me."

They informed me that the prayers were over and I went in while Melvin remained outside. A small light had been turned on in the old nun's cell. I resumed my story and articulated her memory, since she was not allowed to talk.

"I knew at once that you would lead me to Ruth, who had been bewitched. Today I seldom know who is with me and who is against me. You will recall that you asked me if I had come to see Ruth and I merely nodded, for I could not talk then just as you cannot talk now. You told me to follow you, and I was convinced that I was in an enchanted castle and that the flowers I carried had the power to break the spell and put the evil spirits to sleep. You bent over the flowers and smelled them and said, 'What a wonderful aroma. Ruth will be glad. When you are with her, talk to her as if nothing has happened. Don't be afraid. Talk to her about school and about the children.' You led me as far as the door and let me in. I did not hear Ruth's voice. I only noticed the big window and then the door closed behind me.' Then I became aware of a big white pillow with Ruth's black hair spread over it around her face, which seemed unusually small. I put the carnations on the bed as one puts flowers on a grave. 'Here, I brought these for you' was all I said and sat down near the bed, and before I could say anything else you returned [here the old woman nodded her head] and said, 'I have brought a vase for these pretty flowers. Soon you will be able to bring roses that will be as red as our little Ruth's cheeks.' Then you went out again and Ruth and I talked.

" 'Sister Elizabeth is so wonderful. I love her,' Ruth said.

" 'The snow will melt soon; it's already started to,' I said.

" 'The flowers smell wonderful,' she said.

" 'You will get many beautiful presents, Ruth,' I said.

" 'Come to see me every day; I have games that are terribly nice,' she said.

"Then you, Sister Elizabeth, returned and said, 'I am afraid our young friend will have to leave now. He will come back tomorrow. Ruth must have her bath now.' That's what you said."

The old woman nodded vigorously.

"But Ruth began to cry softly. 'I don't want a bath yet. I want him to stay a while longer,' she said. You smiled and put your hand on my head, and I got up and held out my hand to Ruth and surreptitiously looked at the blanket to see whether it was noticeable that her leg was missing. Why didn't she want her bath? Perhaps so as not to have to see the amputation. I recall that I dashed through the corridors and skipped down the stairs and galloped down the gravel path between the chestnut trees. And only when I was outside the hospital wall did I stop, and I swore by the smoke of a passing train that I would never abandon Ruth, never."

The old nun raised her hand as if she were about to say something, but remained silent.

I continued: "Time passed. Do you remember how Ruth matured before her time? Spring came, and then early summer and she sat under the trees outside. I was permitted to visit her at all times, even when other children had to leave. Wrapped in white blankets, she would sit on the grass surrounded by other children like a queen holding court. The old people from the Home used to come to visit with her and, like all old people, they knew many stories."

Sister Elizabeth's old eyes looked at me affectionately. I told her about Ruth's house, which had remained in ruins, and the branch of a tree stretched through one of its broken windows. I told her about the site of the synagogue, where a supermarket was going up. I told her that it was terrible to think that all the people of the generation of atrocities were getting old, and age would endow their faces with an expression of innocence and peace and suffering. Sister Elizabeth began to cry; she nodded her head so that her iron bedstead shook. Then she suddenly cried out in a broken hoarse voice, "All! All! They were all like that! All did it, may Jesus forgive me!" She crossed herself and sank back into her silence.

To calm her as well as myself, I began telling her about the Holy Land and the Vale of the Crucifixion and Nazareth. She relaxed and dozed off. I tiptoed out and two nuns entered. Soon I heard the distant sound of their singing. From the river came muffled sounds of motorboats and the sirens of the loaded barges.

Father Johannes stood near a rosebush. "Where is Melvin?" I asked him.

"He left. He will wait for you in town."

"Is there any transportation to town?"

"By bus."

But when I boarded the bus, all my protecting walls collapsed and I was like Jericho, and a terrible army of conquerors raged on my ruins. The songs of the nuns, Hanukkah songs, words from my marriage service—all became confused in my mind together with wartime commands: "Fire only when they get close! Maintain silence! Don't get nervous! Don't show yourselves when not necessary!" Then, section by section, my mind blanked out like so many cabins in a sinking ship.

52

"Dear man of many birthdays," Patricia said to Joel as they sat in the hospital cafeteria. She handed him a small silver box of ancient Persian make handcrafted with a relief of a galloping wild horse. Inside it was a lock of her hair.

"Why were you alarmed when you saw me?"

"From much happiness. When I see you, my heart pounds so it kills me."

"If you ever leave me, you won't live," she said.

"I couldn't leave you even if I wanted to; and I wouldn't want to even if I could."

She rose and went out for a few moments. "I think you can go up now to see Manheim," she said when she returned.

"The doctors have gone?"

"Yes. Now, go and don't look back. Please."

"Why? After I visit with Manheim I will return here. Wait for me."

"Don't look back. Please, darling. Now, go."

Dr. Manheim's days were numbered. Yet who had counted them and decided that they were numbered? He was sinking slowly toward his end. His thick glasses lay on a stand near his bed, like the armor a knight has discarded. Joel sat down and watched the old man sink into his death. He was little Ruth's father, yet they never talked about her.

"Tell me, my young friend, weren't you planning to be in Weinburg this summer?"

"I changed my plans."

"Good. It's good that you didn't go. Though if you had, you might have been able to locate the manuscripts of my sermons."

"I am sure the Bishop's office will gladly attend to that for you, Dr. Manheim."

"I heard that of all the houses destroyed only ours remains in ruins."

The old man fell silent and resumed his glide toward death. Death must be very deep, for the old rabbi had been sinking into it and still hadn't reached its bottom. A nurse came in and made a sign to Joel to go out while the old man was being examined.

Dr. Manheim is asleep after Patricia gives him an injection. She and Joel sit on either side of the bed, the old man between them like a mediator interpreting their feelings for each other. The two are silent and the soul of the dying old rabbi hovers between them. They whisper:

"How much longer will he live?"

"I don't know. Do you still love your wife?"

"Do you still love your husband?"

"No. I only feel bound to him. He needs me because of what happened to him in the war. Do you still love your wife?"

"We met in the Negev during the war. Once, I returned from a night operation and there she was. She is entitled to have a child by me."

"And when she has a child by you, you will say that you can't leave her on account of it."

"You are my only loved one. This doesn't make sense."

"No, it doesn't make sense. Do you still love Ruth?"

"Without reason."

Dr. Manheim is sinking and his thoughts rise to the surface like bubbles. If only Joel had brought his sermons from Weinburg, as he had promised. That wonderful American lady doctor, like a white angel. "For He will command His angels to be with you." With how many different kinds of garments does God clothe His angels? Should he tell the doctor about little Ruth? Better not. I am going to her but she will not return to me.

Such were the thoughts of the dying rabbi.

But Joel thought otherwise: She returned to me but I am not going where she went. The living do not go to the dead—it is the dead who come back and dwell with the living.

"Where is your wife now?"

"In the kibbutz."

"Will you return to her?"

"No. We are getting divorced. And where is your husband?"

"We decided to get divorced. He is scattered all over the world. Do you know the legend about the mermaid who renounced her fishtail for human feet out of love for a man? Every time she took a step, she felt sharp pain, as if she were stepping on knife edges."

"Yes, I know it."

"This is the way I feel. You never finished telling me the story of little Ruth."

"I will finish it."

They noticed that the old man was sleeping soundly, and went out through corridors built like those of a monastery.

"Dr. Manheim is one of the important witnesses in my life," Joel said. "He is the witness of my childhood."

"Is life for you always a trial that you must have witnesses? Why, this is awful. And who is the judge?"

"You."

"I am a biased judge."

53

It rained and the people of Weinburg stayed indoors. It was a Sunday and everybody rested. But they were only apparently at rest, for in my plan of vengeance I had doomed them to eternal unrest.

Mrs. Metzman received me in her office. "You came at a difficult time," she said. "Henrietta?" She nodded. "The doctor is with her?" "He has already left." Then she inquired about my doings. I answered vaguely, to discourage her. I had been brought up to believe that it wasn't right for a person to perform dramatic and sensational deeds for himself. For dead little Ruth, yes; for the photograph of an unknown woman in a display window, yes. For these I will act. Belated love and pure vengeance are pure deeds, I was convinced. These brought me to the city among the hills of ripening vineyards.

From the moment that I learned to string my actions as one threads a needle, they lined themselves up one after the other, so that soon I will be able to sit aside and watch the chain effect of my deeds, how each brings about the following one. Planting a booby trap is the most detached deed. People conceal the trap and depart from it in space and time. They do not know who will step on it, whether friend or foe, man or wandering beast. Imagine a land mine planted during one war that explodes in the next war, or during the peace that follows war. These are detached acts, for the distance between the doer and what is done is considerable.

I walked up the wooden steps. Sister Maria greeted me. "Quiet. You can come in. The doctors are consulting." Leonora paced back and forth, her skates jingling in a bag slung across her back. She wore a red dress and looked like a crimson angel. "It's good that you came," she said. "Henrietta will be happy to see you. But you look sad."

"Sadness is made of stronger stuff than joy; it doesn't wear out so easily."

I shook hands with her and went into Henrietta's room. Mrs. Munster sat in a corner muttering some proverb about the world which is like a ladder in a chicken coop—too filthy to climb up on.

The old nun came and went mumbling indistinctly. Henrietta whispered, "You still here? Aren't you homesick?"

"No, Henrietta. I am faraway-sick."

"And I am heaven-sick. I long for it. You remember? Every birthday I used to give you a present, and now I owe you many presents for all the years that you were far away."

Mrs. Munster whispered that Henrietta must not be allowed to become excited, but she was already beyond excitement. "How is Uncle Moritz?" she asked suddenly.

"He died in Jerusalem. He is buried provisionally."

"Buried provisionally? In Jerusalem? What does it mean?"

"Until his bones are moved to a permanent location."

"And how are your three spinster aunts—Rosalia, Amalia, and Frieda?"

"They died before the holocaust."

"Please open the window. I want to hear the train go by. The Copenhagen-Hamburg-Rome Express is due now."

Henrietta knows all the trains and all their schedules.

I opened the window and the train rushed by with a wail. The train, too, was an angel, a fiery chariot, determined, purposeful.

The rain stopped.

"Why did you come to Weinburg?"

"To see you and to recall my childhood."

I touched my hand to her forehead and her brittle cheeks. She dozed off. Mrs. Munster, too, dozed off in her corner, which was like the corner of a car in a moving train. The folds of her flesh hung over the edge of the chair and her face was big and heavy, layers upon layers of white and tortured fat.

I went downstairs. Mrs. Metzman dozed over her typewriter. Dr. Messer was reciting the afternoon *Amidah* prayer and, seeing me, he bowed in my direction, as if I were God. I sat down to wait for Leonora. All about me rustled the dead conversations of dead people.

Through the window I saw Leonora playing with Heinrele in the garden and I went out.

Heinrele threw an apple to Leonora and missed. I said to her, "One by one the witnesses to my life are dying." Heinrele saw me and ran up shouting happily. I tossed him into the air twice.

"My witnesses are dying, Leonora. Go up to Henrietta."

"I have already seen her. Why do you need witnesses?"

"Because of the prosecution."

54

From Sibyl I heard that her teacher Madame Von Tuchtolz-Baldheim was organizing a conference of students and intellectuals in her ancient castle near the convent of the silent nuns. Though I was not invited, I went there stealthily.

From the river came the croaking of frogs, and I also heard human voices. I turned off my flashlight and put the map into my pants pocket and took up my ambush behind an apple tree. When the voices receded, I crawled on my belly toward a faintly lit door. A boy and a girl came out in close embrace into the summer night. A door opened and I heard the voice of a speaker inside. A man was delivering a speech and somewhere outside a dog barked. Since no one was around, I came closer. A number of bicycles and motor scooters were parked on a gravel area, as were three automobiles. One of these was covered with emblems and travel stickers; even the windshield had stickers on it, leaving one small opening before the driver's eyes. London, Paris, Tunis, Barcelona, Cairo, Belgrade, Stockholm. I read the names but was not reassured. I said to myself, "I made a mistake; I strayed." I whispered a passage from the confession recited on the Day of Atonement, but could not remember the entire list of sins in that confession. I thought, Little Ruth, I strayed. Suddenly I remembered that once, during the war, my company scaled a hill where, according to the maps, the enemy should have been, but when we got there the hilltop was deserted. My dead friend, on the other hand, went with his company to a hilltop that was supposed to be unoccupied, but the enemy was there and he and most of his company were killed.

I heard water rushing in a toilet. I hid behind a door and shook the dust from my clothes. I combed my hair and checked to see whether my pants were all buttoned.

Someone said, "Come, let's go in. Professor Nidershtatner is talking on 'Anti-Semitism—the plague of Christianity.'" There were some twenty or thirty people in the hall. Some sat on pillows that were scattered about the floor, others stood back to back, each staring before him, and some sat on heavy oaken chairs. Along the walls stood ancient cabinets containing brass utensils. A big old chandelier had been adapted to electric lights that resembled flames. The windows were painted to look like stained glass. Suddenly I noticed Yosel sitting in the hall. His arm was bandaged up to his elbow. I remained near the door. "And where have we gotten?" the speaker was saying. "The answer is well known. Let me illustrate it with a parable. . . ." I didn't wait for the parable, and went back into the garden through another door. It was a warm evening. A train whistle sounded in the distance. Soon the train will pass by Henrietta's window and she will mutter in her sleep, "Paris-Athens, night express."

The garden was big and neglected. Suddenly I heard gay voices and the sound of bodies diving into water. There was a small pool and young men and women splashed in it and called me to join them. I told them I had no bathing suit.

"Nobody has," they cried. "This is a conference of nudists." I undressed. I hoped that the water would calm me. I leaped in. Two arms embraced my hips and tried to draw me farther in. I resisted and a young girl's voice whispered in my ear, "What is the matter with you? What are you doing? We are all in the pool to demonstrate Archimedes' law." Then she left the pool and cried, "Eureka! Eureka!" I, too, left the pool. She sat down on my heaped clothes, naked, glistening wetly in the light of the moon. "Are you one of the lecturers?" she asked. "Yes," I said. She then involved me in a discussion of existentialism until I felt cold. I tickled her to make her get up off my clothes. I dressed in the privacy of a bush and we resumed our conversation. It appeared that she was writing a doctoral thesis on post-despair in the twentieth century. As soon as I was dressed, she jumped into the pool and began thrashing around wildly.

I heard male voices. Two men strolled Socratically among the trees. From their talk I gathered that I was in the midst of a conference of the Society for Science and Religion. From one of the balconies came the sounds of a recording of pre-Gregorian chants—sounds winding about and within one another, yet not touching, and remaining pure and complete without being diluted in the harmony.

One of the doors opened and a group of people poured out. They were arguing about freedom of nations. One of them held a cardboard portfolio stamped with the words "International Conference of Students for the Liberation of All Peoples." I became confused by the many names of this meeting. I raised a glass of wine and cried, "As a representative of the Algerian people, I raise this glass to freedom!" A young man mumbled bashfully, "I thought Moslems didn't drink." I assured him that everything was permissible for the sake of freedom. Then some newspapermen came and interviewed the people about their views on vegetarianism, since this was a conference of vegetarians.

A woman in a wide pleated dress came running and landed near me like an angel. "Have you been assigned a place to sleep yet?" she asked. I informed her that I had no place, and she asked me to follow her. As I followed in the footsteps of her high heels, she told me that she was the organizer of this conference for mutual reconciliation on behalf of UNESCO, the Union of Catholic Students, and the League for Democracy.

We entered a dimly lit corridor and there I recognized her. It was Countess Von Tuchtolz. She did not recognize me because I had put on a false mustache.

"You are a strange people, you Indians," the Countess said. The rest of her words were lost in the night. I stumbled against a suit of armor and then she led me into a large room whose low ceiling was made of beams. A huge bulldog bitch lay on a bed. When we came in, the dog leaped off the bed and rubbed against the Countess's legs. "Poor Pimpenela," the Countess murmured as she patted the dog. "Has everybody been neglecting you? Wait, soon we will organize a conference of dogs." The bitch sniffed at me and I sniffed at the Countess's hair.

We sat down on the bed alongside each other and a number of pamphlets slid to the floor. I read the inscription on the cover of one of them: "Conference of Baptists for Peace." Another proclaimed: "Seminar for International Philately." The Countess picked up a pamphlet announcing a seminar on "Problems of Released Prisoners." We were tired and stretched out on the bed, which was all covered with pamphlets and mimeographed sheets and proclamations and appeals. I turned on my belly and read, "A Call to Vegetarians Everywhere." I could read no more because the Countess, too, turned on her belly. I pinched her behind, which was ample and tremulous.

A door opened and two lanky young men came in talking Dutch. They threw their knapsacks on two beds and paid no attention to us. Just the same, I covered the Countess with a large poster announcing the Interfaith Conference for Interfaith Understanding.

The two young men began undressing, then lay on their beds in their underwear staring at the ceiling. "They are nice boys," I said to the Countess, but she only sneered. I got up and went to the bathroom to wash my face. I looked in the mirror and remembered Ruth.

A little man came in all out of breath. He prepared to shave and meanwhile muttered to himself, "A fine name, a fine name they thought up for the conference." "What name is it now?" I asked. "Symposium on Forgetting the Past," he answered.

I went into the corridor and walked down the creaking stairs. There was dancing in the big hall. The entire conference was dancing. In the corner sat a lean, drunken man murmuring to himself repeatedly, "To forget; not to forget; to forget; not to forget." Then his head sank on his chest and he fell asleep and forgot, but his dreams came to remind him. A gray-haired man asked me, "Do you have the agenda?" A girl was distributing leaflets announcing "Evening Seminars of the Society for the Remembrance of the Past." She was tall and her hair was long. "We must not," she said, "forget what our parents did. My father, too, was an Obersturmbannführer in the S.S. We must not forget."

I invited her to dance the cha-cha. The throb of conscience was like the beat of drums. The voice of forgetfulness was like a clarinet. In one corner an Israeli was holding forth about life in a kibbutz and had distributed photographs of kibbutz life. He pointed to a man in one of the pictures who was washing dishes. "This dishwasher," he declared, "is a minister in the government of Israel." His hearers at once decided to organize a pilgrimage of friendship and atonement to Israel. When they saw me dancing closer to them, they fell silent, for they thought I was a Lebanese. A young Japanese talked about Zen Buddhism. I asked about the violinist with the bandaged arm, but no one knew whether his coming to the castle was in connection with the conference.

I wandered off to a wing of the house that was in ruins. Dates were scratched into the stones of the walls. Many conquerors had passed here. Troubadours went by this way in the Middle Ages, feathers in their caps, their zithers slung on their backs. One tower was undergoing repairs and was surrounded by scaffolding. Near the tower was a sign: "VISITING HOURS 10 TO 2."

I was tired. Tiredness sometimes begins from the feet and moves upward through the body, and sometimes it begins with the eyes. A pair of American twins sat near the suit of armor in the corridor and talked both seriously and frivolously—about a young man who chased one of them and stumbled and fell into a puddle, about the renewed militarism in Germany, about a mad artist in France, about the statues they had seen in Florence. They laughed in unison and disclosed beautiful white teeth.

They pulled me into a room that was lit only by a torch. A woman was reading poems out of a black notebook. I drank cider and listened to her reading. A shutter squeaked, and everybody whispered "Sh-h-h." A young man named Klaus Von Tuchtolz was introduced to me. He, too, was a descendant of the famous knight. Klaus was a medical student, young and enthusiastic. It was whispered that he had once been in a duel over a girl. He told me that he had been in Israel the previous year.

Later warm wine was served. Some played hide-and-seek when the speakers bored them, and there was much running to and fro in the castle. Voices and sudden noises came from all sides. Doors of rooms and closets were being slammed, and the laughter of girls hung in the air like fine perfume. Leaflets in Esperanto floated about like ghosts in the dimmed house. Dr. Menard's lecture on the true essence of democracy was canceled. Wine was spilled and crumbs scattered everywhere. Near the cold fireplace sat a student who declared: "Belief in God is a profound experience. God, who is a product of human imagination, should be put in outer space, like a spaceship, so that He should never return, that He should always circle about us."

While playing hide-and-seek, I found myself together with a student inside a closet filled with women's clothes. We talked until he said warningly, "Hush, they are looking for us." Then we heard the barking of the bulldog and the voice of the Countess: "Pimpenela, you know you mustn't get excited." The student resumed his previous remarks and declared that Professor Tinhaufer was wrong in attacking modern architecture. The characteristic structure of our time says distinctly: You are a man of the twentieth century. and you live in a box, a house that is a box. A modern house means packaging that protects the contents against heat, cold, moisture, and rough handling. It is an efficient container without embellishments. We must aim to make houses easy to pack and convenient to ship, like parcels for the post office. I said, "And what about the human body, which is also constructed to protect against damage but is not rectangular?" "That's precisely the trouble," he answered. "That is why there are disputes and wars." "And what about love?" I asked. "Well, what about it?" he said.

Somebody opened the door of our closet, flashed a light inside, and cried, "Here they are! I found them!" But the game of hide-and-seek had ended anyhow. A ghost passed by in the corridor. I seized it. Under the white sheet was the Countess. There were many confused outcries until finally a decisive voice declared, "Let's resume the business at hand. Cut out the horseplay. Is this what we came here for to the

Congress of German-Jewish Reconciliation?"

The chairs were removed from the lecture hall. The young
Count Von Tuchtolz stood dressed in tight black trousers,
the upper part of his body uncovered, holding a long saber.
He was pale and earnest. There was hardly a hair on his
body. Opposite him stood a coarse beefy man much older
than he and armed with a coachman's whip. At a sign from
the Countess they began their duel. Most of the people in
the room paid no attention to them. But before the young
Count could bring his subtle weapon into play, his older
opponent lifted him off his feet and crushed him in a bear's
embrace. Breathing heavily, Von Tuchtolz cried, "This is
against the rules, you Nazi, you Jew-killer!" "And what
about your father?" his opponent retorted. "Wasn't your
father one of the main killers? Do you give up, you pitiful
plucked chicken?" At this point the Countess intervened. She
tickled the ribs of the big man and he released his terrible hold,
and young Von Tuchtolz collapsed on a sofa.

I went into the garden and I still didn't know what the
purpose of this conference was. From among the trees and
the bushes came snatches of talk that confused me still
more.

"Now touch me here. Yes, here."

"The kibbutz is flexible and constantly changes its form."

"Now here."

"Socialism, perhaps as a moral foundation."

"A great guilt. A great guilt is oppressing. . . ."

"Don't hurt me."

"Christianity disappointed; of course it disappointed."

"You are hurting me. Be more careful."

"And it's strange that there are so many blond children in
the kibbutz."

"Every time you say 'all of them,' you squeeze my
hand."

"That's strange."

"When is the next group leaving for Haifa?"

"Odd how the young people in Israel are so like young people in Germany and in all of Europe."

I went up to my room. Below they were still dancing; then there was the sound of a commotion. But I lay down on my back and stared at the ceiling. The ceiling is everything to me. The two Dutchmen came in and started to undress a second time as they talked in whispers. I got up and took my toilet articles.

55

Now all I had to do was to calm down so that I could return to Jerusalem to my waiting wife in good health and at peace with myself. There were moments when I was overcome by a great longing for the houses of Jerusalem, and for the aromatic eucalyptus trees. Why was I remaining in Weinburg? Perhaps it was necessary to remain a while longer, the way glass is cooled slowly from a high to a low temperature, so that my soul shouldn't crack. There were times as I lay on my back in my hotel room looking out at the St. Mary Cathedral when I was seized with terror that I would never be able to return to Jerusalem. But when dawn came, the fear would vanish and I would think of my home and everything in it, my work, my students, my many friends, and my children which I would beget.

One of the things that relaxed me most was riding in the yellow streetcars of Weinburg. I rode back and forth; I changed cars. The rocking motion was in itself pacifying,

like any rocking chair or cradle. Most of all, I loved to ride
the streetcars on rainy days. I would look out and see
squares and buildings which I remembered from the past.
Sometimes I would close my eyes and see Weinburg as I
remembered it from childhood, for it was this Weinburg
that I had really returned to.

Once, I happened to ride on the No. 7 line, which hugs
the city on the north and returns to the railway station. It
was raining. People got on at the streetcar stops and shook
the water off themselves like dogs; others closed their umbrellas; others sat in silence. Right ahead of us was another
streetcar. I was looking out of the front window. A young
woman stood at the rear window of the car in front. Both of
us were wiping the moisture from our windows. It seemed
she was trying to communicate something to me, but just
then her streetcar turned off on a side track to another street.
I stood near the motorman. From time to time the trolley of
the front car struck sparks from the overhead wire. The rain
beating on the windows blurred the scenes outside. Only in a
dry climate is it possible to accomplish something real. Here
the rain washes everything away. In the desert every person,
every stone, every feature stands out sharply and nothing is
blurred. Everything is remembered forever. Rain and green
plants cover everything with oblivion.

I got off near the station square. The water of Saint K.'s
fountain mingled with the rain and lost its identity. I did not
even stop to look at the Saint's arm raised in blessing. I
walked past Pestalozzi, who had refused to despair of man.
The assistant stationmaster waved frantically at me through
the window of the stationmaster's office. I fled and wandered
aimlessly amid tracks and overpasses and underpasses and
freight cars. I walked in rain and smoke. Tracks gleamed
and trains were shunted back and forth amid a clatter of iron
and steel that resembled the clashing of sword against

sword in ancient battles. Small engines pushed and pulled enormous cars from track to track. Passenger trains maneuvered silently and clicked softly as they passed over rail joints. I crossed a rusty bridge with a soot-covered railing and came to a street where a few laborers stood. Then the rain stopped and children started coming out to resume their games. I returned to the maze of tracks. A refrigerator car stood nearby and one bearing the words "Caution, Chemicals." A row of flatcars were loaded with weird-looking agricultural implements. It is possible that these cars had been used to transport Jews to the extermination camps.

When life first struck Ruth, it was winter and there was snow. Now it is summer, a wonderful summer with showers, a summer of happiness and rivers and gay excursion boats. On this summer I came from dry Jerusalem to take vengeance. I remember Ruth as she stood in our yard near the wall against which branches of the apple tree climbed. Her eyes were gray. I can't remember how she looked in the evening. Children remember each other's appearance only by daylight. Electric light belongs to the faces of adults and causes them to look shiny and sad. Henrietta, for instance, and her kind aunt. They used to knit warm black garments by the yellow light of electricity.

A speck of coal got into my eye and I rubbed it downward toward my nose. A cloud of steam from an engine enveloped me in white—white cerements for all that will never be again. Again I climbed steps and crossed over passes and bridges. Perhaps I will take up residence here. I feel good in the neighborhood of the railway station.

I turned away from the tracks and walked past the municipal gas tanks, enormous containers, and near them heaps of coal glistening wetly. The whistle of a train departing in the distance reached me like a cry from the bottom of the heart, followed by silence, followed by a siren. Was it from a police car? Or from an ambulance? Had something happened that I did not do? Could it be that another man was doing my work of vengeance at this moment?

56

"He is waking," the nurse said. "Go near him; talk right into his ear if you want him to hear you."

But Dr. Manheim wasn't listening. He was muttering, "For Thine is the kingdom, and Thou shalt reign forever and ever."

Then he began saying incoherent things in German. At first he quoted from his most festive sermons: "Bless the old and the young and their posterity whose souls hover about your sacred throne. Raise up those that are bowed, console those that mourn, and give true peace to their souls." Then he suddenly addressed Joel: "Don't be afraid to talk to me about Ruth. There are times when I ask myself whether I did enough to rescue her. Perhaps I should have died with her. Of course, now that I am going to her it does not make much difference. In God's reckoning there is no before and no after. I remember, my dear boy, how you played the role of Judas Maccabeus. Or was it hairy Esau? And you cried out, 'Bless me, too, Father.' Do you remember our house up the street on the hill?"

"I remember the leather upholstered chairs and that the rooms were filled with the smoke of thick cigars."

"I heard that everything has been destroyed there and

rebuilt anew, except our house. I can't recall who told it to me. Sometimes, in my dreams, I am there."

"Ruth used to play a black flute."

"Ruth was covered with slivers of glass on that night in November, 1938. Here I am, bedridden, and instead of greeting you properly I talk about the slivers of glass that covered my Ruth. Here, this book, it belongs to the American lady doctor who works here. Please return it to her. Once, in one of my sermons, I expounded a fine idea. It is written, 'Let us seek our ways and return.' This means that first one must seek a way, or perhaps even construct it, and only then can one follow it. The true return requires both, paving a path and going down it—following it, not merely sitting in upholstered leather chairs smoking cigars. If you had gone to Weinburg this summer, the way you planned, you would have returned to your childhood and incidentally perhaps have recovered my lost sermons. But this is all nonsense, idle talk of an old man."

The nurse came in and motioned to Joel to leave, for the old man had exerted himself too much with talking. It was a long time since he had talked with such force. She gently pushed Joel away from the bed, and Manheim at once dozed off in exhaustion. Another nurse came in and asked whether he was planning to see the American doctor, who had once left a bathing suit with her. Joel took Patricia's bathing suit and the nurse whispered, "I fear he will die tonight. It is a miracle that he survived till now."

He walked out as if in a dream. Ruth at the hour of her death. Now Ruth's father at the hour of his death. He will repeat seven times "The Lord is God," as one does during the closing prayer on the Day of Atonement. Open the gate for us at the time of locking the gate, for the day has turned. Always a gate is being opened or shut.

Dr. Golgolos finally showed up in his office. Though it was late, he was gay and looked fresh. Einat was in the office scanning the proverbs on the calendar pages. Who is a brave man? (Sunday). He who controls his temper (Monday). One who commences a good deed (Tuesday). Is bidden to complete it (Wednesday).

"And now, seriously," he began, "about the divorce."

Golgolos was in high spirits, and joked and offered suggestions for changes in court procedures. "For instance, the matter of taking an oath. Now this is done by placing the hand on a Bible. But why not return to the practice of Biblical days, when oaths were taken by placing one's hand under the thigh of the one to whom the pledge is being made?"

Joel looked at the calendar in Einat's hands. His life was divided; the nights belonged to Patrice and the days to aimless wandering.

Golgolos was swept along by his own witticisms. "There is a great future for the legal profession. Soon no one will stir without a lawyer. Even a person buying a package of butter in a grocery store will have to sign a contract: I, the undersigned, hereinafter referred to as the buyer, receive a package of butter from X, hereinafter referred to as the seller. There will be several lawyers in every grocery store to draw up the contracts."

Then he opened the bottom drawer of one of his filing cabinets and took out a folded white smock. When Patricia had first come to the country, she had once left it there and forgotten about it. Joel took it.

Only to reach her. To retreat from everything else. To curl up and become like a porcupine toward the outside and to open up only in her presence. To break off contact with the enemy. To retire into a fortified city. To enter the city tower, the acropolis, the fortified upper city, and there to wait till the dust clouds raised by the enemy became visible on the horizon. To bolt the heavy gates and be with Patricia forever.

During the small hours of that night, Dr. Manheim died in a hush.

57

Good Henrietta died in the early hours of the day. Good Henrietta, she who told me many stories and who used to tickle me with her long knitting needle till I became oblivious to the entire world out of great pleasure.

Now I must leave Weinburg. With this realization I went from store to store to buy presents for my wife, my mother, my friends. A pipe holder for my friend Itzhak and a folding umbrella for my wife and a nice plate for my mother, and many other things.

With the sudden firmness that is characteristic of undecided people, I stopped a taxi and flung myself into it. The taxi windows were fogged. At first I wiped them so I could see outside, and then I gave up and folded my hands on my knees. What was there to see? I had seen enough already. We got to the hotel and the taxi waited for me with running motor. I skipped up to my room and began tossing my things into a suitcase with the same abandon with which I flung myself into the taxi. Then I went down and paid my bill. I managed to collect a letter which had in the meantime come for me and again jumped into the waiting taxi. "To the station!"

We came to the station square. I collected a quick blessing from Saint K. I paid the driver and ran to the checking window, where I deposited my suitcase so as to be free for my last action. I already felt severed from Weinburg and reserved a plane seat out of Frankfurt by phone. Home! Home! Though at this moment I had no home, having left the hotel but not yet returned to Jerusalem. I felt weightless and valueless, like Dr. Manheim's flying sermons.

The taxi still stood before the station with its motor idling and I jumped in. "To the cemetery," I cried. "Which one? Protestant or Catholic?" "To the Jewish cemetery," I ordered.

The driver did not know the way. I tried to direct him from memory and we lost our way. We asked a policeman and he directed us to the south of the city. We passed by factories and military barracks built of red brick during Kaiser Wilhelm's days.

Finally we came to a rusty iron gate with a star of David on it. A note on the lock said, "I am at the Red Lion Tavern." I dismissed the driver and went into the tavern. The old cemetery guard sat there alone, and was glad that someone had come to visit the Jewish cemetery. He opened the gate and the chain rattled like an anchor chain. Henrietta's funeral should come soon, and I must welcome it. There must be someone to receive it. But the guard knew of no scheduled funeral—he had been informed of none. When I told him that Frau Henrietta was coming, he dashed to his house nearby that was all covered with climbing plants. He returned beaming with relief. "Tomorrow. The funeral is tomorrow."

He told me that on rare occasions someone from America or Israel came to visit a grave. But the number of visitors was decreasing from year to year. The old ones die one by one, and with each death the funerals become smaller and smaller. The last one to die would have to be buried by the guard, without eulogies or anyone else present. Once, he told me, they had occasion to ship a corpse in a brass coffin to Israel. And finally good news: he had a copy of one of the eulogies of His Reverence Dr. Manheim.

He invited me to walk between the graves and see if everything was in order. He was proud of the wonderful order and the scrupulous neatness of the place, of the fine growth of the trees and the precision of the pruning of the bushes. There must be order among the dead, too, so that at the Last Judgment each one should know his place. All the dead here had died of natural causes. Not one had been murdered by the Nazis.

Then he told me that during the High Holy Days he used to help out in the big synagogue. He wore a uniform and was in charge of the cloakroom. He also had to sprinkle perfumed water when all prostrated themselves. Those who fainted from fasting he would bring to the cloakroom, where a doctor attended to them. I told him that my father had been one of the congregation and he apologized for not remembering him.

I strolled among the graves. Everything was well preserved. Not even a stray leaf lay on the path, though it was the end of summer and the trees were beginning to shed their leaves. When the living are neglected, the dead are looked after carefully. I came to the grave of Baron Von Fassen. A scion of an ancient aristocratic Prussian family, he had embraced Judaism. His brother had been a famous general whose campaigns were studied by officers throughout the world, together with the teachings of Clausewitz and Rommel and all kinds of Chinese generals who never won a battle. He died a devout Jew, but was not permitted to be buried in the Jewish cemetery. Only after the Nazi defeat was his body transferred there in accordance with his will.

The guard followed me around. I praised his devotion and loyalty. He referred to the graves by the names of those buried in them. "Moritz, here," he said, "was cracked a little, so I fixed him with some cement. And Ignatz—the flowers don't grow well near him. Wait, you haven't seen Siegfried and Mathilda Hochman yet. Tomorrow Henrietta will be here. Where should I assign a place for her? Near the fir tree, or closer to the gate?"

What should I do with myself until the funeral? I checked out of the hotel, and my suitcase is in the station. I went into a restaurant. Many people were eating and drinking. On a table were big platters of venison and rabbit and other hunters' delicacies—all those who feared and fled and were caught in their fearful flight and died as they were pursued. Me, I eat only sheep led to slaughter, submissive cattle bellowing, stupid chickens which sometimes continue to hop even after their throats have been slit.

58

Joel stopped in a doorway and undid the four knots in the corners of his handkerchief which had served him as a skullcap during the funeral of Dr. Manheim. At the last moment it was his duty to recite *kaddish*, for the dead had left no son and his only daughter Ruth had been burned. The Lord has taken away. He felt that he would have to become a writer. Slow and late, the heavy words rose within him. He would write his sentences laboriously and with difficulty. If only he had time, if only he was not rushed to make decisions, which are the enemies of calm sentences. Rosenbaum, who had also come to the funeral, told him that he had received a telegram from Metzman that Henrietta had died. The witnesses of Joel's life were dying, the partners of his childhood, the emissaries of his father, the messengers of his mother. Manheim and Henrietta died at the same hour, though, of course, one had to make allowance for the difference in time zones.

A group of four blind people walked past, crowding together and holding hands, on their faces an expression of perpetual smile. One of them served as leader and they advanced like a group of dancers.

The turn in his life had taken place. At night the kingdom of Patricia claimed him. Each day at sundown the partition fell; as if in a legend, it happened each day at the same hour. And he knew that the partition between night and day was very thin, and soon she would be his also during the day and all else would sink from view. But he did not yet dare to think of this complete happiness.

Each day he observed himself and seemed to take notes (the effect of the scientist in him) of the stages of his transformation: "At two my hands began trembling. At three Itzhak walked by and I forgot to greet him. At four I daydreamed of being in Venice with Patricia. At six I visualized the face of Ruth, my beloved wife, her braids, her tearstreaked face pressed to the bus window. Then Patricia, and all else is forgotten."

These were the mental notes he made, and this was the way things happened. Manheim's death, too, was a step in his severance from the past, from his parents, from Ruth, and from all the days that were. Now he was available to Patricia.

He approached his apartment. The light was still on in the neighboring grocery store. Announcements of the death of the store's old owner still hung in the window amid special sale prices for margarine and noodles and soap. The owner had been an old man and merely got in the way between his nervous sons and their nervous customers. Age had slowed him down and with his long white beard he had already looked otherworldly during his last days. Outside, cats squatted earnestly near garbage cans.

He stopped before his door and listened. Was Ruth there? Suddenly he wanted to caress her and to speak to her words of love and loyalty: "Ruth! Ruth! My wife, my companion for so long. What am I doing to you!"

59

I went looking for lodging for the night before Henrietta's funeral. Nearly all the hotels were full and those that had vacancies were reluctant to rent a room for a single night. One-night guests are not welcome. They generally use the room only a couple of hours before dawn and then ask to be awakened early. One-night guests sometimes vomit or weep or slit their wrists.

But for some reason I wasn't worried about this one night. I enjoyed being turned down, and also the alibis and excuses that were showered upon me: "A district conference of cattle breeders"; "a seminar for Catholic youth"; "a dog show." I enjoyed the apologies and the shoulder shrugging and the bowing and scraping.

I went to the new central post office and looked at the statue of a woman symbolizing the postal service. I was moved almost to tears at the thought that there was a postal service in the world and women who stand behind grilled windows and hand out letters and parcels. There was a letter for me, too, but it turned out to be unimportant. I sat down on a stone bench near a new church built after the war and took out the airline schedule to see about another reservation. Straight red and black lines connected continents and islands. Then I folded the schedule and made a paper hat of it for Heinrele. Perhaps I'd better take him for a walk so he wouldn't be in the Home while a dead body was there. I went to the Home and found him playing outside and gave him the paper hat. I took him with me and went to the shoeshop to buy another pair of shoes simply to sit down somewhere. I had already been to the barber, and had my shoes shined, but the day was still not over. Shoe boxes smelling of fresh leather were piled up in front of me. Heinrele rode on an elephant while I paced back and forth on the carpet in imitation of going somewhere. Pacing thus I began to think, and dimly remembered the dream I had of little Ruth and buying shoes. It is time to return to where I had the dream, to Jerusalem, and to my wife near whose side I had the dream. Heinrele chattered gaily and I bought him a balloon. Where is my friend Melvin now? Has he perhaps gone to Jerusalem to try to persuade his strange wife to remain with him—the woman who went there to find new life and great love? Jerusalem now has a new role. Not the law but love should come out of Zion. And I have not yet visited the palace garden, and I want to sit for many more hours near the river before going away.

I am losing my bearings. I must go away; otherwise I will not be able to, and won't know where to go. I must return home.

60

He washed his face in the bathroom in his own home. Ruth, his wife, was sleeping in the other room. Her face was happy, though her tears were wet on her cheeks. There was still a chance to turn back. He leaned his forehead against the cool mirror over the sink, and even as the water was running from the faucet the miracle of another chance was his. He could turn time back by a few hours and erase his unexpected return home, and again partake of the grace of the twilight hours with Patricia.

He had been pacing back and forth in the small park near the municipal building. A park? A square of hewn stones, more like a stone platform. There he had waited for Patricia and the miracle of one more chance, the opportunity to return to what might have been. It was a fateful moment of grace, a moment of moving the record needle back so as, with closed eyes, to hear again and again a beloved melody. Fate loves artistic enactment, which is sometimes pathetic and even sentimental.

Thus he paced back and forth at the edge of the city, which was really its center; for it was only the partition of Jerusalem that made this spot seem like the end of the city, or even the end of the world, the way the ancients felt when they regarded the world as surrounded by an endless ocean. He halted for a moment near a small pool in the park. There was no water in it, and its fountain was dry. Close by the pool was a mosaic map of Jerusalem, a decorative map, not one by which one could find one's way around. For him, too, the city was a mosaic of his love, offering little guidance. Here they walked together, there Patricia laughed, at another place she skipped, and at still another they sat on some concrete pipes; here was the square of revelation and there the alley of truth and another place the lane of silence and elsewhere the courtyard of sudden encounter, or of the kiss within which one is lost.

Here he would wait for her. There were few people in the park. Some women belatedly carried baskets and portfolios. Children still played but were gradually sucked into doors and courtyards. Some offices were still lit up. And Joel waited.

Some people wait impatiently and pace back and forth and frequently look at their watches. Others wait calmly with a sense of assurance, so that the waiting becomes a restful end in itself. Others wait with still greater calm, like the ones who await the coming of the Redeemer. Once, late in the evening, he saw Patricia standing near a table in the laboratory where she worked, alone, in her white smock. Because the small park was elevated above the surrounding streets and because it was edged with laurel bushes, only the heads of pedestrians passing in the street below could be seen. The excited voices of children floated up suddenly and as quickly died down. A bird began calling and other birds answered it. They had met here many times before. Once, Patricia came here angry: "Where have you been? You are playing tricks on me. What are you doing to me?"

More birds. One of them was a stranger bird. One could hear that it was a stranger, for it called louder than the others. A prophetic bird.

Patricia appeared suddenly while the stranger bird was prophesying. She approached from the opposite side of the park, slowly, with measured step, as if advancing to have an honor conferred upon her. .

A curl swayed softly on her forehead, like the last ripple of a calming sea, a curving, arching curl; it lent such softness to her face and sweetness to her eyes that Joel felt he would break like a ship that breaks not in a sudden storm but in the middle of a calm sea, that he would break and sink slowly and happily.

They sat down on a stone bench, tired as after a long journey, their knees shaking, like the tremors of falling in love anew, and Patricia shook her head and said, "This can't be. This can't be, that it should be so good."

The prophesying bird called again, a tree rustled, and a child cried out nearby.

She whispered, "Enemy of the people. I bought a tender chicken for you. I will fry it for you the American way." And Joel forgot Ruth and her tear-stained face. As if he had not returned home, as if he had not seen Ruth's happy smile on her sleeping face, as if he did not have to decide, as if the decision had already been made.

And he felt that all his intoxicated decisions would go in one direction, to Patricia.

"What are you doing? When will you come to me altogether? I know you won't. You are afraid of losing everything."

"Till now I have not lived fully. I have been like a man who has learned to use only two of his five fingers, and then he sees others and learns from them how to use his entire hand. Now I live with all my might. What went before was artificial life."

"Pretense?"

"Patrice."

"What?"

"I am hungry. Let us go and eat the chicken."

The moment of grace dissolved. Again children played their wild games in the park. One boy skated. From time to time, he squatted and skated on one leg.

Whence was he coming? And whither should he go? How many times will he have the opportunity to change his mind, to turn time backward, to cancel decisions, to undo what he has done?

61

There was a knocking on the bathroom door followed by Patricia's voice: "Hey, you in there, don't fall asleep and drown in the bathtub. And leave me some hot water. Come out. I'll make coffee." Joel's answer was still on his lips together with soapy water when the knocking resumed: "Have you forgotten your lecture? Or was it all a joke? What? You've delivered it already? You won't go? You're very confusing."

Joel let the water drain and rinsed the soap and kinky hairs from the tub. Patricia came in with a rush, her head slightly bent forward, like a battering ram about to knock down the wall of a besieged city.

"Beast! Kodiak bear!" She began to undress and his attention became fixed on her movement as she pulled her black blouse over her head. Her voice became indistinct. If only she could remain fixed forever in this motion of self-liberation, of appeal and of helplessness. Then he shaved while she refilled the tub and sat in it and chased little ripples toward her throat. In the mirror he saw her head above the water, her eyes closed, and he whispered to himself, "Because you love you shall be loved, and in the end your lovers will drown."

"What are you whispering?" she asked.

"I was only mumbling."

"Translate it for me."

"I will remember Jerusalem at the height of my joy."

"What does that mean?"

"It is written on wedding announcements. It means that Jerusalem should weigh heavily on joyful occasions."

"Tomorrow I will make you a nice breakfast. You know, we must learn to be more ruthless."

"Yes, Patrice, in dealing with life."

For a moment there was only the splashing of the water; then she said quietly, "I know you visited your wife. You must love her; her name is the same as little Ruth's. I am not complaining. I understand you and I hate your weakness—and mine, too."

"We must not lose each other."

"The honest finder will be rewarded."

"To whom should he return the loss?"

"You to me and me to you."

Patricia rose from the tub and water dripped from her. Her body was like the bodies of the women of ancient Greece; her hair was gathered up on top of her head.

After she dried herself, they sat naked in the kitchen. The coffee began to bubble in the glass percolator. She sat opposite him and, putting down her cup, she touched the tip of his nose with her finger. "You still have ancient jars and broken pottery and idols and excavations in your head."

He pursued the thought: And broken columns and brass utensils; all these become valuable after they have been in the ground a long time. Patricia's head, which he held in his arms, was only for him and only for this time. It was wonderful to be with her, wonderful beyond all desire. But it would also be wonderful to leave her now. This would be an opportunity to go on living after death. Soon she will sit up and deliver one of her orations on the loneliness of her life before she met him. But loneliness is also a fruit of life, a sweet fruit at the end of a branch. "You are innocent," he will say to her. "I, innocent?" she will ask with wonder. "Yes, despite everything."

Later Joel walked through half-deserted streets to the bus station, where the floor was greasy with black lubricating oil. In the adjoining garage buses were being washed down and he could hear the streams of water beating against their metal sides. The station manager sat bowed over his time-tables. The last bus for the night stood near the platform, its motor idling. Only about half its seats were occupied by sleepy passengers.

He assisted Ruth into the bus and put her suitcase on the overhead rack. A man blind in one eye was selling pea-nuts.

"I am leaving, and this time will be the last. No more coming back. You rejected me. You are fed up with me."

"I neither rejected nor am I fed up."

"I don't know what happened to you. You are not the same."

"I will be going up to Mount Scopus."

"You told me already. Take care of yourself there."

Tears rolled slowly down her cheeks. The motor began to roar. The conductor passed through the bus and asked, "Are you going or staying?" Slowly Joel walked out of the bus, as if against his will and simply in obedience to the conductor. The big vehicle started to move jerkily. Joel stood looking at Ruth's face—she who had been with him in a small tent in the Negev, who had waited for him at the entrance to the wadi, who had come to him from the torrid Jordan Valley, who was the daughter of his admired commander, who was his love and his witness. Now she was leaving, "her tear on her cheek," the phrase from Lamentations came to his mind.

The bus moved out and disappeared.

At once he jumped into a taxi as into a last lifeboat and fled to Patricia.

"You came. You came," she whispered, and she was like an animal that had long lain in ambush. "You are a bad agent, man of many terrors. You have betrayed your trust. The lock doesn't work, the toilet seat is broken, the Venetian blind is loose."

"I am going up to Mount Scopus."

She made no comment and drew him farther into the apartment. They sat opposite each other and listened to music. On the wall above them was a woodcut of a Jerusalem alley—a bent old man on his way to prayer. On the opposite wall hung a Chinese print of a dreamy fisherman in his boat suspended between reeds and the moon. A guitar hung on the third wall.

"My mad friend was here. She buys a guitar after every unsuccessful love affair."

She talked of many things without order or sequence—what she had done in the hospital during the day, how she would set up a mink farm, and other wild ideas—and her laughter poured out like wine. Then she sat at her desk and went over some notes that she had been preparing, while Joel waited for her to finish and paced back and forth, and noticed that the contents of a suitcase which had spilled on the floor remained scattered.

And without turning to him she said, "I knew it would be like this, that you would tear me to pieces."

62

I walked along the walls of public parks over which branches hung. Weather vanes turned. This was the day of Henrietta's funeral. I had spent the previous night alone near the river. Now I kept walking so as to forget my weariness. If I sat down, I would fall asleep. I approached people in the street and asked them for directions, and about strange places and what was the meaning of the inscriptions I saw. I got them involved in arguments about the best way to get to places and left them while they were still arguing.

Time stretched but the city diminished, for I remembered it as a child and it was the recollection of small feet. I called the Home for the Aged from a phone booth to find out the hour of the funeral, but the answers I got were confused and contradictory. Mrs. Metzman said that the funeral would apparently be postponed for another day. I couldn't understand why.

Finally I came to the Palace Park. For some reason I had postponed visiting it from day to day. It was here that I first learned about Ruth's accident and it was this park that we passed through every day on the way to and from school. Now that I finally came to it, the cycle of my childhood would be completed and my blood would come to rest.

The big gate was a network of black iron in all kinds of shapes—a crown, a cross, and a shepherd's crook—to symbolize the secular authority of the bishops who were also princes. Iron deer and lions were caught in a tangle of flowers and wheels and laurel plants. Standing before the gate, I put my hand on my heart and looked inside. The garden was unchanged, but I was not the same. At twilight a bell rings to warn the visitors that the gate will soon be locked. It rings a long time so that even those who hide in it or are caught in its tangles can't miss the sound. When we were children, this ringing of the bell used to fill us with delicious terror. What if we were to remain in the park for the night? The old guard would come with his heavy keys and the last visitors would slide through the closing gate. Oh, to remain once for the night, to be locked in, forgotten, among the trees.

My return to the Palace Park of my childhood was, I thought, another doomed attempt to regain the lost Eden. Man conceives of many Edens, and the gates of all are guarded by angels with flashing swords. Now, as I slowly walked into the park, I knew that there was no returning. I have always known this yet am always surprised anew.

My Indian friend once told me: "Our memory tells us that the Nazis had murdered so-and-so many Jews and that the city was destroyed by the American army. Crime and punishment. History will describe the events otherwise. It will say: 'So-and-so many Jews and Germans were killed in the great war.' Here will be a balancing and equalizing of oppressed and oppressors. More distant history, which has to embrace many generations and wars, will say: 'In the middle of the twentieth century a great war raged and so-and-so many people perished in it.' Archeology of times to come will define the event as follows: 'It appears that toward the end of the second millennium or the beginning of the third millennium of the Christian Era a great catastrophe occurred marked by many conflagrations. This is proved by a black, fire-scorched layer and numerous broken iron objects that have been uncovered. The city appears to have been rebuilt.' "

Thus spoke my Indian friend. Now I turned back to look

at the gate one last time. It was still wide open. When it closes behind me, I will know that little Ruth is locked in this park of our childhood amid the fountains of death and the lawns of conflagration, and beneath the clouds, one of which is hers because it was formed from the smoke of her burning body. I walked down an alley bordered by citrus trees in huge pots. These trees seldom produce fruit, and when they do it doesn't ripen. But I was happy with these trees which come from my homeland, like Jesus, who is also from my country.

I heard the voices of children pleading with their parents: "A little longer. Let's stay a little longer." I descended slowly in the glory of my sorrow, like a monarch of sorrows, down a broad stairway bordered by engraved red sandstone columns. My feet remembered and led me to a plaza surrounded by a hedge. Stone benches formed a circle and in the middle was a stone platform with a balustrade. Here a military band occasionally played for the public. I sat down on one of the benches. Once, when I was still quite small, I witnessed here a fatal battle between a butterfly and a hornet. At first the two insects were a tangle of legs and wings struggling madly. Then the triumphant hornet ripped the wings off the butterfly. The branches of a chestnut tree waving softly cast a pleasant speckled shadow on the battle whose image sank deep within me.

At that time I still believed in reward and punishment. Near this plaza there was a maze of paths, and it was here that I was told of Ruth's accident. During the first moment of shock, I feared that the accident was part of the system of reward and punishment, for Ruth had invited handsome Heinz to her Hanukkah party but not me, because of the squabble we had had when I accepted the role of Judas Maccabeus against her advice that I reject it proudly.

From a pool rose a boulder covered with dripping green

moss. On it were statues of cloven-hoofed satyrs carrying heavy-fleshed women struggling in terror and lust not unlike the butterfly in its battle with the hornet. Once, as I was staring entranced at this group, my school principal passed by and I failed to notice him and to tip my cap in greeting. "Come here," he ordered me. I went to him expecting a slap in the face, but instead of raising a hand against me the pedantic principal smiled and asked, "What's the matter? Do you have birds in your cap you're afraid will fly away if you take it off?"

I took out some bread crumbs from my pocket and stood motionless with outstretched hand. A red-breasted bird approached. It flew around me cautiously and finally landed on my hand with small nervous feet, and tickled my palm as it pecked at the crumbs. In his day, my father was an expert at bird feeding and it was he who taught me how not to frighten them away.

I heard my name called. Mrs. Metzman approached leading Heinrele and asked me to look after him. When would the funeral be? The time hadn't been set. Relatives might perhaps come. Heinrele stretched out his hand and I put some crumbs on it, but he was afraid of the birds and they didn't come to him. I shut my eyes and almost dozed off standing, for I had not slept for twenty-four hours. Then we walked by the duck pool and the oak trees. Here we used to collect acorns to feed the squirrels. "Now let's go up," Heinrele cried, pulling me up the path. The Palace Park was built on two levels, the lower one being on the ancient city wall. Europeans are lucky—they transform their fortresses into municipal parks. In Jerusalem we preserve every fortress and city wall and all reminders of war.

The smell of smoke assailed me, not the smoke from the crematorium where Ruth was burning but the smell of the first autumn leaves burning. Soon the Jewish New Year would come around. A stone sculpture group along the path showed a child playing with a lion, as in the prophecy of the end of days. Another stone child held up a bunch of grapes while his little stone brother reached for it. "When will the little boy get the grapes?" Heinrele wanted to know. I lifted him up and put him on a stone dog, and he began to cry. Ruth and I used to divide people according to the way they cried. The more aristocratic wept quietly, their faces calm, the tears rolling down their smooth cheeks from beautiful eyes. Ordinary people wept loudly, sobbing and wailing at the top of their lungs. Heinrele was scared.

I recalled the time when it was dangerous for us to go through this park, for the pupils of a large Christian school named after Pestalozzi lay in wait for us and attacked us near the statues, and when they did so we ceased being the heroes of our fantasies and became ordinary children pursued by gangs of Nazi youngsters. Young Wolves, and Hitler Youth, and Young Germany, and tribes and gangs and leagues and unions. When we succeeded in escaping, they would shout after us, "Jew swine! Isaac go to Palestine!"

It started to rain and we stood under a chestnut tree. It was like the rain in Zurich on the first evening of my arrival in Europe. Now, on my last evening, I again heard the rustling of the raindrops on the big finger-like leaves, and thus the cycle of my journey was completed.

Sibyl, who knew that we were in the garden, came and stood with us in the rain. Then I handed Heinrele over to her to take him back to the Home. I wanted to remain alone with the last of my love for little Ruth.

Heinrele cried again and I tried to console him with words, but he was too small to accept words in consolation.

The children left, looking like a brother and a sister in fairy tales, and I sat down on a bench under a tree and the rain stopped. When a man sits on a bench without any purpose, his inner thoughts come to the surface like blood from a cut. I took out pen and paper to write down a number of things before I forgot them. Just then the sun broke through the clouds and the pen flashed back a ray.

I got up. Now I was through, altogether. I crossed the shadows of the trees and they did not hinder me. Nothing would again keep me in Weinburg, neither the trees nor their shadows, nor people and their shadows, neither the living nor the dead.

The bell rang. In half an hour the park gate would be locked for me forever.

I went out into the streets which had new names and new residents. A rustling of paper in my pocket jogged my memory. Of all Manheim's sermons I retained one. I also had a copy of the Gestapo decree expelling the Jews of Weinburg.

I walked in the direction of the Home for the Aged and on the way passed for the last time the site where our house had been and where now stands the big international students' house. I raised one hand as if asking the chairman for permission to speak, while with the other I made a gesture refusing the permission. What was there left to say? And to whom should I speak in this place? I turned right to avoid the ruins of Ruth's house and came to the wall of the Jewish hospital. Before me walked a man whose keys fell to the sidewalk; first he seized his head in despair and only then did he bend down to retrieve them. I entered the yard of the hospital even as I did on the day of my arrival in Weinburg. The chestnut trees confirmed my return. Seeing this, a host of disconnected words flooded me, words like "forever," "for ever and ever," "never again," "till eternity." The words then dropped off like leaves without meaning and without any connection to other words. It was getting dark.

Mr. Cohen's dogs barked in their shed. The dining room was dark, for this evening there would be no TV program. The old people must have gone to bed early, and now they no doubt lay on their backs with open and sleepless eyes. In Henrietta's room lay the body of the old woman, her chin tied in place and her eyes closed after they had been shut.

I sat down in the dark dining room. The clatter of a plate and a fork came from a distant kitchen, then silence. I sat in one of the old folks' chairs. Here I would remain for the night; I would not return to the river. A train passed with a prolonged wail and blurred lights. Tomorrow I would be in such a train on the way to a city where there is an airfield. I thought of my suitcase in the baggage room with a numbered tag on it. Suddenly I thought of a poem I learned as a child, a poem by Goethe about *Der Erlkönig*, the wizard king of the trees, and a sick child whom his father held before him in the saddle on the way home. The trees, the wizard's daughters, wanted to play with him, and the feverish child said to his father again and again: "Father, don't you hear? Father, don't you see?" The father tried to calm him, saying that it was only the rustling of the branches. Finally they reached home, the child dead in his father's arms.

Then I thought of all the expressions used to describe death: "deceased," "departed," "the late . . ." Many words, but death is the same for all men.

I went up to the second floor, where Henrietta's room stood open. Her body lay on the floor and a candle stuck into her Sabbath candlestick burned at her head. In an upholstered chair in a corner Mrs. Munster bulked like a huge mass. She was asleep and snoring, and a woman's prayer book lay open on her knees. She read it the way sleeping people read. Only now did I look at Henrietta's dead face. All my childhood was concentrated in this peaceful face, the street of my father's store was impressed on Sibyl's face, and the face of my wife held all my life in Israel, the wars, the desert, the happiness of the hills of Jerusalem and the shores of the sea. My life is becoming ever more concentrated, and from now on it will only be necessary for me to look at a few faces to have it before me.

Mrs. Munster in her dark corner began to utter slow, heavy words. A freight train carrying loads wrapped like corpses passed outside. "They go and go," Mrs. Munster said. "This is their punishment, that they should be moved about and around. How do they say it? Turn the other cheek. Touch Henrietta's cheek."

I touched the dead woman's cheek. The skin was cold and the flesh underneath seemed to have sunk out of reach. "When is the funeral, Mrs. Munster?" I asked. "Tomorrow morning—on account of the relatives."

She has no relatives. The soul of her husband may come. He was in Theresienstadt, and they didn't let him return to the camp when he came back from a funeral, and they sent him *there*.

I didn't know what more to say, and sat down on a stool near the wall where my picture hung. In this picture I was six years old and stood in the entrance of a *sukkah* holding a small *lulab*. I confessed to Mrs. Munster that as a child I used to steal the pictures of athletes from packages of margarine. The corpulent old woman said, "What for? All those who took part in the show 'Eliezer at the Well' are dead— Eliezer and Laban and Rachel and Rebecca and Esau and Jacob. And Judas Maccabeus, too, and Lysias and Antiochus and Esther and Ahasuerus. The heroes of all the shows are dead. All."

I said, "In the Bible and in shows everybody dies at the end."

She said, "But not of typhus and not in the snow. The

trains were running then and soldiers were being moved and the prisoners were freed. Only a single Russian officer stayed with me and told his friends to go on and not to wait. My daughter Clara died on my knees. The officer told me: 'Think of yourself.' He spoke Russian and I don't know Russian, but I understood him just the same. Then a high-ranking officer came and shouted and the young officer shouted and pointed at me, and I shouted and pointed at Clara. We all shouted but each for a different reason, just as everyone died from different causes."

I went out and then returned to Henrietta's room for one more glance at my childhood reflected in her face. The candle had burned out and a new one was lit. The dark bulk of Mrs. Munster said, "Listen, you are Clara's friend; here I have a train timetable. I can tell you which train to take after the funeral."

Now I noticed that the book on her knees was not a woman's prayer book but a German summer railroad timetable. We turned its pages and planned and calculated like a couple of cabalists.

Sister Maria came in, silent and bat-like. "I am glad you are here," she said. "Sister Elizabeth sent you this snapshot of Ruth." I took the picture and walked out, for I didn't want to turn on the light in the room where Henrietta lay. I went into the bathroom. The glazed tiles and the mirror doubled the light. It was a picture of Ruth taken on the day of her deportation. Her face was rounded and her cheeks looked childish still. There were shadows on her temples. Her eyes looked straight forward, clear and proud and courageous. The woolen scarf around her neck was carefully and neatly arranged, as was her custom. Her hair was combed back behind her ears, and curled forward under her ear lobes. On her chest was a small sign with her number and the number of her transport, not unlike the numbered tag on my suitcase in the checkroom at the station. She wouldn't get lost. Who claimed her after she died? Who came with a checking stub and claimed her ashes? On the lapel of her coat was a star of David with the word *Jude*.

The instructions given to the deportees were precise. The star had to be a prescribed size and sewn on at a precise place between chin and belt. The small sign given to the deportees was already punched in two places. "Each deportee must provide his own string," the instructions read.

I put the snapshot in my pocket and wiped my tears off. The tears were really not mine—merely a matter between my eyes and the yellowing snapshot, just as Ruth was now merely a piece of cardboard in my hand.

I turned out the light in the bathroom and returned to the two old women, one dead, the other not yet dead. Once more I touched Henrietta's rough cheek. Mrs. Munster said, "And now we will try the case and hear witnesses." The nun said, "All are guilty." Ruth confirmed, "All are guilty," and gave the names of people. A train passed outside. Trains don't mention names; they only click as they pass over track joints. "Anyone want to add something?" Mrs. Munster asked. Then she herself added: "The water is flowing; the waters are rising; a fisherman sits on the bank." "This is by Goethe," Ruth said quietly. The nun said, "He who does not eat his bread in tears, may the powers of heaven not know him. This, too, is from Goethe." I said, "The child died in his arms. This also is by Goethe."

Ruth suddenly reminded me that I once cheated her in a game of marbles. "That's not so; I did not cheat," I protested. "You haven't changed," she said. "That has nothing to do with this trial!" Mrs. Munster cried. "You are evading the issue." "The priest is to blame; he hid in his vestments," the nun announced. "Clothes make the man," the old woman quipped. Ruth remarked, "Soon it will be fall; they are already burning leaves down the street. No one pitied me when I went to the train in the fall and leaves were being burned. I was among the last, on account of my leg, because I limped."

A tear rolled down Mrs. Munster's dead cheek. Ruth whispered, "It is artificial, like my leg." The old woman began to rock back and forth like a keener of ancient times.

63

Where did the seashore smell of sand and salt come from suddenly? Joel lay on his back in Patricia's small room and covered his eyes with his arm. He heard the ticking of the clock and water dripping from a faucet and knew that Patricia had not yet returned. Many times he had come to her apartment to await her return from the hospital. Strange, he thought, that we were never together by the sea. All the time we have remained in Jerusalem, locked in this little apartment of the Kleins'. We were neither by the sea, nor in Venice, nor in railway stations, nor at airports where we would have to shout at each other over the roar of jet engines. Nor did we lie together in the warm sand, and I did not see her on the yellow sand, her knees drawn up, her legs like a tent in the heat of an afternoon.

He daydreamed about the tourists' Venice. They sit together in a café, and a young waiter, curly-haired and insolent of face, a mixture of angel and billy goat, waits on them. Or another fantasy: Patricia suddenly returns. "Patricia?" "Yes." "I went to the hospital and the doorman wouldn't let me in." "I am glad you are here. Let's be quiet." " 'My true love'—isn't that how you say it in English?" "Yes, 'My true love.' " "Meaning that there is also another kind of love?" "People say I am destructive. You look like a Roman." "When in Rome, do as the Romans do." "When in Rome, do as Joel does."

Thus Joel's waiting heart dreamed. He will forget her clothes, her colorful skirts, her underthings of all kinds, starched and lace-trimmed or made of net cloth so that when she walks in them she seems to be floating, and he will forget her blouse which buttons in the back, and the golden thread woven into the sleeveless black blouse; he will forget how she pulls the blouse over her head and how on warm days she goes about in a blouse that covers very little, how she slips out of her skirt so that it lies about her feet like a pool of cloth and she steps out of it and her bare feet slap against the cool floor. He will forget how she closes the zipper at the side of her skirt, and her somewhat old-fashioned blouses with collars firmly buttoned; the sound of her sandals as she throws them to the floor when she is tired, and the click of her high heels as they beat against the stones of Jerusalem. He will forget her manner of speech and how she laughs and cries alternately. That is, he will not forget all at once. At first he will simply forget to remember, and then he will forget altogether—her wide sailcloth skirt and her white summer things; the skirt with a broad Spanish sash that reaches almost up to her bosom; her happy skirt and her sad one, and the lace skirt enclosing her wild brown body which suggests a peasant woman and also an untamed mare. He will forget the clothes that cling to her body and those that are wide and airy and cool, and the winter sweater of Scottish wool, thick and soft, its turtle neck flaring widely. He will even forget the white handkerchief which she inherited from her grandmother and of which she would say when they lay naked together, "What can one cover with it?"

He heard the key turning in the lock and pretended to sleep. He heard her go into the bathroom and then tiptoe into the room where he lay. Near the bed, she knelt and folded her hands because of much happiness. He heard her walk out and saw her come back with a green towel. Then he heard her undressing until it seemed that the whole room was filled with her clothes.

"Where have you been?"

"You scared me, darling. I thought you were sleeping. I was by the sea. Why don't you come with me sometime?"

"Let me smell you. You are tanned. There was a smell of the sea here all along, before you came."

"Jealous? Silly. There is no one but you."

She shook sand out of her hair and her skin was hot and smelled of salt.

"You are jealous of the sea?"

"Just jealous."

She showed him the new sandals she had bought, with rope soles and gold straps.

She went out again and he heard the rustling of her movements. When she returned, he again pretended to have dozed off, and as she quietly seated herself near him he seized her about the hips and with a single motion of his arms pulled her down on the bed. She laughed and sighed. No, no, and they struggled and wrestled, as on the first night when he was a bull and she a matador, for in a strange way their love preserved the way of that first night when, in their great confusion, they did not know how to begin touching each other.

And they tried to cause each other pain, and the laughter died out, for the sense of pain remained the only thing that could still measure up to their love. She embraced his head and whispered, "Mine, all mine, I have a right to you, to your arms and belly and eyes. You are mine; I won you in a deal with life."

He tickled her and she became a fish struggling in a net. And she called him names, "Wild bull, buffalo, big bear." He seized her hair and pulled her head backward so that her chin rose, and he bent over her heavy and big and powerful and came to her, and then they lay spent and the smell of the desert mingled with the smell of the sea and she curled up like an animal and fell asleep.

Joel got up, driven by the vision of the tearful face of his wife Ruth in the bus window. Without waking Patricia he went out into the street on the way home. His attention was alert as he looked about him. A traffic signal stood bent from a collision a couple of days before. Footsteps echoed in the deserted side streets. The later the hour grew, the more fateful and final and uncompromising these steps became. Many times during the night, he walked between his home and Patricia's apartment. Once, he noticed the light from a shuttered window fall in stripes on the pavement. Another time, the clicking of high heels against a sidewalk receded and was lost in the silent darkness. Cats wailed and prowled around garbage cans. A breeze came from the unseen valley. Invisible bicycles rang their bells in the distance. Someone was staying up very late; someone was up very early. In a fish store which he passed, water whispered in the live fish tank. Over the door hung a sign showing a fish dressed as a waiter serving a fish on a tray.

And as he went back and forth, he was aware of stones—stones in the walls and stones on the ground, stones within stones, big soft ones and small hard ones, stones for headstones and stones for stoning, pebbles thrown by hand at cats and dogs that miss their mark and rocks flung in impotent rage, stones that are precious and stones that are not.

At dawn the dairy truck was already parked near the entrance to the alley, and white bottles were handed to the delivery carts. Not a soul was seen; there were only the bottles being passed from one vehicle to another and the forlorn sound of their tinkling. And once he stood near a window in his home holding a couple of screws that had come out of a piece of furniture, and these, too, testified to his anxiety and struggle. Only after it became light did he return to Patricia and they slept. Once he awoke and an unuttered cry filled him: "My God, my God, why have You forsaken me?"

64

Once I awoke with the cry "My God, my God, why have You forsaken me?" And immediately after I cried, "My God, my God, why have You not forsaken me? Why didn't You leave me in my peace, without vengeance and without love?" My bones ached and my heart was empty, and I rose to my feet in confusion.

I saw that the gates of the hospital were open and the pallbearers came carrying the coffin. Mr. Metzman and some of the construction workers from the neighboring building carried it. Mr. Metzman was the only strong Jew left in the city, and therefore the assistance of German laborers was needed to bear the coffin to the black hearse. Some of the old people touched the coffin, thus fulfilling the commandment to honor the dead. A train passed and let out a cloud of steam which enveloped everything. When the steam cleared, Henrietta's meager funeral cortege had already passed. It was just as well that they hadn't noticed me, for I didn't want to take part in the funeral.

Henrietta! Henrietta! You are being carried away from here, and so am I. You are being carried to the abyss of absolute certainty, while all my life is a constant falling from one error into another. Go, go, Henrietta, reminder of my good childhood. Your life was sad and your cheeks were never soft and smooth. Your eyes spoke of the weight of exile. Go, belated victim of the death camps. The number tattooed on your arm will stand you in good stead where you are being taken.

Then I went to the railway station and took a last look at Saint K. pouring his blessings, together with water from his fountain, with great love. I picked up my suitcase and walked through the underpass. The shoeshine man was not there. I stood on the platform awaiting the train that would carry me away like a flowing river. I no sooner stepped into the car than the train started. I looked out of the window and saw Melvin come running and waving his arms. I was glad of the chance to see him one last time. He shouted something but I couldn't make out what because of the noise and the growing distance. I despaired of hearing him and allowed the city of Weinburg to slip behind me.

On the outskirts of the city, the train came to a sudden halt. The tracks were apparently being repaired. Another train slowly passed by us, and the faces of its passengers looked at me out of their remote lives. They were going to Weinburg, while I was going away from it. Again the train moved slowly. Laborers stood near the track. The good river alternately approached and receded. The first forest came into view. Another group of workers stood watching the passing train as if it were fate passing before their eyes. The woods and the fields provided a wonderful backdrop, but I no longer believed in forests and lakes and pastures or in women hanging out the wash. We entered a tunnel, and when we emerged from it the landscape had changed and become more hilly. Then the train stopped at a station near a small town.

I saw myself picking up my suitcase and getting off the train that was to have taken me to the city where the airport was. Then I was asking when the train to Bachfeld was due and I was informed that in a quarter of an hour a mountain train for Bachfeld would be leaving the station. I phoned the airline office postponing my flight again. I was becoming fearful that I would never get back to Jerusalem.

The mountain train pulled up at a little-used side platform on a narrow-gauge track and I was on my way to Bachfeld, where my grandparents had lived and where my father was born. It was a small train consisting of three cars. Every so often it halted at villages and scattered estates, and the passengers who got off were hailed with love and cries of joy— uncles and aunts, grandchildren and suitcases and crates. Each station manager was also ticket seller and inspector, and after he passed through the cars and greeted his acquaintances he would look at me in surprise, don the official manager's cap, blow a whistle, and the train would move on. Branches of trees nearby touched the windows as our train climbed grunting and screeching. I saw my reflection in the window move over the receding trees. The peasants spoke with a special German accent, and I found it difficult to understand most of what they said. A child stood in front of a white house and waved a flag to the rhythm of my heartbeat. Over and over, I thought of the great error in which I lived, a recurring error, until death comes and erases all the errors in one sweep. Who knows whether all the people whom I know are not really other than I know them? Even my wife Ruth might be an entirely different woman, and I will discover this when I return to Jerusalem. For Thine is the error, and Thou shalt reign forever. God rules only by means of an error, and leaders of nations rule as a result of error in identity. Because of all these errors, the reflection of my wan face is now being moved over the trees. What strange notion possessed me to change trains at the junction? We arrived at Bachfeld, the native village of my grandparents, and I would have forgotten to get off, except that this was the last stop on the line. I was the last to detrain. The dark forest reached to the very station. When I got off, the station manager removed his hard uniform cap and became an ordinary human being. He shut the ticket window and locked the station doors, for there would be no other train till the following morning. Then he said something to me but I could not understand him; I could only distinguish here and there expressions like "God willing," and "in God's name." In these districts people often mention God and His will. What is God's will with me here among the aromatic fir trees of Bachfeld?

I walked through the streets of Bachfeld. This must have been God's will. I passed by plunging little streams that tumbled down impatiently from the mountains. I crossed small bridges where I put my suitcase down for a moment to rest and listen to the gay bubbling below. Now I came to the village center and I passed by the few stores that follow the same order in all villages: bakery, butcher shop, tavern, drugstore, dry-goods store, tavern, and finally church. This is an orderly country and everything is in its proper place—mountain, estate, forest. Though I did notice some modern houses and two American soldiers coming out of a bar.

I went into the Deer Hotel instead of the Post Hotel. Near the entrance, a sign proclaimed that this hotel was approved by the Society of Followers of Dr. Kneip's Therapy. I didn't know what this doctor's therapy consisted of, but I figured that no therapy could do me harm. I entered the hotel restaurant. A fleshy pink waitress was setting the tables for dinner. From the keyboard I noticed that there were no vacancies; therefore I was particularly firm when I ordered, "A single room, please!" The woman became flustered and declared that though the house was full she would arrange quarters for me in an attic room. She smiled and added by way of explanation that people from all over the world came here. I informed her that I, too, came from all over the world. This pleased her and she called to a girl who was helping set the tables to finish up and show me to my room. The girl led me up stairs that creaked anciently and pleasantly to a door that groaned as it swung on its hinges, and into a room with a sloping ceiling. Lena, for that was her name, opened the window and the room was filled with the smell of firs and grass and manure, in addition to the smell of wood and starch that hung in it from before.

Lena went out and soon returned with a large porcelain jug and a towel, which she placed on a low stand. "Goodbye, Mister from all over the world," she said, "and if you need anything, ask for Lena." She went out and I remained by the window, my suitcase still unopened and the folded towel on the stand. The lowing of cattle and the sound of playing children reached me. Near the basement of the hotel was a barn and near that a slaughterhouse; in this hotel people not only lived and ate and drank but also milked cows and slaughtered and butchered them. There was, too, a tavern and shouting over beer and noise from TV. (Eat and drink, for tomorrow we will eat and drink again, and the same on the day after tomorrow.)

In an interval between the roofs I recognized my grandparents' house and yard. I must have looked at it before without noticing it, for I had been standing by the window for quite a while, and only now my heart opened to the view of the narrow alley paved with round stones and the outdoor steps that led to Grandfather's house. There had been a barn on the basement floor which was reached from the house by a trap door from the kitchen. There used to be light in the living room and people sat quietly at table around the cheerful lamp. Night mist would drip down from the mountains around the village, and outside there would be the sound of wooden clogs and carts passing.

Grandma died long ago at the hands of God and not at the hands of beasts against His will. Her death began with an incident that occurred during my childhood. Once I visited my grandparents during the winter, and Grandma filled a hot-water bottle to put in my bed. Somehow it slipped out of her hands and my feet were slightly scalded. Ever since then, her hands shook and the process of her death began as God willed it. Maybe I will visit the house tomorrow.

But what have I to say to those below who are now bent over their dinner around the heavy table like a conference of the dead?

Lena knocked on the door. "Mister from all over the world, do you want to come downstairs to eat?" I asked her to come in. She looked around and clapped her hands "You haven't even unpacked your suitcase. Let me help you." I refused her offer and followed her downstairs. The hotel owner greeted me at the door. "You are lucky," he said. "Today we slaughtered some animals and there is fresh bloodwurst. People come here from all over the world." A big wolfhound confirmed his master's information, and the man cried, "Tasu! Tasu! Here. Come here!" And to me: "I like a dog to be strong and vicious and aggressive." Then he opened the dining-room door for me.

I saw heads floating amid clouds of steam and tobacco smoke, and sat down in the only vacant place. My neighbor was a manufacturer who had become wealthy during the *Wirtschaftswunder*. He said, "Every year I come here to the mountains and fir forests to rest and to take Dr. Kneip's water treatment." Somewhat later we were joined by a young Norwegian who was a gliding enthusiast. Near Bach-feld there is a mountain from which gliders take off.

Later, when the hotel guests settled down in a semicircle around the TV, I went outside. Lena saw me going out and said, "Going for a little walk in Bachfeld?"

"Yes."

"A walk all over the world?"

"A walk through all the worlds."

A light was on in Grandma's house. Along the outside wall still stood the bench on which the old people used to sit at twilight until the aroma of the earth from below and the night from above closed in on them and silenced them. I walked on till I came to a small square; many lights and voices poured out of a milk bar where all kinds of strange juices and ices were served in peculiarly shaped glasses. "Oh, this generation," an old peasant who had stopped alongside me muttered. "They no longer know the taste of good beer. Call these young people? Not our kind at all."

I sat down among young people and American soldiers and drank a foamy strawberry milk shake topped with cream and thought that these young people had done nothing during the time of the Nazis. So I drank a chocolate milk shake with cherries. Then some young glider enthusiasts came and talked in many languages, and I, who came from all over the world, understood all of them.

I wiped the foam off my mouth and resumed my wandering in the village. Unlike Weinburg, little had changed here since my childhood. Here is the house of Mr. Katz, who served as teacher, cantor, and ritual slaughterer. I can still see him leave the classroom near his house to go into the kitchen and put a pot of milk on the fire, because his wife was too busy with their numerous children. And opposite is the house of Aunt Yetchen, Grandma's younger sister. Her house was always spotless; no one sat on its chairs or cooked in its dishes or slept in its rooms. Two weeks after her wedding, her husband was killed in the war.

I returned to the hotel. Near the keyboard was a sign: "Tomorrow we will celebrate the fiftieth anniversary of the founding of the Bachfeld Sports Society with a gala field day." Some of the drinkers and smokers still sat about the television set in the dining hall. Somebody won a basketful of canned goods in a quiz. He dropped the basket and the cans rolled all over. Then they switched to a broadcast from a circus in some big city. There was Leonora in the circus performing on her skates. She doubled over, then shot forward and circled the arena peacefully. From now on, whenever I suffer from insomnia, I will think of Leonora gliding on her skates. What are her plans now? I miss her even though I did not fall in love with her.

I left the dining hall and asked Lena to prepare a warm bath for me. She took her bunch of keys, and we went down to the basement where the facilities for Dr. Kneip's water therapy were. We passed through corridors paved with white tile. Now and then a door opened and someone would totter out on wooden clogs wrapped in a huge bath towel. Then the hallway widened into a small room. Here a number of men and women circled round and round in a small shallow pool. The men had their trouser legs turned up; the women held up their skirts. It appeared that this was part of the Kneip treatment and helped regulate the circulation and calm the nerves. I stopped to watch them walking in the water and I observed their earnest faces. Then we turned in to another hallway where steam issued from under the doors and alarm clocks rang. A man in a white smock said to Lena, "Number seven has finished." Lena reset the clock with the number 7 on it and said to me, "Now you start. Use your time well. The clock will wake you."

We returned to the pool by way of the corridor. On a

bench lay a man, his skin all flushed, and crouched over him, like Cain over Abel, another man in a white robe kneaded his back. In the pool the water walkers had changed. Three young girls now circled in the water, raising their skirts higher than necessary and certainly higher than prescribed by Dr. Kneip, who was a good Christian and a moral man. The treatment booths were now emptying. Alarm clocks sounded like mad birds in a forest of streams of water, and steam rose up like a fog. Herr Keitel, owner of the local garage and vice-chairman of the Bachfeld municipal council, emerged from the Turkish bath sighing in contented exhaustion. Over all was the smell of dampness and forests after a rain, and of wet boards, steaming damp towels, and sweat-absorbing powders.

As I went into booth No. 7, I heard Herr Keitel talking to the three girls and heard their ringing laughter and screams of delight as he teased them about participating in the field day as wrestlers.

The water in the bathtub rose and lulled me pleasantly till I sank into the depths of memory of what I had done and into the abysses of what I had not done. Then I stepped out of the tub and wrapped myself in a toga like a Roman and recalled that strange last evening in Itzhak and Mina's house, when all my friends had seemed like Romans before the decline, and within me had ripened the decision to flee my sinking life in Jerusalem and go to Weinburg to exact a belated vengeance and then to return to Jerusalem strengthened and unraveled like a complex riddle that had been solved. The three girls and Herr Keitel now quietly circled the pool in accordance with Dr. Kneip's instructions, and I went up to my attic room with the sloping ceiling. The lights in the house had already been turned out and I literally climbed into bed over a towering mound of pillows and sank into it.

According to the testimony of the calendar and the list of phone calls I made to the airline, it seems that I stayed in Bachfeld another two or three days. During that time, my only human contact was with Lena. She was nineteen years old and could not have taken part in the hounding of the Jews. So I could resign myself completely to the landscape and my childhood without having anything to do with any other people. I walked in places that bore strange names like the Red Swamp, the Black Forest, Deer Crossing, Rabbit Run, Cross Height, Mary's Hill, Elm Heights, Black Well, Valley Mill, Watch Hill. I lay in forests and listened to sounds made by gay or frightened creatures; the sounds are the same. Pine needles gave off their aroma as I crushed them. A pine needle, I was taught long ago, was a leaf that had become hard and sharp for purposes of survival. What form will I acquire considering that I do not wish to survive in this form? My life is too short for me to become hardened and sharp. I remain a leaf which will shrivel and fall off and be borne by the wind aimlessly and to no purpose.

65

During the last days before he went up to Mount Scopus, Joel used to wake at dawn and at once begin to seek for words such as, "These are the last days, Patrice." Or, "It's the end, Ruth; this is the end." The words did not come from inside him. They seemed to lie outside and he reached for them with sudden awakening the way a man alarmed out of his sleep feels around in the dark for his shoes and clothes.

The scorching days of late summer had lost all shape for

Joel. Day became mixed up with night and the hours lost their sequence. All that remained was his grasping after the last remaining reality, Patricia's body. There were days when his life was completely automatic, the way it is described in foreign-language primers: "He gets up in the morning. He washes his face. He combs his hair. He eats breakfast. He takes his briefcase. He goes out. They go out."

On one of these dream-like mornings he attended a staff meeting of the archeology department. The discussion revolved about plans for the next season, and also about his going up to Mount Scopus: what he would have to look for, what to pack up for shipment below, what conditions of the place to note. What was to be done in the future? They had already explored all the ravines, examined all the caves, climbed into mountain crevasses with torches. They had unearthed the spearheads and the pottery shards and the blackened layers of cities that had been burned in a single night. They had climbed on rope ladders to inaccessible peaks and had been lowered by rope to the depths of the earth to disturb the past from its sleep.

Joel said, as his arm rested on the map table like a strange limb not of his body, "Archeology is a science that thrives on wars and on the dead, like the hyena or the hawk. A city that is destroyed by instant catastrophe leaves traces and 'finds.' A city that grows slowly and dies slowly disappears without trace, like the body of a happy man."

They accused him of nihilism and destructiveness and defeatism and indulging in love affairs and neglectfulness. And Yoske remarked that Joel might yet become a poet, like Imron.

But Joel thought, Love leaves no remains; only the remains of war are left in the earth.

It would be strange to be on Mount Scopus once again. He could often see the white buildings on the mountain shining in the light of the setting sun but separated from him by all sorts of mine fields and no-man's-land strips and enemy areas. Jerusalem preserves everything, including a university campus with no students and a hospital without patients. It is not necessary to dig in Jerusalem.

He was given instructions like a man being sent to another planet. Somebody remarked, "Final instructions," and the others laughed, but for Joel this laughter opened doors and gates and extended into hallways and corridors in all of which he looked for Patricia.

The first clouds of summer's end, which that year came early, cast their shadows on the city and on its hills, so that Jerusalem seemed camouflaged for war with spots that moved constantly.

All this Joel noticed as he sat at the meeting; then he went out into the city swept along by his blind search. It was very hot. If it wasn't for this blazing heat, he thought, it would be easier to think calmly and reach decisions.

Klein had returned to Jerusalem alone. His wife remained abroad. The end of the world and the blood bath which he had prophesied had not come to pass, and he returned wearing a bow tie and rimless glasses.

Since Klein had come back, Patricia left the apartment and returned to the little hotel surrounded by jasmine bushes. There Joel sat with her on the balcony while a curly-haired and insolent-faced waiter served them cold drinks. Then she would disappear from his sight, or he from hers, and the blind search would start over again. Thus, wandering around, he once came to the end of the city opposite the Old City wall and stood on the bridge spanning the Sultan's Pool. The dogs in the nearby animal hospital howled. It was a late Friday afternoon and the streets were empty; the houses had soaked up all the inhabitants. One man stood shaving near a window in the last house; then he pulled the shutter closed and the hillside was completely deserted. A field of thorns on the opposite side stretched as far as the proud gray wall of the Old City that had been built by Saladin.

Near a gas station a hearse stood parked. And not far off was the little synagogue bearing the name "Peace and Friendship." A thin wall separated the synagogue from the sooty military shower room used by soldiers stationed here during emergencies. A garbage pit was filled to overflowing. An institution for abandoned children bore the sign "OUR HOPE" over its door. A torn placard announced the death of Dr. Shlesinger, a friend of Joel's dead father. A generation is dying. No man dies alone or loves alone; his generation is born with him and accompanies him in his loves and in his death.

As he sought Patricia, he learned much about Jerusalem, discovering devious paths through yards of hallways. Finding himself in one quarter of the city, he might pass through a hallway and cross a balcony and be in another quarter. He walked through fields of thorns and bent low as he passed under lines of drying wash. Children played near an empty house and one of them discovered the carcass of a dead cat. They formed a circle about it and sang at the top of their lungs. Where is Yosel now, he wondered, the man with the mermaid tattooed on his arm to cover his concentration-camp number? Einat, too, seems to have vanished, and also Mina, and Itzhak was abroad on some mission. Where are they, all those who had been swept up by the wave of his generation, full of the joy of life, arms waving, crying out to one another? They had been like the heads of swimmers in the sea. Heads rising out of breakers. Now the wave had smashed against the shore and everyone was on his own, looking out for his personal salvation or attending to his individual joys, and the roar of the breakers deafened and further isolated them.

A crazy beggar came along and a crowd of children at once surrounded and taunted him. Children are like hawks and hyenas, who smell a carcass from a distance; they sense the unusual and the weak spots in the armor of the grownups. Madmen and beggars are weak spots through which the children break through. First they test them with simple questions: "What time is it?" "Where does this road go to?" "Where is the bus stop?" Then follow insults and taunts, and finally stones.

A couple of the children scanned Joel and returned to taunting the crazy beggar. Joel is still armored with the aura of respect and does not have to fear the children's instinctive discovery that he is sinking.

How was it then? How did it feel when his hands held her thighs? It is impossible to reconstruct such sensations, even though within a few hours one is to experience them again. Everything that is done becomes absolute past, not as in the English language, which offers possibilities of escape into continuing pasts and futures, and past within past, and past within future. In Joel's awareness the past moment was like the past of thousands of years ago. For was he not an archeologist? And tomorrow he would go up to Mount Scopus. To prolong the time, he divided it into hours—another twenty hours, another fifteen. Then he divided the remaining time into quarter hours, thus causing an inflation of time; he arrayed the remaining minutes as one arrays an army in the face of enemy fire, and though the casualties are heavy, sheer numbers make the enemy appear remote.

He got as far as the Sports Club, which was surrounded by tall pine and eucalyptus trees. Once upon a time, this was an aristocratic establishment. Officers and officials of the mandatory government played cricket and tennis here. In the days of its glory the club had eight tennis courts. Now Joel entered through one of the numerous breaks in the fence. These breaks lent a certain pathetic irony to the main gate. The club itself had not changed, but the paths on the grounds revealed the anarchy that reigned during the last days of the mandate. Branches that had fallen off trees in preceding winters blocked the paths between the courts. The courts themselves showed the effects of the inroads of children playing soccer, of dogs, and of pairs of lovers. The courts had also become the stamping ground of street urchins and the hoarse young people of the youth movements.

He distinctly heard the sound of the slamming of a racket against a tennis ball. He could not see the players. They could have been ghosts playing, the ghost of the British District Commissioner MacShaw, and the ghost of Judge Pearson, and the police supervisor Smith, or the Anglican priest with the white collar who had been an inveterate tennis player.

In the prevailing silence, the sound of the racket against the ball was like that of a bowstring sending an arrow on its way. Open ditches led as far as the fence. Several children resumed their soccer game on one of the courts whose edges were already crumbling while the middle still remained firmly packed and red from Jerusalem's earth and dust, which the winds and rains of many seasons had drifted on it. Bicycles lay on their sides. Shrubs grew wild, and the well-ordered and straight paths were reverting back to the state of desert paths, as ownerless dogs slowly revert back to a state of wildness. One tennis court was already largely covered with junk, broken stoves, rusty bedsteads. The people of Jerusalem use their beds intensively.

Joel went into the clubhouse. The Sudanese waiter was there as in the past dressed in white jacket, black trousers, and black bow tie. He is the only one left. Some people sat at table playing cards, slamming them down firmly and occasionally arguing excitedly and briefly. Standing by the win-

dow, Joel saw Patricia returning from the only court that
was still undamaged. She noticed him and broke into a run.
He jumped out of the window to meet her and sat down on a
damaged bench. She squatted at his feet and turned her face
up to him, and he raised her up like a king crowning his
queen and set her down on the bench near him. Whom had
she been playing with? He did not ask. Perhaps with her
husband Melvin, who had arrived from Germany, or perhaps
with Major Patterson, who waved his racket from a distance
and cried, "Tomorrow. Tomorrow I will see you at the
Mandelbaum Gate."

The Sudanese waiter brought them coffee, then lit the
lamps over the card tables. Patricia was a woman of summer's end, and summer, exhausted, was now approaching its
protracted end. The earth lay on its back weary and breathing heavily; having contended with the summer for many
months, it now awaited the first rain.

"You are a woman of summer's end."

"You can have me forever. I am flesh and blood, and I am
yours in all seasons."

They left the club and easily slipped through the broken
fence and went to her hotel. Patricia stared forward and did
not see his face, whether it showed signs of staying or of
departure. In the hotel the lights were already on in the
large chandelier.

That night they attained perfection in their love. There
was no postponement by resort to violence as on the other
nights. Life was no longer either vengeance or compensation, but great reconciliation and great peace and endless
love, till the olive trees before their window turned gray in
the first dawn.

66

Some hours later, holding a small suitcase, Joel stood in the plaza at the Mandelbaum Gate alongside the line-up of policemen, U.N. officials, and soldiers of Israel and the Arab Legion. He bought a drink from the woman who was licensed to run a shop in no man's land, a kind of sad and aged Rahab between the fortress walls. His mind was clear. Patricia's words were in his mind like the secret combination to a locked safe. There was that time when she waited for him, seated on the edge of the sidewalk under the light of a street lamp, pleading, "Take me. You can't just pick me up and put me away like some object. Come, we will raise mink; we will start a school for outlandish tongues." She cried then, and her eyes were like messages in the rain. When was that?

Sere grass and thistles grew in the devastated yards on both sides of the border. Major Patterson completed the formalities of changing the police shifts and turned to Joel. They exchanged a few words about Mina, and then Joel was the last to enter the armored car, which was crowded and dark. The trip to Mount Scopus, the mountain of good advice, seemed to last endlessly.

Having arrived, the police lined up in two files, and an official registered their names on a paper which already showed the date of their return to the city. He explained to Joel that the moment one reached Mount Scopus instructions for the descent are given, how and where to turn in mess kits and borrowed books. Slowly Joel walked down the main road of this place he hadn't been in for years. He passed by the abandoned botanical garden, and a building whose construction had been halted midway. He got as far as the National Library without encountering a soul. There he stopped and looked down on the city which lay below, pink and yellow and gray and frozen in its countless stones. He sat down on a stone bench which bore an inscription in English and Hebrew stating that it had been set up in memory of some woman who died in a faraway country.

Having removed their uniforms, the police were dashing about amid the neglected buildings and gardens lugging sacks of flour and crates of vegetables and containers of bread, meantime shouting gaily or irritably. The officer in charge of arrangements found Joel and invited him to a meeting in the office of the commander of the mountain. Such was the title of the man who was in command of this strange island, and there was something ancient about it: the old man of the mountain, the man of the mountain, the king of the mountain, recalling far-off days when every mountaintop had its king. Still busy with his lists, the officer assigned Joel his living quarters in the science building. Huge piles of books were heaped in the room and a head of Einstein looked down from the top of a box. On the blackboard were crude pictures of nude women drawn by the policemen at various times, and the bulletin board still carried yellowed announcements from before the war: a professor of chemistry announced the postponement of his lecture, which was now delayed forever. Joel unpacked his suitcase and on the board he wrote the names of Patricia and Ruth in the form of an equation. Then he erased the names, patted Einstein's forehead, and went outside. From his desk, the officer pointed with his pencil in the direction of the meeting. Smoke, together with the smell of fresh bread, drifted out of what had once been a storeroom. The baker, a fat man, greeted him: "Hello, Mr. Professor. Come have some fresh bread. And you can always get hot water for shaving here. Don't let the commander impose his rules on you. You are not a policeman." He pinched a piece off a fresh brown loaf and held it out. Joel accepted it and walked in and sat down on the baker's bed. Like Joel's bed it had once been a hospital bed and could be raised or lowered as needed. From an adjoining room came the sound of kneading and the slap of dough against a board.

The meeting was held in what had once been the zoology building. Along the walls still stood moth-eaten and ragged specimens of stuffed animals. Most of the people asked to attend were already there and watched Joel from the balcony as he ran up the steps.

Exactly at the appointed time, a door opened and the commander of Mount Scopus walked in. Without looking at those present he walked up to the table and sat down, and only then did they sit down, too. He put his stiff military cap on the table, his officer's stick on the cap, and then scanned his motionless guests with a severe and contemptuous glance. He cleared his throat with a brief barking cough. One of his eyes was artificial and a scar extended from it down to his ear. He was small and totally bald. Steps were heard on the stairs and the doctor entered. In the same barking tone, the commander called the doctor's attention to his tardiness and added that here on Mount Scopus the regimen was strictly observed and everybody must obey instructions— not excepting civilians, he added, glancing at Joel and at the doctor, who had turned pale. "Is that clear?"

Then followed brief and precise instructions. Everyone had to keep the commander constantly informed of his whereabouts. Certain areas were off limits. "I can be very unpleasant," he warned the assembled. At this point he dismissed Joel and the doctor with the warning "And there must be no tardiness."

The little man coughed, and Joel and the doctor went out. A policeman came to report himself sick, and the doctor went with him. The officer at the door raised a finger in silent greeting. Strange how the medieval knightly custom of raising the visor in token of peace became transformed into the military salute and finally reduced itself to a mere raising of a finger. Only the gesture remained. And this, too, is all that will remain of Joel's love. The embrace will become a mere lifting of the hand in greeting, the memory of an embrace, and then a memory of a memory, an echo of a memory, an echo of an echo.

He stood in the area between buildings that had been built for other purposes and sensed the great idea embodied in this mountain that overlooked Jerusalem and the wilderness of Judea. Dry grass and a small yellow flower grew at his feet, a last attempt of a tortured earth to prove that it was not yet entirely dead. He walked by laboratories whose windows were caked with dust and dry leaves and pine needles. Smoke rose slowly from a nearby valley, and above it the blue sky, which was not really blue but a mere void that rose eternally like the smoke. He passed through an unkempt wood till he came to a rock from which he could observe an Arab village that spread out on the opposite slope. It was a big village crammed with houses and stairways. A caravan of camels and donkeys was entering the village. An old woman sat at the entrance to a hut and ground something in a hand mill. He decided to adopt one of the village houses for special observation. Two young women were leaving it and he watched them. They walked up the slope, disappeared in an alley, then reappeared again and stopped to chat. A window opened over them and a woman's head appeared in it. She said something to the two women beneath her, and they at once walked away till they came to a white house. A dog looked from a window. Another woman shaded her eyes from the setting sun. Two men wearing black headdress were coming up from the valley below the village. They walked together like brothers. Soon they would encounter an old man wearing a white skullcap, who was descending cautiously. Finally they would meet the two young women. Joel watched impatiently for this meeting and meantime he assigned them names.

Then he went down to the amphitheater east of the campus. Grass and thistles had grown on the steps. He sat down and looked at the stage ringed by pillars. Somewhere among the barren hills, someone sang in a gay yet weepy voice. It was a man's voice, the voice of absolute man, whose weeping resembles his gaiety. Here he would sit and contemplate and understand. Here he would examine his life without restraint and separate the places where he had pleasure from those where he suffered pain. For this is all there is to man. As he walked about on the mountain, he found a chair in a wood, a classroom chair with an armrest. On it he would sit and contemplate and be calm and alone and remote from everything, from Patricia, from Ruth, as if these two had canceled each other and he remained alone, purified.

In an inner court some policemen were whitewashing porch pillars and tree trunks. Soldiers and police always whitewash things. Crows cawed overhead. A wheelbarrow lay overturned. From a room nearby came the sound of an old typewriter. The officer had made a mistake in the alphabetical listing of the people who came up the mountain and was retyping his lists. People were shouting advice to a white auto that was backing up: "Hey! Turn right, right—now left."

Joel went down to the avenue of cypresses, then entered the archeology building. In the twilight he saw crates and wrapping paper and jars and statuettes with broken noses. Suddenly he heard footsteps and then a dry cough. The commander stood behind him. "Everything is neglected, eh?

You people can't organize your affairs. Last time we had a professor of zoology here, and he locked himself in the laboratory from the moment he came up and only went out for his meals. You seem to be enjoying all this."

"Yes, a forgotten and abandoned world."

"And you enjoy it?"

A ray of sunlight glanced off the commander's glass eye and emphasized the shadow of the scar. He coughed dryly. "I think very highly of your discoveries of two years ago."

"They were not mine. My teacher Professor Oren made the discoveries."

"Nonsense. Don't be too modest. I know it was your work. Why did you come up to the mountain? Some assistant could do this work."

"I wanted to run away for a while."

"And how do you react to the regimen here?"

"Very well. It gives me a chance to rest. It's like a cast on a broken leg."

The commander laughed and put his hand on the head of a goddess from the Hellenistic period.

"She, too, has to put up with the regime. Also I suggest that you read the permanent regulations; they save much speculation and prevent doubts. Nonetheless we have to be prepared at all times for a sudden breakdown of routine, for a total disarray of all order, for madness."

"Which means that the permanent regulations here are merely a cover for madness?"

"Yes, there **is madness** beneath all the order on this mountain."

His glass eye glinted. Then he struck his stick against one of the crates, raising a cloud of dust. At the door he turned and remarked, "By the way, in half an hour there will be hot water for the officers' shower. You may come. Also, every day between ten and eleven, between checking equipment and inspecting the kitchen, I have a free hour. I'll be glad to see you."

He coughed and went out. Joel remained in the dim room amid antiquities and crates and dust colored by the rays of the sun. A great happiness filled him and he blessed the commander of the mountain whom everybody feared and hated, for he, too, had opened for him many highroads to people and to the world—not only the road to Patricia and to Ruth, to his past and to his childhood, but also to his friends. His anxiety dissipated and he hummed a favorite tune as he began classifying items, and everything seemed clear and resolved and extending to endless horizons.

Then he began writing a letter without a salutation; without addressing it to a single person.

"It seems to me that I have been here in this weird monastery a long time. I share a room with Einstein. His wise head may be having an influence on me. Sometimes I come in my imagination to our room. Sometimes I wait for you to return from the beach. Once you waited for me after a night battle, that time when Avraham was killed. You stood at the entrance to the wadi when we returned at dawn. It was then we decided to be man and wife if we remained alive. We survived and we got married. If I was a physicist like my roommate, I would draw some conclusions from the past few weeks, my wandering from one home to another, my great love for Patrice. Are you still waiting for me? Are you waiting? I have become a gambler with fates. Now, at night, when the police are away at their posts, I am calm and have only to listen to the rustling of the trees. I think of my life and of the upside-down order which it followed. When I was young, I was earnest and dedicated and responsible and mature and wise. Perhaps it was the war, and the unit for which I was responsible, that made me thus, as it did others of my generation. And now that I am successful and enjoy some public recognition, I am an ardent youth again, falling in love and casting everything aside, torn inside and enslaved by passions and swept toward the big sea."

The next day, he again worked in the archeology building, then walked through the neglected garden to the up-to-date hospital buildings, which were also in a state of neglect. Out of curiosity, he looked into the nursing home. In one of the rooms a closet stood open and a pink ribbon still hung from the doorknob. In the hospital garden he sat on a bench overgrown with jasmine and stared at an unfinished building across from him. Heaps of lime lay there and the cement had hardened in its paper bags into solid rock.

A cough interrupted his reverie. The commander stood behind him ominously twirling his stick. His face was severe: "What are you doing here? Don't you know? Haven't you read the permanent orders? What the devil!" He turned away and Joel regarded him as some angry angel, for he had not resisted temptation and had entered the forbidden garden. The following day, when he came to the commander for the appointed conversation, the door was not opened for him, and during the afternoon meeting the little man made some cutting remarks, though without naming names, and he scolded the police officers for the untidy state of their men's quarters and he reprimanded two individuals who were caught shaving with hot water obtained from the bakery, and he threatened severe measures.

Joel again went down to observe his Arab village. This time he concentrated on the school. The school bell could be heard distinctly from where he sat, and he could see the children filing into the building with the teacher at their rear. Two boys who were late came running down the hill. Fatima—that is what he named one of the young women—stood on the roof of her house holding an infant. Then she left the house, still carrying the baby, and walked toward a yellow house. Joel saw her knock on the door but knew that no one would answer, for he had seen the people of the house go out earlier. Nearby a group of men were discussing something; then they dispersed and shortly met again before the coffeehouse. But the door of the yellow house opened after all, and Fatima went in. A few minutes later, a woman dressed in black walked out of the house with Fatima following her, the child asleep on her shoulder and her steps short and gay, as if she were mocking her old mother-in-law. One man was busy digging a pit. At the other end of the village, a man was raising a pile of earth. Shepherds returned to the village in the middle of the day. They left their sheep in charge of a boy. They must have something to tell. From time to time a child came out of the school. Order everywhere. Somebody walked through the olive grove. The olive trees are ancient and half dead; the man walks energetically and turns his face happily toward the breeze. Three women dressed in black leave the village on the road to town. Goats have entered a grove of fruit trees. The village alternately fills up and becomes empty, according to some law of tidal rise and fall, as in a staged ballet—a set of rules governing beat and rhythm, tying and loosening, weaving and unraveling.

In the course of time, he learned to know many of them, the sociable ones and the loners, the unyielding ones and those who walk on their way lightly. And many sounds reached his ears as he watched the village from behind a fence: the sounds made by dogs and the sounds of children at play, the sounds of quarreling and the sounds of song. "What is all this about?" he wrote to Patrice. "What is all this about?" he wrote to Ruth. He wrote: "Some come bringing things and others return them; some pick up and others put down; they pass alongside each other, they form groups, and then they part. They stop for a moment, then flow on; they are swallowed by houses, then are spat out again. What is all this about? I am in a strange world, a world of demonstrated laws, like a laboratory. I feel calmer than usual." "Ruth, I heard that I can get this letter to you through our friend Major Patterson, who is expected here soon. I have recovered a sense of bond with people. I have changed greatly. I realize that doubts may assail me again." "Patrice, there are times when I think I would have to be an artist to act out my decisions."

To Ruth he wrote: "I am here as on a ship. I am returning to you on this ship which is Mount Scopus."

And to Patricia he wrote: "I miss you. I remember the delicate veins on your thighs. Do you remember how we made love on the open suitcase? Where are you now? Mount Scopus is a watershed geographically. A fine parable of my life, Jerusalem on one side and the desert on the other."

To Ruth: "I sit on a schoolroom chair among pine branches that the storm broke off last winter."

To Patricia: "I hung my towel to dry on Einstein's head. The room is large and books lie around in heaps. My bed is a hospital bed. My power of attorney over you is still in force and will never expire. You should hear the yelling and the shouting here. I try to obey the regulations of the little commander in order to placate him. Today I used the wooden shack which serves as latrine, instead of urinating outside. The little man, who is my great friend, happened to pass by and smiled, a severe but almost forgiving smile. I hope that Patterson will give you my letter. You will no doubt ask what my decision is. I love you very much. You have turned my life into a wide-open space where I can gallop. I feel clear inside my heart. My heart is like crystal. I have changed."

Such were the letters and scraps of letters which he wrote. At moments he thought of confiding his problems to the

commander of the mountain, then decided to be content
with his friendship; it was sufficient that there should be a
man like him nearby, a man who makes his rules and announces his regulations and imposes his orders all about
him.

The day came when Major Patterson was expected to arrive in his white U.N. car. Joel was in a cheerful mood. All
his past life seemed like a strange and remote dream. The
heat had subsided a little. Winter would come after all. At
the daily meeting, the glass eye of the commander suggested
reconciliation and affection. Joel wandered through the
overgrown botanical garden. The names of the plants had
faded from the signs, and all the plants were nameless, as all
people are anonymous, their names but weak echoes. He felt
the letters in his pocket which he had prepared for Patterson
to take to town. Through the trees he glimpsed the Dead Sea
far away, and he felt so light and relaxed that he knew anything he might decide would be right. There was not a stir of
motion aside from some branches close by. For Yours is the
kingdom, he thought. I am at peace with myself and with
the world. There was an expression of exaltation on his face.
He believed he would survive till winter.

Just then a mighty explosion rocked the mountain and a
cloud of dust and smoke rose. Far below in the city the echo
of the explosion was heard, but it was thought to be only a
blasting of rocks for a foundation, a sound common during
these days of unbridled construction.

There was the sound of nailed boots running and alarmed
outcries and terse commands. At that very moment Major
Patterson's white car drove in and he rushed to the site of
the explosion. There were calls for the doctor, for a
stretcher. "Careful! There might be more mines!"

The commander made his way to the scene of the blast,
disregarding the shouts about him. After him came others.

When they reached Joel, he was already dead. The doctor knelt near the body; then he raised his face and shook his head sadly. The commander and Major Patterson watched in silence. Then Major Patterson went to his car, where the radio transmitter was already nervously crackling, and spoke quietly: "No, no . . . we don't know. . . . A lecturer in archeology . . . An old mine . . . No, not marked on the map . . . An old mine . . . from another war apparently . . . not of this time. . . ."

67

As I sat in the small peaceful square in Paris at the end of summer, a great forgetfulness descended upon me like grace. This beautiful city was the last stop on my journey. It seemed to me that I had already died and was in a different world. Nor did I know what it was that I forgot, or whence I came. I did know where I was returning—home, to Jerusalem, to my wife, to my friends.

I sat dunking a crumbling crescent roll in my coffee. Now I was alone and no one knew me. Soon I would be among many who knew me and loved me. There was still a little time before the plane took off. I gazed upon the square as I sat at the iron table, the only customer, the only person around, for it was Sunday morning.

How did I get to Paris from Bachfeld? How did I leave Weinburg? How did I leave Jerusalem? Perhaps I left like a glider which has to be pulled at first until the air grasps it under its wings and lifts it up. I, too, was given a lift to go on with my life, to attain peace. And here I was in this small square. It was the end of summer and everything shone with a delicate gold. Here and there the leaves were beginning to put on color in anticipation of falling.

Why was I flying from Paris instead of from Frankfurt, in Germany? One might have thought that I was still pursuing Nazis who had scattered all over the world. But it was also possible that I came here to leave Europe with the taste of Paris in my mouth, just as I had spent some days in Zurich when I came to Europe.

These were good days. Yesterday I checked my suitcase at the Gare des Invalides, the station which serves the airports in the city. I checked my suitcase a day earlier than necessary so that I could leave this beautiful city on foot. It is fitting to depart on foot from a city where one has stayed, to be a wanderer as in olden days.

I did not have to return to the hotel—I had already paid my bill for the two nights I stayed there—so I went for a stroll along the river. Justice, too, is a large flowing river. People pour their petty vengeances into it but its surface remains unruffled, bearing no trace of the fury of action and the rage of violence. It flows calmly and bears on its surface an endless parade of skulls.

Strolling thus, I came to the Gare des Invalides. In contrast to the Sunday-morning quiet of the rest of the city, an inferno of confusion prevailed here. People shouted; baggage was being weighed; children and dogs were underfoot. I went up to the desk with the sign that showed my flight to Tel Aviv and had my suitcase weighed. It was very light; but when I looked for my ticket I could not find it. I searched in all my pockets, I took off my jacket and shook it, I ransacked my belongings, but it was not there. Cold sweat covered me. How could this have happened? The people behind me began to mutter. The clerks became angry and looked at me suspiciously. The big terminal and all the moving things in it were growing dim before my eyes. I stepped aside to let others come up to the desk. What would happen now? I had no money left and the plane was leaving soon. And even if they checked at the office and learned that I had bought a ticket, it might be too late.

At the far end of the swaying tunnel of moving people, I beheld, as in a vision, the face of a woman, and at once my anxiety turned into a great and profound peace. This was the woman from the photographer's show window in Jerusalem, the unknown woman whose hair was piled high on her head and whose lips were full. She looked at me from a great distance, caught by my gaze as by the beam of a projector. We both stood transfixed. I put my hand over my heart; it was the only gesture I was capable of at the moment, and I felt my airplane ticket in my vest pocket, yet I thought that I had looked for it everywhere. I took it out without removing my eyes from the woman at the end of the hall. The bystanders laughed and congratulated me. Someone cried, "A miracle! A miracle!" In a moment, it seemed, some old woman would kneel and bless the Lord and His Son for the miracle. I picked up my suitcase and, my eyes fixed on the woman, I made my way through the sea of humanity, which parted before me.

"Excuse me," I said after a moment's hesitation. "Excuse me, haven't we met in Jerusalem?" She shook her head. "No," she said, and her lips trembled; then she added in a whisper, "But I am coming from Jerusalem. I got here only an hour ago. I am going to the United States, where I live. Possibly we saw each other in Jerusalem during the summer." I told her that I had not been in Jerusalem all summer; I must have seen her face in a photograph. Yes, she agreed, she had taken some pictures in Jerusalem and over her protests her picture was put on display. Now I noticed that she wore a lace blouse of old design and a tight skirt. I raised my hand to replace my heart, which had leaped out.

Together we went into the airline bus which took us to the Orly airport, from which she would take off for New York and I for Jerusalem. The bus left the city. We did not speak. Signs addressed us all along: "Drive Slow! Curve Ahead! Buy . . . Buy . . . Save in the . . . Bank . . ." Red lights detained us and green ones impelled us forward. Then more signs and warnings. There are no prophets in the world today as there were in the days of the Bible, but prophecy remains and has been passed on to warning signs: "High Tension! Caution! Crossroad! Slow Down! No Left Turn! Stop! Go! Go!"

We approached the airport and my throat was full. Flags waved at the entrance, some to welcome a minister, others to bid another minister farewell. The fluttering flags showed the direction of the wind, as did the scarf on the neck of the woman alongside me. A straying curl softened her forehead. We passed the taxiing area, which was full of confusion, the roar of engines tuning up, ear-splitting noise. A plane approached and landed. Near its open door the passengers were still one group, but as they walked toward the building they broke up and separated into slow and fast groups. They were recognized and greeted with a wave of a hand, with a shout of welcome, with wild waving of umbrellas and newspapers; they were being swallowed and absorbed in the passport and customs inspection rooms, and channeled into pipe lines that fed them into their private lives. Never again would they be a company as they had been inside the plane that brought them.

The American woman accompanied me to a desk where I had my passport and ticket stamped. Behind us, waiting passengers sat on upholstered benches apart from one another, staring before them. They had not the strength to approach one another.

We stood near a railing as on the deck of a ship and watched my suitcase moving forward, one among many others. Then we, too, sat down.

I said to her, "Let us go and eat and drink. Let us eat and drink and think." We went to the restaurant. Many sat at the tall narrow tables and ate and drank, yet did not die. Opposite us sat a Japanese in a black suit. Out of a drinking straw he made a stork standing on one leg; then he took the tinfoil from his package of cigarettes and made little beakers and silver mice. These he brought and, without saying a word, put down before us, like a sacrificial offering to save himself from his terrible aloneness. People like him sit in airports all over the world. In all the airports there are glass walls and loudspeakers, for airports are all alike and it does not matter whether big cities or high mountains, forests or factories, are outside of them.

"The Japanese in transition. The American woman in transition. I in transition," I said, "for all have the same expression of looking for something." She turned her head toward me and said that people make many mistakes and are often lost, and have no other assurances than the food in their mouths. All else is uncertain. Then she added, "Your jacket is stained, with plaster it seems," and she wiped the stain with movements that were like sobs.

I went down to the washroom simply to assure myself that there was still time to experience the surprise of seeing her there. I stood between six glass walls. I washed my face six times, and six times I wiped my hands; then I came back. She had not vanished. She was real. She was eternal. For what is eternity in the life of man if not to see for a second time one's childhood, or a woman, or a place?

We ate and drank and had some left over. "You are sad," she remarked. "No, I am not sad," I answered. "It's on account of the thoughts. The thoughts are not sad in themselves, but the process of thinking produces an expression of sadness, no matter what one thinks."

I looked at my watch; there was still time. "Will you ever return to Israel?" I asked.

"I couldn't. It would break my heart. Pay no attention to what I am saying. I am still intoxicated. I don't remember a thing."

"We are in flight and in transition and in retreat."

"Yesterday I was in the Café Dôme drinking all morning."

"I was there, too. Strange that we didn't see each other. But I didn't drink; you shouldn't drink."

She didn't answer. One perfectly shaped tear rolled down her cheek.

People were looking out at the runways. The woman's voice did to my heart what the wind did to her hair. The loudspeaker alerted the passengers for Tel Aviv. We put down the little cups we held and heavily got off our high chairs. A considerate customs official allowed her to accompany me through the barrier. A march was being played in the distance. The minister had arrived and people rushed in his direction. Carpets were spread out. Everything became dim.

We passed through doors bearing the inscription "OUT-SIDERS NOT ALLOWED." Two people like us are never outsiders. Where were we going? How far would this woman be permitted to accompany me through the maze of partitions and barriers and turnstiles? We went down an escalator, and then we were in the final glass cage beyond which was the airfield. My fellow passengers were all here and ready, but I had eyes only for this woman who was not coming with me.

The glass doors were opened and the people began to file out. I opened my briefcase and the wind lifted a sheet of paper from it and blew it away. An official ran to retrieve it, but I motioned to him that it didn't matter. It was Manheim's last sermon, which had remained with me by chance. Rummaging in the briefcase, I came across Clara's comb which Mrs. Munster had given me. Once I had given it to Leonora, but she must have returned it to me without my remembering it, the way Joseph surreptitiously returned the money to his brothers when they came to Egypt to buy food. I gave Clara's comb to the woman. I wished to tell her its history, but there wasn't time. We went outside; but an official would not permit her to go beyond the glassed-in area. I looked at the clouds the way a sailor returning home examines them. The woman said, "One who looks at clouds with such interest will never suffer from hardness of heart or from bitterness." I said, "Soon the flowers will bloom on Jerusalem's hills."

My fellow passengers were already going up the gangplank. I kissed her lips and a tremor passed through me.

I hastened to join my fellow passengers. Mechanics in white overalls were all around like so many angels or doctors, the healers and angels of my life. On the top step I turned around. She still stood in the glass doorway. I entered the plane and took a seat near a window. She was still there. We sometimes talk about a look being returned, but it is never really returned; it is a different look, unlike the young one we sent out.

The engines roared powerfully. The plane was like a man testing his muscles before a wrestling match. The plane was now alone, far from the tower and the terminal, and engrossed in its own affairs. All at once it began to mount its strength and move forward on the ground. A few moments later its roar and trembling increased, and it was like a bull preparing for the final plunge. There was great trembling and wrath and fury in it, and with a force that was unnatural, that was more like the force of angels, it tore itself from the earth and rose. At once we were away from the airport. Below us a shepherd stood wondering as he leaned on his staff. We barely reached our elevation when preparations for the landing began. We had to fill out various forms and did so with great earnestness, avoiding all thought. The hostess talked to me in French as if she were reading from a French primer. I opened the air vent. The woman near me said, "I am not at all impressed by flying; I feel just as I would in a café." These days everyone wants not to sense what is happening to him. On ships the sea is concealed from the passengers so that they should delude themselves that they are in a floating hotel. In planes they are isolated from the air. And love is concealed from lovers.

Such were the thoughts that clustered in the forecourt of my mind. Only as we passed the Alps and flew over a huge cloud that was rent with lightning and thunder did the gates open to my inner mind.

What would have happened had I remained in Jerusalem this summer? Thoughts of what might have been at first filled me with rending pain, which then gave way to a sense of consolation and warm happiness and prayerfulness.

Beneath us was the blue sea, which turned greenish, then white near the shore. Here and there a cloud covered a town or a mountain like a kindly white hand. From time to time we were informed about our elevation and what time it was and over what shores we were passing. Flying over the islands, I was suddenly filled with pride that I had survived the summer.

In Athens we stopped for an hour. We had coffee and I bought a pipe for a friend and perfume for my wife, which I added to the other presents I had been buying for her along the way. These presents were like signposts pointing the way back for me. People talked Greek, and I was glad that I did not understand them and that I was alone. It was hot and we boarded the plane again. Late in the afternoon we passed over an island, and I thought that perhaps someone lay on his back on this island and looked up and said, "Here are some clouds, and a small dark plane," and his thoughts would have matched mine. Then we passed over clouds that were reddened by the sunset, and beneath them and above them it was already night.

Returning, again and again. He who does not go forth cannot return. That which is not begun cannot be finished. To live means to commence and to complete. I felt very light; nothing bound me and I bound no one. Only people like me should fly. I dozed off, then woke again. I opened my briefcase, took out the letters that had been held for me in General Delivery in Paris, and opened them. I regarded them as directives for my return.

There was a letter from Melvin in which he said that he had finally decided to divorce his wife. They would meet in New York, and there make all arrangements for the divorce. I was not surprised. There was also a letter from the Indian. He had been called back to his native land to assume a high government post, but had managed to complete his study of Western despair. Mr. Metzman wrote that a handsome headstone was set up on Henrietta's grave and he thanked me for my donation to the Home. Leonora, it seems, continues her circling and travels with circuses.

I was surprised at myself that I did not feel agitated. All this was so remote, as if I hadn't met these people even in a dream. And already there were cries of "There are the lights of Israel!" Then I opened the last letter, which was from my wife Ruth. She was happy that I was coming back, she wrote, and among other things she informed me that Mina had again returned from a trip abroad. When I fastened the seat belt, I could see my life as from a great height, from its beginning to the end, which was still shrouded in mist.

The plane began to descend gently. How will my life be from now on? Will it be stormy and fateful, or calm with endless peaceful thoughts?

About the Author

Yehuda Amichai was born in Würzburg, Germany, in 1924, and emigrated to Israel in 1936. He was educated in Israeli schools, and later taught in them. Mr. Amichai served in the British Army in World War II, and afterward in the Palmach (commando troops) of the Haganah underground. He saw active service on the Negev front in the Israeli War of Independence and later in the Sinai Campaign. He has published several collections of poetry and short stories in Israel, and has had his plays produced there. His radio play *Bells and Trains* won the Israeli Radio Play Prize in 1962 and has been broadcast in translation in ten European countries. He represented Israel at the Spoleto Festival in 1966, and the International Poetry Festival in London in 1967. In America his work has appeared in several magazines, including *Commentary*, *Midstream*, and *Atlantic Monthly*. *Not of This Time, Not of This Place* was published in Israel in 1963.